ELECTRONIC
GAMES

WALTER H. BUCHSBAUM
Electronics Consultant

ROBERT MAURO
Manhattan College

ELECTRONIC GAMES

Design, Programming, and Troubleshooting

McGRAW-HILL BOOK COMPANY

New York St. Louis San Francisco Auckland Bogotá Düsseldorf
Johannesburg London Madrid Mexico Montreal New Delhi Panama
Paris São Paulo Singapore Sydney Tokyo Toronto

Library of Congress Cataloging in Publication Data

Buchsbaum, Walter H.
   Electronic games.

   Includes index.
   I. Video games—Equipment and supplies
I. Mauro, Robert, date.   joint author. II. Title.
TK6681.B83   668.7'4   78-16655
ISBN 0-07-008721-0

1234567890   KPKP   765432109

The editors for this book were Tyler G. Hicks
and Joseph Williams, the designer was Elliot
Epstein, and the production supervisor was
Thomas G. Kowalczyk. It was set in Palatino by
University Graphics.

Printed and bound by the Kingsport Press.

Contents

Preface, ix

1   ELECTRONIC GAME FUNDAMENTALS   **1**

1.1   *Games We Have Always Played, 1*
1.2   *Electronic Game Block Diagram, 4*
1.3   *Controls, 7*
1.4   *Displays, 8*
1.5   *Potential Problems, 9*

2   TV PICTURE PARAMETERS   **11**

2.1   *Essential TV Receiver Functions, 11*
2.2   *Monochrome Picture Tube Basics, 14*
2.3   *Horizontal and Vertical Scanning, 16*
2.4   *Monochrome Video Signals, 18*
2.5   *Synchronization, 20*
2.6   *Color Picture Tubes, 22*
2.7   *Color TV Signals, 25*

3   VIDEO EFFECTS   **29**

3.1   *TV Game Block Diagram,   29*
3.2   *Display Circuits for Fixed Patterns, 33*
        Analog Method
        Digital Method
3.3   *Display Circuits for Moving Patterns, 40*
        Analog Method
        Digital Method
3.4   *Color Display Circuits, 43*
3.5   *Special Display Effects, 45*
3.6   *Typical Display Circuits, 48*
3.7   *Troubleshooting Display Circuits, 50*

4 SOUND EFFECTS FOR ELECTRONIC GAMES **53**

4.1 *General Aspects of the Sound Synthesis Procedure, 54*
4.2 *Specific Circuits for Sound Effects Generation, 51*
4.3 *Generating Specific Sound Effects for Video Games, 69*

5 MICROPROCESSOR FUNDAMENTALS **79**

5.1 *Introduction, 79*
5.2 *General Microprocessor Architecture, 81*
5.3 *Subroutines, Nesting, and the Stack, 84*
5.4 *Microprocessor Execution of a Sample Program, 86*
5.5 *Interfacing Microprocessors to I/O Devices, 90*
5.6 *Special Microprocessor Control Signals and Operations, 92*
5.7 *A Sample Microprocessor—The 8080, 95*

6 PROGRAMMING **103**

6.1 *Introduction to Programming, 103*
6.2 *Flowcharts, 107*
6.3 *The 8080 Microprocessor Instruction Set, 112*
      Data Transfer Group
      Arithmetic Group
      Logical Group
      Branch Group
      Stack, I/O, and Machine Control Group
6.4 *Programming Examples, 134*
      Example 1: A Random-Number Generator
      Example 2: Packing the Deck
      Example 3: Electronic Craps
      Example 4: A General-Purpose Time Delay
6.5 *Software Debugging Techniques, 148*

7 PROGRAM STORAGE TECHNIQUES **153**

7.1 *Introduction, 153*
7.2 *Semiconductor Memory: ROM and RAM, 157*
7.3 *Microprocessor Memory Interfacing and Addressing Techniques, 163*
7.4 *Digital Data Recording on Magnetic Tape, 167*
      Data Recording on an Unmodified Audio Cassette Recorder
      Direct Digital Recording on Magnetic Tape
7.5 *Microprocessor Interfacing to Magnetic Tape I/O Devices, 178*

8   MICROPROCESSOR APPLICATIONS TO GAMES   187

8.1   *Microprocessor Refresh Techniques For Raster Scans, 187*

8.2   *Hardware-Software Trade-offs, 199*
           Joystick Interface
           Keyboard Interface
           Digit Scan
           A Software UART

8.3   *Microprocessor control of Video Effects, 211*

8.4   *Sound Effects, 219*

9   ELECTRONIC GAME PARAMETERS   227

9.1   *Games of Physical Skill, 227*
           Tennis
           Battle
           Roadrace
           Common Features
           Key Electronic Functions

9.2   *Games of Mental Skill, 232*
           Nim
           Guess the Number
           Common Features
           Key Electronic Features

9.3   *Games of Chance, 235*
           Draw Poker
           War
           Common Features
           Key Electronic Features

9.4   *Educational Games, 238*
           Multiplication
           School House
           Common Features
           Key Electronic Features

10   DESIGN EXAMPLES   243

10.1   *Pit and the Pendulum—An All-Hardware Electronic Game, 243*

10.2   *Software Implementation of Pit and the Pendulum, 252*

10.3   *Blackjack—A Full-fledged Microprocessor-controlled Video Game, 262*

11 TYPICAL ELECTRONIC GAMES   **283**

Code Name: Sector, 283
Chess Challenger, 285
Missile Attack, Autorace, and Football, 286
Indy 500, 288
Odyssey 2000, 4000, and 5000, 290
Studio II, 291
Channel F, 292
Video Computer System, 295
Telstar Arcade, 296
Tic Tac Quiz, 297
"Fonz", 299

12 TROUBLESHOOTING TECHNIQUES,   **303**

12.1 *Basic Troubleshooting Techniques, 303*
12.2 *Symptom-Function Technique for Electronic Games, 306*
    Typical Uses in Board Games
    Typical Uses in Coin-operated Games
    Typical Uses in TV Games
12.3 *Signal-tracing Techniques for Electronic Games, 312*
    Oscilloscope Signal Tracing
    Using Logic Probes
    Word Generators and Logic Analyzers
12.4 *Voltage-Resistance Technique for Electronic*
    Games, 318
12.5 *Substitution Technique in Electronic Games, 320*
12.6 *Most Frequent Defects in Electronic Games, 323*
    Display Effects
12.7 *Intermittent and Hard-to-Find Defects, 323*

Appendix, 325

Index, 331

Preface

Games have been part of every civilization throughout the ages. It is no wonder, then, that electronic games have been developed in our time. Integrated circuits and the microprocessor have brought an endless variety of electronic games within the reach of everyone who has a TV set—and that includes almost every household in the United States.

The technical aspects of electronic games involve a number of specialized fields within the electronics technology. Basic television principles, both monochrome and color, must be combined with digital display techniques and, most important, with an understanding of microprocessor and computer elements. Engineers, students, technicians, and competent hobbyists who already know electronics will find in this book all the information they need to design, program, maintain, and troubleshoot all types of electronic games.

Television, digital displays, and even microprocessors are covered in many different books, but *Electronic Games* is the first practical book that deals with all technical aspects of electronic games. Clear and concise chapters cover each of the essential elements of elec tronic games, including the home TV types as well as other types of games. The emphasis throughout this book is on the practical technology as it applies to existing and future games. Typical hardware and software are discussed in practical terms, with a large number of illustrations, backed by information from the service literature of the major game manufacturers.

This book starts by presenting electronic game fundamentals in the form of block diagrams, concentrating on the essential circuit functions. TV picture parameters, including basic monochrome and color TV circuitry, are reviewed in Chapter 2, and video effects related to games are covered in Chapter 3. Sound effects and the special circuits used to generate them are the topic of Chapter 4. The next four chapters deal with microprocessor fundamentals, programming, program storage, and microprocessor applications to games. These chapters give the reader an insight into how microprocessors

work and how they can be programmed to provide endless variations of all types of electronic games.

Chapter 9 deals briefly with the fundamentals of games, their
rules, and their appeal to different players. Typical electronic games
are discussed in Chapters 10 and 11. Design examples for a relatively
simple game, Pit and the Pendulum, and a microprocessor-based
game of chance, Blackjack, are presented in Chapter 10, while Chapter 11 covers typical electronic games from the major manufacturers.
Chapter 12 completes this book with troubleshooting techniques
designed specifically for electronic games, from the simplest to the
most sophisticated.

We hope that these twelve chapters, together with the references
cited, will provide a complete source of technical information on
electronic games to all of our readers. Because we have emphasized
both essential elements and actual circuitry, hardware and software,
we are certain that advances in electronic game design will not
render this book obsolete for many years.

Walter H. Buchsbaum
Robert Mauro

ELECTRONIC GAMES

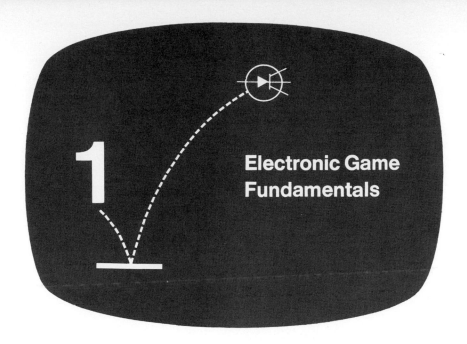

1

**Electronic Game
Fundamentals**

1.1 GAMES WE HAVE ALWAYS PLAYED

The importance of electronics in our daily lives continues to increase every year. The TV system uses electronics to extend our vision, as the name "television" implies. Public address or intercom systems extend the range of our voice, and remote control systems extend the range of our arms. A moment's thought will convince you that electronics, in practically all applications, is a tool used by human beings to improve, extend, or magnify the capabilities of our senses. In the design, manufacture, and troubleshooting of all these electronic devices, we have to have some fundamental understanding of these senses. In Chap. 2, a brief explanation of some of the characteristics of human vision is included as part of the explanation of how TV pictures are generated. Every hi-fi fan knows about the frequency and dynamic amplitude range of human hearing. In electronic game design, some of the principles of vision, hearing, and manual dexterity are, of course, an important part. But, as we shall see below, when electronics is applied to games, new and quite different dimensions have to be considered. Before we start with the technical aspects which are the topic of this book, we want to look very briefly at some essential nonelectronic concepts.

1

Games occupy a very special place in our life. Games have been studied on a sociological, psychological, and cultural basis, and we know from history that they have been an important part of all civilizations and cultures. Games involving competition among individuals, both in a physical and mental way, have been known throughout recorded history, and there is good reason to believe that even cave dwellers threw stones or shot arrows at targets for the fun of competition. The people who enjoyed these games could always be divided into players and spectators. The spectators participated in games by putting themselves into the place of the players. Even in today's televised football games, the viewers seem to suffer or enjoy the hard knocks of the players on the screen.

All of the games known today can be divided into two broad categories. There are games of skill, physical or mental or both, where the key element is the competition between players and the need to win. In the second category are games of chance, where the key element is the player's belief in luck, intuition, or some special, magical quality. In this type of game, too, the object is to win. As a matter of fact, "winning" is common to all games, and it is this key element that generates the anticipation, excitement, joy—for winning—and sadness—for losing. This common element of games, the emotional involvement, is the key difference between electronic games and all other applications of electronics. Our emotions aroused by a TV or radio program have little to do with the electronics, but depend primarily on what the studio transmits to us. In electronic games, however, the emotional involvement is, at least in part, influenced by the game design itself. It is the first time that engineers have had to design for emotional response.

Let's think about this new design requirement for a moment. Instead of designing only for simple tuning, clear pictures, true colors, realistic audio reproduction, low noise, etc., we must now make our product appeal to some specific human emotions. What are these emotions? What specific features must our electronic game have to arouse and then satisfy these emotions? Without getting into psychology, let's briefly look at the emotional aspects of games.

As we pointed out before, the key object in any game is to win. Whether we win over a human competitor or win over what we think of as the goddess of luck or, in the most recent type of electronic game, win over the computer, one key element is uncertainty. If the outcome of a game were known in advance, neither the players nor the spectators would have any interest in it. If you know what cards everyone will get, if you know the cast of the dice in advance, there will be no interest in playing. This point, the element of uncertainty, is an essential element in designing electronic games. It is a new departure for engineers because, ordinarily, engineers design for certainty.

The element of uncertainty can be introduced into an electronic game by the uncertain skill of the player or it can be introduced by the game itself. Different players will have different motor and mental skills, and these skills vary from moment to moment in each player. Our dexterity in turning knobs, concentrating on the display, guessing our opponent's moves—all these things contribute uncertainty. In most games additional elements of uncertainty are introduced by, for example, varying the trajectory and the speed of the ball, etc.

In the case where the game itself provides the uncertainty, as in games of chance, random actions are generated electronically. When the dice player throws the dice, many random factors, such as the bouncing, the speed, and the surface, interact on each other to produce the winning or losing number. Randomness means that events occur in a sequence that is not prearranged or predictable. The events that occur may be limited, such as the 11 numbers in dice or the 52 cards in blackjack, but their sequence must be random. As we shall see in later chapters, the generation of random numbers is not as simple as appears at first thought. To produce a long string of random numbers using only the numbers from 2 thru 12, as they apply to a dice game, requires careful design.

While uncertainty is probably the major element in a game's emotional appeal, two other aspects are also essential. All games require certain rules on which the players have to agree in advance. Sometimes these rules are so complex as to require judges or umpires to interpret them. We need only think of the simple rules for tic-tac-toe and compare them to the complex rules of baseball or chess to realize that, without knowledge of and adherence to the rules, games simply couldn't be played. In electronic games these rules are, of course, known to the players, but they must also be a part of the game itself. As we shall see later in this chapter, the rules must be incorporated in the electronic game control circuits along with the elements of randomness. In the more sophisticated electronic games, where a wide variety of different games can be programmed, the rules for each game occupy a designated portion of the program memory.

"What's the score?" is the perennial cry of every spectator and player. Knowing the score is essential for the player in deciding future actions. In electronic games this need to know the score means that some circuitry must be included which keeps count of the winning and losing actions of each player. This information must then be displayed in the format appropriate for the particular game. A moment's thought will convince you that the scorekeeping circuitry must, in some way, be connected to the circuits that "know" the rules. We also realize that the scorekeeping circuitry will have to "know" when the game starts and when it is over.

The display of the score can involve considerable circuit complexity for all those games that use a TV display. It is one thing to display lines, dots, and simple objects, but displaying the whole set of alphanumeric characters—that requires sophisticated electronics. To avoid this, most of the inexpensive TV games display only numerals which can be composed of the seven segments so familiar from the light-emitting diodes (LEDs) used in digital watches and pocket calculators. When you see "YOU LOSE TURKEY" displayed on a TV screen, you know that a sophisticated microprocessor-based electronic game has told you your score.

To sum up this brief, nontechnical discussion, now is the first time that game designers, electronics engineers, and technicians must consider the emotions, not only the senses, of their customers. The rules of the game and the score are also essential features, common to all electronic games. The TV viewer believes that the action on the TV screen represents reality. When we are watching a football game we can believe, at least for the moment, that we are at the stadium. We know that what we see is really happening. When we really get involved, we can almost feel the tension and we become part of the action on the playing field. This element of emotional involvement is, of course, also important for the success of electronic games. The viewer has now become a player who is trying to win. As we have seen, the uncertainty of the outcome is one of the key elements in any kind of game. This uncertainty must be assured either by the player's own actions or by some contribution of randomness contained in the electronic game itself.

1.2 ELECTRONIC GAME BLOCK DIAGRAM

Figure 1.1 shows the complete block diagram of any kind of electronic game. You will notice that it includes the player. The player has, like the electronic game itself, an input and an output. In this simplified version, the input is visual and the output is manual. The player watches the game display and acts on it by manipulating the controls. The electronic game's input consists of the player's action on the controls, and its output is a TV screen. Between the player controls and the TV screen is the real heart of the electronic game, the control section. As we shall see in later chapters, this control section can consist of a single integrated circuit (IC) or, in more sophisticated electronic games, it can contain what is in effect a small computer.

In reality, there is a great deal more in each of the blocks shown in Fig. 1.1. The player's input is not limited to the TV screen. The player may receive audible cues and may also use his or her own brain, a very sophisticated computer, to introduce variations of the game rules. The manual activity, the player's output, may range from pushing the button to manipulating a complex "joystick" or two. Dexterity, practice, and nerve-muscle reaction time, are only a few of the elements the player adds to the game. In Fig. 1.1 a single player is shown for simplicity's sake, but several players usually compete against each other, either by manipulating the controls sequentially or by using individual controls.

Figure 1.1 depicts a closed-loop system. This means that, in order for the system to function, all of its elements must be able to interface with each other correctly. If the display is too fast or too slow, too bright or too dim, for the human player, the system will not work. If the controls are too difficult or too easy to operate, if they are too large or too small, or if they do not correctly control the display, the system will not work. As we shall see in later chapters, definite limitations exist concerning the speed of the action and the amount of information that the display can present to the players.

Most electronic games can be categorized as coin-operated, arcade-type games, board games, or TV games. Both arcade and TV games use a TV screen as the display, but the TV game includes an RF link so that it can be added to any home receiver, while the arcade game contains its own TV monitor. Board games usually use LEDs as

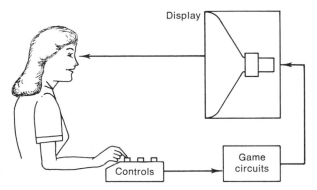

Figure 1.1 Basic electronic game.

displays, while the game is actually played by moving figures on a board, as in chess.

Figure 1.2 shows the block diagram of a basic TV game. Two players are shown here, each with individual controls which signal to the control logic section. The master control lets us select the type of game we want to play and choose its key parameters. It is possible, for almost all TV games, to determine the speed of the ball, the size of the racket or bat, the type of trajectory, whether the game is to be played on a novice, intermediate, or expert level, etc. The output from the master controls goes to the control logic portion, which is the center of the electronic game itself. Depending on the level of sophistication, this control logic may be a single, special-purpose IC, or it may be a microprocessor with memory and other additional functions. In either event, signals from the control logic go to the display circuits where they are converted into TV signals. These TV signals are then modulated on an RF carrier and sent to the antenna switch. As explained in some detail in Chap. 3, this switch allows the viewer to select regular TV broadcasts via the antenna or connect the TV signals from the game, which are then displayed on an unused

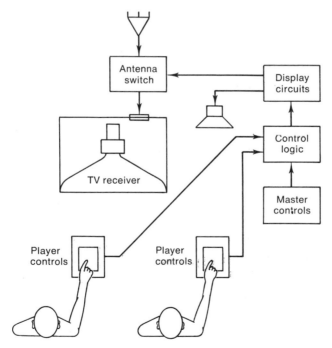

Figure 1.2 TV game block diagram.

TV channel. In this arrangement the TV set serves as display and requires no modification.

The major difference between TV games and arcade or coin-operated games is that the display circuits of the arcade game (Fig. 1.2) drive a monitor. There is no RF output and no antenna switch, and the power switch is controlled by the coin collection device.

Each of the functions shown in the simple block diagram of Fig. 1.2 is covered in some detail in this book. The player controls and the master controls are described in this chapter, as are some of the most frequently used non-TV displays. Because of the importance of TV displays, both monitors and TV receivers, Chap. 2 is devoted to this topic. The antenna switch and display circuits are the topic of Chap. 3, and sound effects, indicated by the loudspeaker of Fig. 1.2, are the topic of Chap. 4. The simple box marked "Control logic" is so important that its description fills Chaps. 5 thru 8.

1.3 CONTROLS

As indicated in the block diagram, two types of controls are provided with every kind of electronic game. The master controls, usually a set of toggle, rotary, or thumbwheel switches, are used to select the type of game and its key parameters. Player controls range from simple pushbutton switches or a complete keyboard, to potentiometers, joysticks, and combinations of potentiometers and switches arranged in some unique ways. The early TV games invariably used simple potentiometers to control the vertical position of the racket, bat, etc. In more complex versions two potentiometers, sometimes mounted on concentric shafts, were used to control both horizontal and vertical motion.

Another degree of complexity is added with the joystick. This arrangement essentially consists of two potentiometers located at right angles to each other which are driven by a two-dimensional mechanical arrangement. One potentiometer turns when the joystick moves front to back, while the other moves when the joystick moves left to right. When the joystick moves in the diagonal direction, both potentiometers are driven by the gear mechanism. In the Fairchild Channel F game an ingenious mechanical arrangement allows the player to hold the control handle in one hand while moving a knob as a joystick, rotating it, and using it as an up-down pushbutton control. These complexities increase the required manual skill and are potential trouble sources due to contact wear.

Probably the most reliable type of player control is the pushbutton keyboard. In the RCA Studio II games the keyboard is used for all control functions, even for positioning the racket or bat, and for moving the pointer in the games of Doodles and Patterns. Different keys, designated by appropriate arrows, control motion as long as they are depressed.

Potentiometers are fine for those games that do not use a microprocessor as control, but pushbutton controls are more economical for microprocessor-controlled games because the information they generate is already in digital form. When potentiometer controls are used with microprocessor games, the analog voltage due to the potentiometer must be converted into a digital quantity in order to be entered through the microprocessor system.

1.4 DISPLAYS

The vast majority of electronic games rely on a cathode-ray tube—a TV picture tube—for their main display. This includes the TV games and almost all coin-operated games. There are some pinball machines that use the conventional multicolored flashing lights and

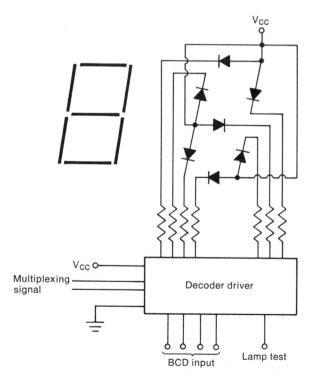

Figure 1.3 LED driver system.

incandescent displays. All of the board games usually offered by the toy industry use the familiar seven-segment numerical display found in digital clocks, watches, hand-held calculators, etc. These numerical indicators are available as LEDs, gas-discharge devices (Nixie for example), and liquid-crystal displays (LCDs). The LED, the most popular, features low voltage, relatively high current, high visibility, and relatively low price. The gas discharge type of display requires a higher voltage, usually above 100 V, and low current and is equally visible and inexpensive. LCDs act as light valves and depend on reflected or transmitted light in order to show the numeral. LCDs require moderately high ac voltages at very low currents and they cost slightly more than the other two types.

LEDs are most widely used in those electronic games which do not rely on a picture tube. Figure 1.3 shows a typical LED driver system. Note that separate resistors go to each LED segment from the decoder/driver circuit. The desired number is entered in binary-coded-decimal (BCD) format, and the correct segments are automatically illuminated. ICs are available that can drive as many as four to six 7-segment LED numerals. The Parker Bros. game Code Name Sector includes the driving circuits for six LED numerals and four LED dots in the single microcomputer game IC. In some games the current to the LED is switched on and off at a rapid rate, to save power. Since this switching or multiplexing occurs very fast, the numerals appear as a steady display.

1.5 POTENTIAL PROBLEMS

Like many new products, electronic games face a number of problems, mostly in the merchandising, pricing, and promotion field. Three technical problems have surfaced so far. While solutions have been found for all of them, their existence cannot be ignored.

The first problem concerns a characteristic of cathode-ray (picture) tubes. When a fixed pattern is displayed for a long time at high brightness and contrast, the phosphor screen will "wear" more at the bright areas than at the dark ones, causing the pattern to remain visible, even when other pictures are displayed. This problem does not normally occur in TV receivers because pictures change continuously. In some early studio monitors the station test patterns did become permanently fixed on the screen. The same thing happened in some of the early coin-operated games because a particular game pattern could remain stationary on the picture tube screen for many hours. All of the newer coin-operated electronic games eliminate this potential problem by continuously changing the display patterns when the machine is idle. In home TV games this problem of "wear" during long periods of fixed game pattern display has been solved in several ways. The owner's manual usually contains advice to the user to turn the set and/or game off when not in use. Some games automatically change patterns, and in all of them the level of modulation of the RF carrier is deliberately set below 50% to reduce the contrast between the light and dark portions of the screen.

The second problem concerns FCC regulations for "Type Approval under Part 15" of any Class I TV device that is coupled to a TV set with a modulated RF oscillator. This means that every TV game must have type approval, requiring RF emission tests conducted in an elaborately instrumented test facility. Possible interference with nearby TV receivers is the reason for this requirement. This interference can originate in the RF oscillator chassis itself or in the cable connecting it to the TV set; in the worst case, the RF signal could be radiated by the antenna that is connected to the TV set. Since the first few TV games were refused approval by the FCC, the industry has learned how to eliminate or greatly reduce all unwanted radiation. Technical details are covered in Chap. 3 in connection with the RF oscillator and the antenna switch.

The third problem concerns electrical safety and involves the ac power line. Many TV receivers do not use isolating transformers and have one side of the chassis connected to the power line. A potential hazard exists if the electronic game chassis is also connected to the power line and if the two ac plugs make the TV and the game chassis "hot" with respect to each other. All of the TV games now on the market use either batteries or an isolating transformer. In addition, the external surfaces of all ac-operated games are well insulated from the power line. When you are troubleshooting a TV game, it is still a good idea to check if there are any points where the power line could connect to the chassis.

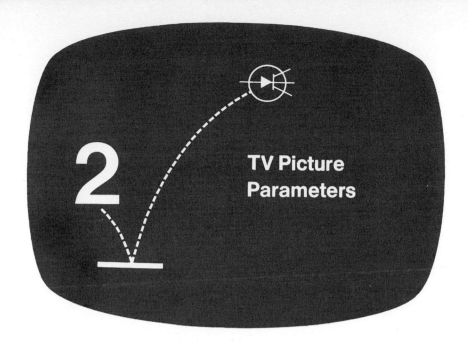

2

**TV Picture
Parameters**

The vast majority of electronic games are used with standard mono-chrome and color TV receivers, and unless you know how this equipment works, you'll be tapping in the dark when you are trying to design, program, build, or troubleshoot an electronic game. This chapter contains the essentials necessary to understand what each TV receiver stage does and why, the critical signal characteristics, and a very brief explanation of monochrome and color picture tubes.

2.1 ESSENTIAL TV RECEIVER FUNCTIONS

Commercial TV transmission in the United States uses a total of 82 assigned channels, each 6 MHz wide and covering portions of the VHF and UHF spectrum. Electronic games which are connected to the TV receiver antenna terminals use either channel 3 or channel 4 because there is practically no location in the United States served by both of these channels. TV transmitters operate essentially on a line-of-sight basis, and stations in adjacent areas generally are assigned alternate channels.

Figure 2.1 shows the TV channel spectrum and illustrates the key features of TV transmission. We see that the video and the audio signals are transmitted on two different carriers. The video information is amplitude-modulated and, as explained later in this chapter, requires a bandwidth of about 4 MHz, while the audio signal is frequency-modulated on a separate carrier with a bandwidth of 50 kHz. As illustrated, the audio carrier is 4.5 MHz higher in frequency than the video carrier—an essential feature, as we shall see below.

To save precious spectrum space, the lower sideband of the video carrier envelope is suppressed. This particular arrangement is called *vestigial sideband suppression.* For channel 3 the video carrier frequency is 61.25 MHz and the audio carrier is 65.75 MHz. Channel 4 is exactly 6 MHz higher in frequency. There is an anomaly in the frequency assignment of channel 5. Its video carrier is at 77.25 MHz and its audio carrier at 81.75 MHz. The 4-MHz gap between channels 4 and 5 explains why both of these channels are frequently assigned to TV stations in the same service area. You may encounter adjacent-channel interference from channels 2 or 4 if your electronic game operates on channel 3, but it is almost impossible to get channel 5 interference on channel 4.

The block diagram of Fig. 2.2 illustrates the essential monochrome TV receiver functions. Color operation requires additional circuitry, and these functions are discussed at the end of this chapter. The RF signal enters from the antenna and is selected by the tuner. Standard superheterodyne circuits are used, with the local oscillator higher in frequency than the incoming signal. Because of the difference between VHF and UHF circuits, separate tuners are used, with mechanical and electrical coupling. The output of either tuner is the IF signal, which has the video carrier at 45.75 MHz and the audio carrier at 41.25 MHz. For monochrome receivers the video carrier is 3 dB below the peak, and the audio carrier is 40 dB below the peak video response. In color receivers the audio carrier must be about 60

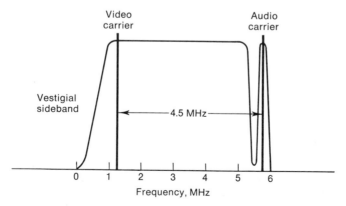

Figure 2.1 TV channel.

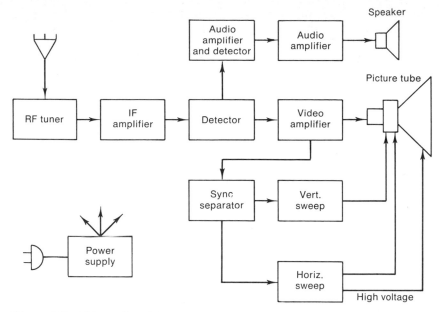

Figure 2.2   TV receiver block diagram.

dB below the peak to avoid audio interference in the picture. Special tuned circuits in the IF amplifier section reduce the audio to these levels.

A simple diode detector removes the video signal from the carrier and also produces a 4.5-MHz FM audio signal as beat between the audio and video IF carriers. This 4.5-MHz audio, often called the *intercarrier* or *second sound IF signal*, goes to an amplifier and FM detector. The resultant audio is then amplified and drives the speaker. The video amplifier produces the final video signal, which must be about 40 to 60 V peak-to-peak to drive the picture tube.

A portion of the video signal is supplied to the sync separator section, where the vertical and horizontal synchronizing pulses are removed and separated. More about these signals is discussed in Sec. 2.5. The vertical and horizontal sweep sections generate the signals required to form a raster on the screen of the picture tube, and these functions are discussed in some detail in Sec. 2.3. The picture tube itself, monochrome and color, is such an essential element for both TV games and the arcade-type games that Sec. 2.2 is devoted to monochrome picture tubes and Sec. 2.6 to color picture tubes of all types.

TV receivers generally operate from the power line, and a regulated power supply provides the needed dc potentials. These functions present no special problems, but the very high anode voltages required by all picture tubes are obtained from the horizontal sweep section, and this function is discussed briefly in Sec. 2.3.

2.2 MONOCHROME PICTURE TUBE BASICS

The TV picture tube can be described as a large glass bottle, evacuated to a very high degree, which has an electron gun at the neck and a phosphor screen at the other end. A thin beam of electrons originates at the electron gun and strikes the phosphor screen inside the glass envelope. The viewer sees a small dot of bright light. When the beam is rapidly moved both in a horizontal and vertical direction, a raster is generated on the screen. To obtain a picture, it is necessary to vary the brightness of the moving dot.

Figure 2.3 shows the basic elements and voltages required to operate a monochrome TV picture tube. A filament-heated cathode emits electrons, and the grid bias controls the number of electrons which will strike the phosphor screen. An accelerating anode focuses the electron beam. After the electrons strike the phosphor screen, they are attracted to the second anode, usually a conductive coating on the inside of the picture-tube envelope. Typical second-anode voltages range from 12,000 to 25,000 V, with the higher voltages usually used for larger-screen-size picture tubes.

Picture-tube type numbers start with the diagonal size of the screen as the first two digits. A 19-in picture tube, for example, may be a type 19 GP4. The last digit, the 4, indicates a television-type, fast-decaying phosphor. The phosphor designation number for color picture tubes is a two-digit indication, such as 22.

TV screens have an aspect ratio of four units wide by three units high, but for many electronic games only a portion of the screen is

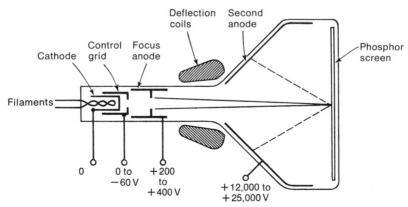

Figure 2.3 Picture-tube cross section.

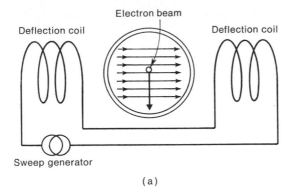

Electron beam

Deflection coil

Deflection coil

Sweep generator

(a)

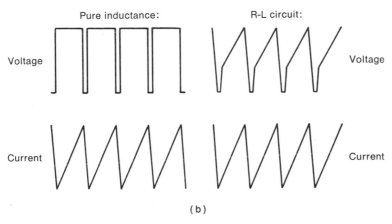

Pure inductance:

R-L circuit:

Voltage

Voltage

Current

Current

(b)

Figure 2.4 (*a*) Magnetic deflection and (*b*) current-voltage waveforms.

used. This means, of course, that a portion of the TV screen has to be blanked out. Because the TV raster is made up of fine horizontal lines and because the same number of lines is present on every TV screen regardless of size, the size of the screen determines the minimum viewing distance. This distance is approximately eight times the height of the screen. If you watch a 10-in-high screen, you have to be at least 80 in away to avoid seeing individual lines. Many viewers have a tendency to sit close to the screen, particularly in playing games, and this often results in eye fatigue.

In Fig. 2.3 we have indicated the location of the electromagnetic deflection yoke which controls the motion of the electron beam. Small cathode-ray tubes, such as those used in oscilloscopes, employ electrostatic deflection, but all TV picture tubes, monochrome as well as color, use electromagnetic deflection. Vertical deflection is obtained by means of horizontal magnetic flux lines, as illustrated in

Fig. 2.4a. Similarly, vertical magnetic flux lines deflect the electron beam horizontally. The deflection yoke is mounted on the neck of the TV picture tube and consists of one set of horizontal and one set of vertical deflection coils. The horizontal deflection coils are located at top and bottom, while the vertical coils are on both sides. Because much more horizontal deflection power is needed, as explained later in this chapter, the horizontal deflection coils are on the inside of the yoke, closest to the electron beam.

To generate a TV picture, the electron beam must be moved at a fixed rate from left to right and then returned, at a much faster rate, from right to left. At the same time, the beam is moved downward for the next line. After the desired number of horizontal lines has been "painted" on the screen, the electron beam must return rapidly from the bottom of the screen to the top. The magnetic flux lines vary in sawtooth fashion, both for the horizontal and the vertical deflection coils. The magnetic flux generated by a coil is a direct analog of the current flowing through this coil. The current and voltage through an inductance, however, are not identical. Figure 2.4b illustrates the relationships between current and voltage through a pure inductance and (the actual case) a combination of resistance and inductance. The voltage waveform becomes particularly significant when we consider the relevant time it takes the electron beam to "paint" a line and to fly back or retrace.

2.3 HORIZONTAL AND VERTICAL SCANNING

All TV games depend on horizontal and vertical scanning characteristics to generate the display and, in the case of some of the target games, to receive information back from this display. For this reason, we shall discuss this important topic in some detail. The TV picture actually consists of a dot of light which covers the entire screen 30 times per second. A complete TV picture, monochrome or color, is "painted" in one-thirtieth of a second.

Motion picture projectors show 24 frames, or complete pictures, each second. To avoid the appearance of flicker, the motion picture projector contains a rotating shutter so that each frame is actually flashed on the screen twice. For motion picture projection, then, 48 pictures per second are shown. In TV systems the 30 complete frames per second are also broken up by an electronic "shutter" to result in 60 "fields" per second.

A complete TV picture consists of 525 horizontal lines. To avoid the flicker effect, this 525-line picture or frame is broken into two fields of 262½ lines. One field will scan all of the odd lines, 1, 3, 5, etc., and the next field will scan all of the even lines, 2, 4, 6, etc.

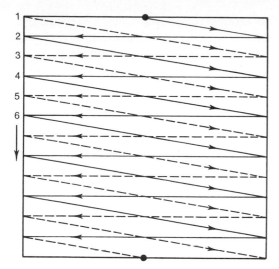

Figure 2.5 Interlaced scanning. *(Adapted from Buchsbaum, Fundamentals of TV, Hayden Book Company, 1970.)*

Figure 2.5 shows, in simplified form, how this interlaced scanning pattern is generated. The vertical deflection current must repeat at the rate of 60 times per second, but the horizontal deflection frequency is 15,750 Hz, generating a total of 525 lines 30 times per second or 262½ lines 60 times per second. As illustrated in Fig. 2.5, the odd scanning patterns start in the upper left-hand corner while the even scanning patterns start in the upper center of the screen. It is obvious that something has to be set up in the vertical deflection system to assure that alternate vertical scanning periods start at different points. We shall see in Sec. 2.5 how this is accomplished.

While the total number of lines is 525, not all of these lines contain picture information. Between 7 and 8% of the lines are used up during the vertical retrace portion, when the electron beam returns from bottom to top. In addition, some of the top and bottom lines are normally blanked out. In standard commercial TV transmission only 483 to 490 scanning lines actually carry video information.

The amount of video information contained in a complete frame determines the *resolution* or *definition* of the picture. A picture showing the very maximum resolution would consist of a fine checkerboard pattern, with each square being the width and height of each individual line. To display such a high-resolution picture would require a bandwidth of approximately 4 MHz, as indicated in Fig. 2.2. Most commercial TV receivers have a video bandwidth of approximately 3.2 to 3.8 MHz but are usually so limited in focus and alignment that most fine detail is missing. Misadjustment of the vertical synchronization of most TV receivers has accustomed viewers to accepting a picture which actually consists of only 262½ lines, rather than a full 525. TV games do not require fine detail, and their synchronization circuits do not provide the necessary shift in the vertical synchronizing pulse, as described in Sec. 2.5, to generate interlaced pictures.

In commercial TV transmission a special blanking pulse is transmitted during the retrace period to cut off the electron beam and thereby eliminate the appearance of retrace lines. Horizontal retrace lines are normally invisible because of the close spacing between the horizontal lines, but during the vertical retrace period, when the electron beam moves from the bottom to the top of the screen, they are visible unless they are blanked out.

Scanning at the rate of 15,750 Hz, each horizontal period lasts 63.5 μs. About 10.5 μs of this is blanked, including the time the electron beam returns from right to left and a short period at the beginning and end of each horizontal scan to assure even edges on the picture. This means that approximately 53 μs of actual display time or video information is available in each horizontal line. This also means that a 5-μs-wide pulse, displayed on a 12-in-wide (30 cm) screen, will result in a 1¼-in-wide (3 cm) bar. As discussed in Chap. 3, the time periods involved in TV displays determine much of the electronic game circuitry.

Before discussing the other aspects of video signals, one characteristic unique to television should be mentioned. The magnetic energy built up in a deflection coil during the video portion must be suddenly reversed to return the beam to the left. This results in a very high reverse voltage during the horizontal flyback period, and this flyback pulse is used to generate the second anode voltage for the picture tube. A special transformer, appropriately called the *flyback transformer*, provides this high voltage. Various signals required for other portions of the TV receiver are derived from this flyback transformer because no video information is transmitted during the flyback period. Defects in the horizontal deflection system, particularly the high-voltage flyback transformer, often mask other problems which may affect a TV game display.

2.4 MONOCHROME VIDEO SIGNALS

A normal TV picture has a range of different shades of grey, from a total black, when the screen is dark, to the maximum brightness, or white. Figure 2.6 illustrates a typical video signal for one TV picture

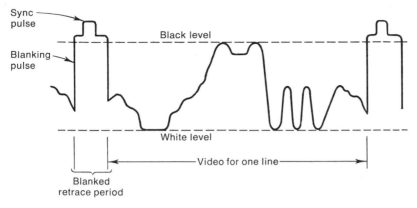

Figure 2.6 Video signal for one line.

line. Note the synchronizing and blanking pulse at the beginning of each line and the various levels of grey, from the black to the white levels. The blanking pulse, of course, goes beyond the black level to make sure that the picture tube is completely cut off during the flyback period. Neither the black level nor the white level of the video signal should exceed the linear range of the cathode-grid characteristics of the picture tube. For most monochrome picture tubes, this linear range is approximately 60 V, and this means that the video signal applied between cathode and grid must be linear within those values. Many TV games, particularly the simpler ones, operate only with black-and white signals. If the relative amplitudes between the blanking pulse and the white level generated in a TV game are incorrect, the resulting TV picture cannot reproduce the desired game pattern.

The frequency response of the TV receiver is quite important, even for the simple black-and-white patterns usually provided by TV games. A bandwidth of at least 60 Hz to 3.5 MHz is required to reproduce both low-frequency and high-frequency components of the TV broadcast signal. To assure the correct frequency response, the IF bandwidth is at least 3.5 MHz, and the video amplifier section contains high- and low-frequency compensating networks. *L-R* circuits enhance the response at the high-frequency end, and *C-R* circuits make sure that the response at the low-frequency end is also satisfactory. Poor low-frequency response is often caused by defective coupling capacitors and is made apparent in a TV game pattern display by a whitish smear in the area where white and black areas meet. Poor high-frequency response appears as loss of fine detail. Typical high-frequency and low-frequency compensating circuits are shown in Fig. 2.7.

determine the correct response for the 60-Hz or the 15,750-Hz signal respectively. Vertical deflection circuits operate directly from the vertical sync signal but horizontal deflection circuits, because they operate at a higher speed, depend on an automatic control circuit. This circuit compares the received horizontal sync pulses with a horizontal pulse obtained from the flyback transformer and generates an error voltage which provides the automatic control to the horizontal deflection oscillator. The horizontal automatic frequency control (AFC) is one of the critical parts of a TV display, and defects in this circuit can often lead to problems which may be blamed on the TV game itself.

2.6 COLOR PICTURE TUBES

The color TV system in use in the United States is based on the fundamentals of colorimetry and the characteristics of the human eye. In brief, we are able to integrate different-colored elements into a single pattern. We can see a combination of blue and red dots as purple, for example. For a more detailed discussion of colorimetry and the so-called tristimulus system, the reader is referred to the many excellent texts on color TV.

All color TV receivers reproduce the color picture by creating patterns of red, green, and blue (RGB) dots of light which we then perceive, from the proper viewing distance, as "natural" colors. In TV picture tubes transmitted colors, as opposed to reflected colors, are used, and it is possible to obtain yellow from a combination of green and red light. When the proper intensity or brightness levels of red, green, and blue dots are generated, we see white. Depending on the overall intensity level of this mixture of colors, we can see various shades of grey. A very wide range of colors appearing in nature can be generated by the three-color TV picture tubes. Whether they use a single electron gun or three separate electron guns, all of these picture tubes generate the same red, green, and blue "primary" colors.

A description of these colors in terms of physics and mathematics is beyond the scope of this book, but the RGB color system can also be presented in terms of brightness, hue, and saturation. The term *brightness* indicates the intensity of the light. The term *hue* (or *tint*) refers to the shade or dominant color as it appears to the eye. The term *saturation* refers to the purity or, more precisely, to the amount of other colors present. White, for example, has zero saturation, and all three primary colors are present. A pastel pink may have 50% saturation. Beige, light green, sky blue, etc., are pastel colors, with specified amounts of saturation of their primary colors.

The basic elements of a three-gun color picture tube are shown in Fig. 2.10. As the name implies, it contains three separate electron guns, each with its own filament, cathode, grid, and screen grid located on the inside neck of the color picture tube. Each electron gun has its own dc (brightness) and video signal amplitude (color intensity) control. A common focus element varies the potential between the three screen grids, the focus element, and the second anode, called the *ultor* in color picture tubes. The three electron guns are aligned within the glass envelope so that one electron beam will strike the red phosphor dots on the screen, another the green, and the third the blue. Many of the older color picture tubes use the so-called shadow mask, which is, effectively, a metal screen with one hole for each triad of individual red, green, and blue phosphor dots. When the green and blue electron guns are cut off and the red electron gun is set for normal brightness, only the red dots should light up on the screen. When all three electron guns are set to the correct intensity, the screen should be white.

Section 2.7 deals with the color signals required to generate the color picture, but the essential dc voltages can be seen from Fig. 2.10. The second anode or ultor is set at 25 kV, a typical voltage for almost all types of color TV tubes. Note that different dc potentials are applied to the red, green, and blue screens. This is because unequal amounts of intensity of the RGB primary colors are required to produce white or grey. With the screen voltages of 470 V (red), 600 V (green), and 430 V (blue), the result will be a neutral, grey picture-tube screen.

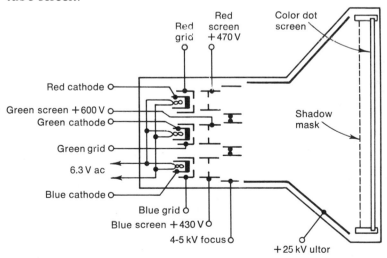

Figure 2.10 Basic three-gun color picture tube. *(Adapted from Buchsbaum, Fundamentals of TV, Hayden Book Company, 1970.)*

Color picture tubes using three electron guns are available either in the delta system or in the in-line system. The first, the *delta system*, is the older and features the three electron guns spaced in an equilateral triangle configuration, just like the three phosphor dots which they illuminate. In the *in-line system* the three electron guns are located on a single line. The major advantage of the in-line system is the relative ease of alignment of the three electron beams so that each strikes only its respective color dots. There is also a difference in the shadow mask. In the delta system the shadow mask always has round holes, but in the in-line system vertical slots or a vertical grid are often used. In-line color picture tubes sometimes feature a three-color screen consisting of vertical RGB stripes instead of the triad color dot pattern.

To make sure that each electron beam strikes only the dots or stripes of its respective color, a variety of adjustments are necessary. The largest number of adjustments is required for the delta system and the smallest number for the single-gun color tubes discussed below. Figure 2.11 illustrates the external components necessary for a delta system color picture tube. Mounted directly behind the deflection yoke is the convergence coil and magnet assembly. This provides static (dc) and dynamic (ac) adjustment for each of the three beams over the entire screen. If you have ever adjusted a color TV set using a delta color tube, you will know that there are three static adjustments consisting of rotating magnets in each of the three convergence coils. In addition there are separate dynamic convergence adjustments for vertical and horizontal, tilt and magnitude, for

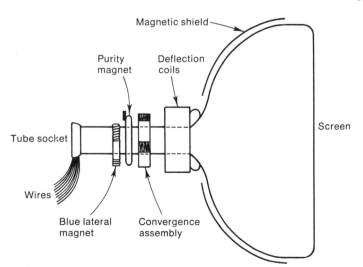

Figure 2.11 External components for delta color tube.

each of the three colors. There are also some master convergence adjustments, all mounted on a panel containing as many as 12 different adjustments.

The purity magnet with its adjustment tabs affects all three electron beams but is usually set for optimum red purity. The delta system also requires a so-called blue lateral magnet, a separate external magnet which affects primarily the electron beam from the blue gun so that it can be brought in line with the red and green.

With in-line three-gun color picture tubes, many of the convergence adjustments described above are eliminated. There is no lateral blue magnet, and the convergence adjustments are greatly simplified. Single-gun color picture tubes, such as the SONY Trinitron, avoid most of the problems of convergence and purity altogether. These picture tubes always use a vertical-stripe color screen, but they require an additional deflection signal (discussed in Sec. 2.7) operating at 3.58 MHz, the color subcarrier frequency. This signal is necessary to switch the electron beam between the red, green, and blue strips on the screen in synchronism with the three color video signals. Just as in three-gun color picture tubes, the single-gun picture tube must reproduce the three color signals virtually simultaneously.

For TV games which feature color, the type of picture tube used is only important as far as troubleshooting and alignment are concerned. Manufacturers' data or any of the many texts on color TV servicing should be consulted for these tasks.

2.7 COLOR TV SIGNALS

As discussed at the beginning of this chapter, the video signal is amplitude-modulated on the carrier, and the audio signal is frequency-modulated on another carrier, 4.5 MHz above the video carrier. These parameters must remain the same so that all monochrome receivers are able to receive color TV signals and display them in monochrome. To transmit the additional information required for color, however, it was decided to use the third possible modulation scheme, phase modulation, and a special color subcarrier to minimize interference to monochrome receivers.

Theoretical analysis and spectrum analyzer pictures show that the monochrome video signal is not a continuous band of frequencies but rather consists of bursts of energy spaced 30 Hz apart and clustered about the harmonics of 15,750 Hz, the horizontal scanning frequency. A simplified spectrum chart is shown in Fig. 2.12. When color TV standards were established, this characteristic was utilized to modulate color information on a subcarrier which is based on a

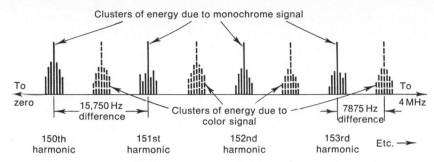

Clusters of energy due to monochrome signal

To zero

15,750 Hz difference

Clusters of energy due to color signal

7875 Hz difference

To 4 MHz

| 150th harmonic | 151st harmonic | 152nd harmonic | 153rd harmonic | Etc. → |

Figure 2.12 TV signal spectrum. *(Adapted from Buchsbaum, Fundamentals of TV, Hayden Book Company, 1970.)*

15,750-Hz rate but designed so that its bands of energies would fall between those of the monochrome signal. The dotted bands of energy in Fig. 2.12 are due to the color signal. This process is called *interleaving* and permits the transmission of a 3.579545-MHz color subcarrier which is not usually visible on monochrome receivers.

Figure 2.13 shows the phase relationship in vector form between the key portions of the color signal. We can see that the RGB color difference signals, the color signals with their brightness components Y removed, are transmitted as a change in phase and amplitude from the reference signal burst. This reference burst consists of 8 cycles of the unmodulated color subcarrier transmitted during the horizontal blanking pedestal, as illustrated in Fig. 2.14. In actuality, two different signals, the I and Q vectors (shown in Fig. 2.13), are detected to indicate the hue and saturation of the color signal.

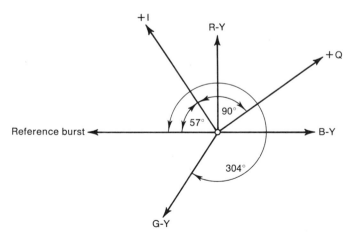

Figure 2.13 Subcarrier vector diagram.

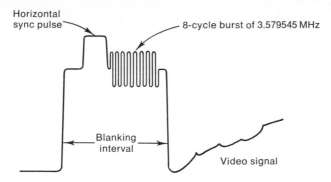

Figure 2.14 Color reference burst.

As explained at the beginning of Sec. 2.6, the red, green, and blue color signals can be converted into their brightness, hue, and saturation components. This is done according to the following formulas:

$$E_Y = 0.30E_{red} + 0.59E_{green} + 0.11E_{blue}$$
$$E_Q = 0.21E_{red} - 0.52E_{green} + 0.31E_{blue}$$
$$E_I = 0.60E_{red} - 0.28E_{green} - 0.32E_{blue}$$

The brightness component is transmitted as the monochrome video signal Y, and the hue and saturation components are encoded on the color subcarrier. Because the fine detail of the color picture is provided by the monochrome video signal in this scheme, the hue and saturation information contained on the color subcarrier now requires much less bandwidth.

The block diagram of Fig. 2.15 shows the functions of the color circuits found in color TV receivers. These circuits are required in

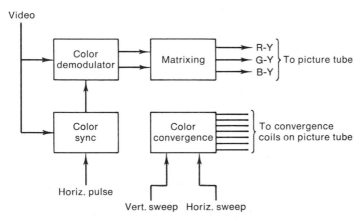

Figure 2.15 Color circuit function block diagram.

addition to the conventional monochrome functions shown in Fig. 2.2. From the brightness amplifier (the video amplifier in monochrome sets) video signals are supplied to the color demodulator and the color sync section. The color demodulator consists of a special amplifier for the 3.58-MHz color subcarrier, which is then phase-demodulated by a color reference signal. This is locally generated, but phase-locked to the color reference burst described above and shown in Fig. 2.14. After the color subcarrier is demodulated, the resulting signals are matrixed by voltage addition and subtraction and amplified to provide the red, green, and blue color difference signals, which are then used to drive the electron guns of the color picture tube. The Y or brightness signal (the monochrome video signal) is usually added in the electron guns. In some systems the color difference signals and the brightness signals are added before they reach the color picture tube. The key element is that, at the color picture tube itself, the three separate color signals, RGB, must be available to generate the color patterns on the screen.

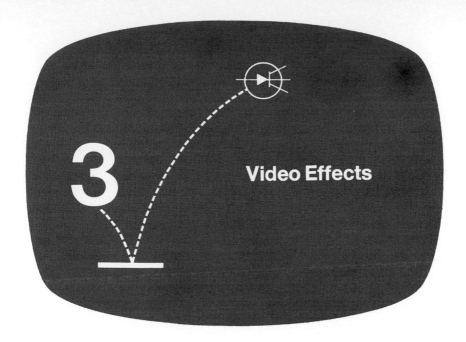

Video Effects

The circuits and functions described in this chapter provide the display for all types of electronic games. Coin-operated games connect the video information directly to the picture tube, but in the so-called TV games, the connection is made through one of the unused television channels. The special requirements for this type of game, including the parameters which need FCC approval, are taken up first. Then this chapter covers analog and digital circuits used in sophisticated, microprocessor-based games. Color display circuits and special effects are also discussed. Two typical display circuits are described, and a section on troubleshooting all types of display circuits completes the chapter.

3.1 TV GAME BLOCK DIAGRAM

Figure 3.1 shows the fundamental blocks that are required for any type of electronic game intended to work with a standard TV set. The game logic, master controls, and player controls, as well as the display circuits, are required for any type of electronic game. In order to feed the antenna terminals of the TV set, the video signals from the electronic game must appear at the TV set in the same form as those from a TV station. That means that the video signals must be modulated on an RF carrier, following approximately the same modulation standards as those described in Chap. 2. Typical circuits for the RF generator and modulator are discussed below.

The modulated RF signal must go through a special antenna switch to the antenna terminals of the TV set. When the antenna switch is connected to the TV antenna, the signals from the electronic game should, if possible, be shut off. When the TV game is connected to the TV set through the antenna switch, there must be at least 60 dB isolation between the signals from the RF generator and modulator and the TV antenna. This isolation is necessary to avoid radiating some of the signals generated in the TV game over the antenna and thereby causing interference with other TV receivers. TV games require FCC approval, and the main concern of the FCC is the possibility of interference originating in the electronic game. Even a 1-mV signal applied to the TV receiver can radiate an interference signal which can be picked up by neighboring TV antennas. For that reason, the 60 dB isolation between the RF signal path from the RF generator and modulator contained in the game and the TV antenna is absolutely essential.

Another important characteristic which FCC approval is intended to assure is the output amplitude of the RF generator and modulator. If several volts of RF were available from that point, even the 60 dB isolation of the antenna switch might be insufficient to avoid inter-

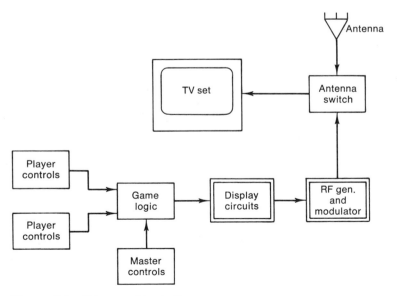

Figure 3.1 TV game block diagram.

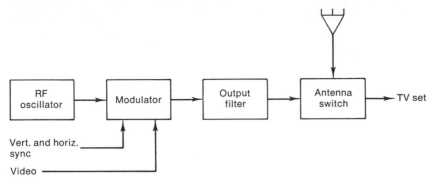

Figure 3.2 RF interface for TV games.

ference. Most TV game manufacturers limit the output of the RF generator and modulator to less than 500 μV.

Before describing actual circuitry, let's look at Fig. 3.2, which shows the basic functions of the block marked "RF generator and modulator" in Fig. 3.1. The RF oscillator in Fig. 3.2 is a single-transistor oscillator which may operate at either channel 3 or channel 4 (selectable by a switch), depending on the location of the viewer. Some games provide a choice between channels 2 and 3. The sine-wave RF signal from the oscillator goes to the modulator, where the vertical and horizontal synchronization signals are combined with the video signals and amplitude-modulate the RF. The modulated signal is then passed through an output filter which limits the output to the desired TV channel frequency band. In more sophisticated TV games, the color subcarrier and the audio carrier are also combined in the modulator section.

A typical circuit for an RF oscillator-modulator and output filter is shown in Fig. 3.3. Transistor Q_1 is the oscillator for channel 3 or channel 4. For channel 4, the higher frequency, the resonant circuit consists of the adjustable coil L_1 and capacitor C_1, going from the collector to the emitter. When S_1 is closed, capacitors C_2 and C_3 are connected across C_1. This will lower the frequency of the oscillator close to the desired channel 3. The trimmer capacitor C_3 permits precise adjustment of the oscillator for channel 3.

While some TV games use diode modulators, the circuit shown in Fig. 3.3 modulates the RF oscillator's amplitude directly by applying the combined video signal across the emitter resistor R_3. The video signal and the vertical and horizontal synchronizing and blanking portions are obtained from the integrated circuit containing the display portion. These signals are combined at the base of transistor Q_2, which acts as emitter-follower, to drive the emitter of the RF oscillator Q_1. The output filter is comprised of L_2 and C_4 and is, in effect, a low-pass filter. It eliminates the higher harmonics of the oscillator. Because the modulator in this circuit varies the RF oscillator amplitude directly, fewer harmonics are generated. In diode modulators, the generation of harmonics can be much more of a problem, and the output filters for those circuits are generally more complex.

The problem of interference is usually attacked by a combination of shielding, grounding, and filtering. Most of the antenna switches are shielded, and most of the RF generator and modulator sections of electronic games are also shielded, with all of the shielding connected to a common ground. Some TV game manufacturers have included the power switch for the TV game in the antenna switching box. This means that, when the switch is closed to connect the TV antenna to the TV set, the electronic game power is automatically shut off. This approach eliminates the possibility of interference when the viewer is watching a local channel, but it does not eliminate the possibility of interference with other TV sets when the viewer is using an electronic game. As previously explained, it is necessary to limit the output of the RF oscillator section to less than 500 μV. It is also necessary that the RF isolation between switch contacts exceed 60 dB. Some leakage will occur on account of the chassis mounting, the proximity of components, etc. Needless to say, the RF connection from the modulator output filter to the antenna switch should be a well-grounded coaxial cable. In order to

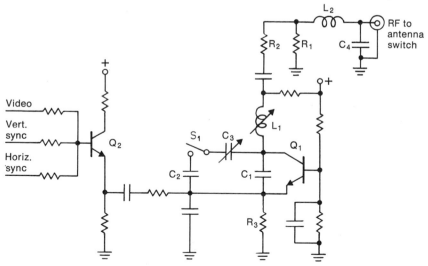

Figure 3.3 Typical RF interface circuit.

gain FCC acceptance, screen-room measurements at all TV frequencies may be required to assure that all radiation is within the specified limits.

3.2 DISPLAY CIRCUITS FOR FIXED PATTERNS

We will approach the generation of displays in a gradual way. First we will see how fixed patterns, such as the borders of a playing field, are generated, and then we will discuss how moving patterns are obtained. The two basic approaches to display generation are the analog method and the digital method. Many of the simpler electronic games use the analog method, while almost all of the microprocessor-based games use the digital method. For purposes of explanation, however, the analog method gives us a better insight into the principles of display circuits.

Analog Method

We know from Chap. 2 that the horizontal sweep circuits operate at 15,750 Hz and that this means an approximate horizontal sweep time of 64 μs. As illustrated in Fig. 3.4, the period between successive horizontal blanking and synchronizing pulses is 64 μs. In actual broadcast TV, this time period is slightly longer, but for TV games 64 μs is a convenient time frame. Six μs of the horizontal period is not used for video information because that is the time it takes for the electron beam to "fly back" from the right to the left side of the screen. This interval is known as the *horizontal blanking period.*

In Fig. 3.4 we have shown how a vertical line on the screen can be generated by the use of 2 one-shot multivibrators with a differentiating network between them. At the input to the first one-shot, point 1, the horizontal sync or blanking signal is applied to trigger the one-shot. The duration of the pulse generated by this multivibrator is determined by potentiometer A. As illustrated by the waveforms of Fig. 3.4, this results in a rectangular signal having a duration A. When this signal, appearing at point 2, is passed through the differentiator, it looks like the signal shown at point 3. At the rising edge of the pulse, the differentiated signal goes positive, and at the falling edge it goes negative. The second one-shot is driven by this signal and is arranged so that it fires on a negative-going pulse. Potentiometer B determines the width of the pulse generated by this one-shot. The output of the second one-shot is shown at 4.

To generate a complete video signal for one line, the horizontal sync and blanking signal appearing at 1 must be combined with the video signal appearing at 4, and this is done through a simple amplifier, with the resulting waveform shown at 5. Note that the horizontal blanking pulse is a positive-going pulse, while the video signal is a negative-going pulse. The distance between the horizontal blanking pulse and the start of the video pulse is determined by potentiometer *A*, and the width of this video signal is determined by potentiometer *B*.

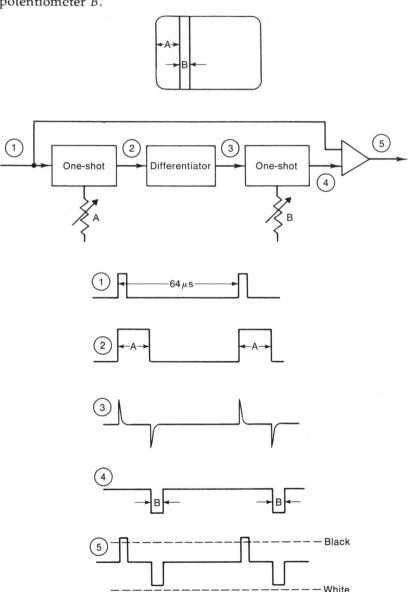

Figure 3.4 Vertical-stripe generator.

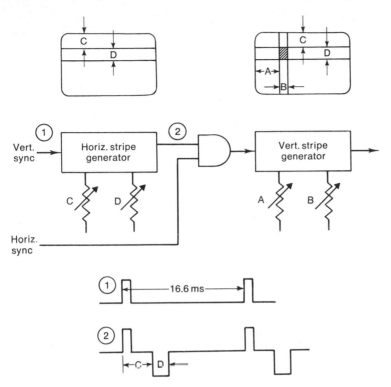

Figure 3.5 Rectangular dot generator.

Therefore, with the proper polarities arranged in the TV set, a vertical line will appear with a width B at a distance A from the left side. Every horizontal line will go "white" at the same point, and this, of course, results in a white vertical stripe. Additional white vertical stripes can be generated either by providing additional one-shots or by arranging for the first one-shot to be triggered from the output of the second one-shot as well. Another method would be to have each one-shot arranged as a fixed-period multivibrator, operating at a multiple of the horizontal synchronizing and blanking pulse and locked to this pulse. Some of the pattern generators used for aligning color TV sets operate in this manner.

Vertical lines are generated by triggering multivibrators from the horizontal synchronizing signal. Similarly, horizontal lines can be generated by triggering one-shots from the vertical synchronizing and blanking signal as illustrated in Fig. 3.5. Here you see the same kind of setup as shown in Fig. 3.4, triggered by the vertical sync and having two potentiometers, C and D. This results in an output at point 2 (Fig. 3.5), which contains a video pulse located C μs away from the top of the picture and D μs wide. The vertical frequency is

60 Hz, which means that the period between vertical pulses is approximately 16.6 ms. Again, a number of variations of the circuit can be used to generate a number of horizontal stripes.

If we wish to generate a rectangular dot, such as the one used to indicate the paddle in a TV ping-pong game, we can combine a horizontal-stripe generator and a vertical-stripe generator as illustrated in Fig. 3.5. The same circuit, depending on the setting of the potentiometers, can, of course, also generate a square dot. The combination of the horizontal-stripe generator (triggered by the vertical sync) and the vertical-stripe generator (triggered by the horizontal sync) only requires an AND gate, which allows the horizontal sync to enter only when the horizontal stripe is being generated. It is possible to build a complete game of tennis, hockey, squash, etc., out of a one-shot assembly of horizontal- and vertical-stripe generators. In actual TV games, as we shall see in Chaps. 10 and 11, many simplifications and component-saving circuits are possible.

Digital Method

In the digital method, the same displays are generated, but instead of being based on the duration of one-shot multivibrators, adjustable by potentiometers, these displays are based on digital counters. Again, a single horizontal line requires 64 μs including the retrace. If a 2-MHz clock is used, it will generate 0.5-μs pulses. If these pulses are fed into a digital counter or divider which can count up to 128, it is possible to define 128 dots in each horizontal line. In actual practice, of course, we have to account for the 6-μs retrace time, which means that twelve ½-μs pulses less are available.

We know that there are 262½ lines in every field and that there are 60 fields per second. This means that for a 2-MHz clock, a total of 33,536 clock pulses occur for every TV field. If we had a digital arrangement that would permit us to determine which of these 33,536 clock pulses would appear as a bright dot on the screen, any pattern could be displayed simply by gating the desired clock pulses through a video amplifier, which would then produce a bright spot at that time. While this may sound very complex, digital counters are important elements of microprocessor-produced TV displays.

The key digital logic block in all digital display systems is the programmable decoder. This logic function can select any of the 33,536 clock pulses, and a simplified explanation of how it works is contained in Fig. 3.6a and b. The four flip-flop stages shown at the top of Fig. 3.6a represent a simple binary counter or divider. Each flip-flop divides the input signal by 2. Figure 3.6*b* shows that the square wave applied at point *A* is twice the frequency and half the duration of that at point *B*, the output of the first flip-flop four times that of the second flip-flop *C*, and so on. While only the basic divider connections are shown in Fig. 3.6*a*, actual dividers or counters include additional gates for isolation, reset, etc.

Only a simplified portion of the logic is shown as the programmable part of the decoder in Fig. 3.6*a*. At the output OR gate, only those signals can appear which have been enabled by the control inputs 1, 2, 3, 4, and 5, as illustrated in the examples of Fig. 3.6*b*. If only *A* and *C* are enabled, double pulses at the original frequency will appear for each positive-going *C* portion. When *A*, *B*, and *C* are combined, the result is a single-pulse output at the *C* frequency because the nega-

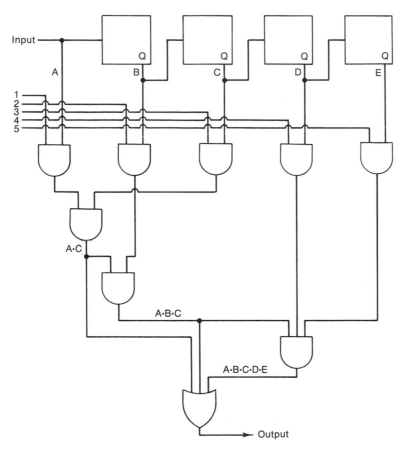

Figure 3.6a Simplified programmable decoder logic.

tive-going portion of the B signal eliminates the second A pulse. We can see from these examples that by proper application of the control signals 1, 2, 3, 4, and 5, any combination of outputs is possible. In a typical 10-bit programmable decoder the logic is much more complex and extensive, but the basic elements, a binary divider and a set of logic gates to control the output of this divider, are always the same.

All of the functional blocks required for digital monochrome video signal generation are illustrated in Fig. 3.7. Assuming a 2.0-MHz crystal-controlled clock, we can see that the divide-by-128 counter generates the video detail on a per line basis. The output of this divider is the horizontal synchronizing frequency, and that is applied to the divide-by-262 counter, which determines on which lines the video signal will appear. We have shown the outputs of the divide-by-128 counter to be from 2 to 128. In most simple TV games, the fine detail is limited, and that means that 0.5-μs pulses are not required. If 1.0-μs pulses are required, the smallest output into the logic section will be the clock frequency, 2.0 MHz, divided by 2. In the horizontal line counter, the divide-by-262 clock, we have shown only lines 40 through 234 because the lines from 1 to 40 and from 234 to 262 are usually blanked out, either as part of the vertical retrace or as the top and bottom blanking of the screen.

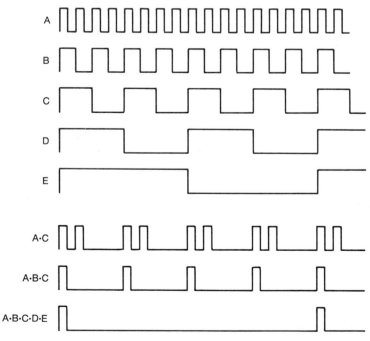

Figure 3.6b Output waveforms for Fig. 3.6*a*.

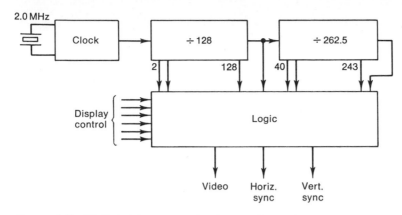

Figure 3.7 Digital video generator (monochrome).

The block marked "Logic" in Fig. 3.7 will contain a large number of gating circuits, but the input marked "Display control" does not have to have as many lines as might be expected from the illustrative example of Fig. 3.6. If 1.0-μs detail is displayed, you may think we need 64 display control lines to select the spots where we want to brighten the screen. Fortunately, 64, a binary number, can be expressed by six control lines. When we use six control lines to select any of 64 output pulses, we utilize the same binary logic principles as in the binary counter or divider. In a similar way, only eight control lines are required to determine the vertical location in terms of 256 horizontal lines. The digital video output will be a single line, with all of the various logic outputs summed up into the final video signal.

Two special logic circuits, not affected by the display control, are also contained in the logic block. One of these provides the horizontal sync and blanking signal, while the other provides the vertical sync and blanking signal. Both of these signals are obtained by taking the output of the 128- and the 262-dividers, respectively, and combining them with the appropriate pulse-width signals.

Although the logic block in Fig. 3.7 appears quite complex, modern large-scale integration (LSI) techniques permit all of it to be contained on a single IC. In some of the TV games even more circuitry, not part of the video display generation, is contained on a single IC.

So far we have considered only monochrome displays, but we know from Chap. 2 that, in order to generate color pictures, a 3.579-MHz color subcarrier must be phase-modulated and included in the transmitted signal. For TV games a 3.58-MHz crystal-controlled clock, as illustrated in Fig. 3.8, is used as the source for all of the TV signals. As mentioned above, a single IC usually contains all of the

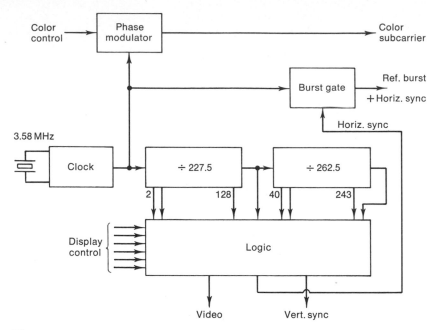

Figure 3.8 Digital video generator (color).

circuitry shown in Fig. 3.8. Note that, because the clock frequency is 3.58 MHz instead of 2.0 MHz, the clock signal is divided by 227.5 to get the horizontal scanning frequencies. To maintain the precision required for color TV, the vertical divider is also more precise and goes to 262.5. The logic and display control circuitry is essentially the same as for monochrome, but two additional components are required for color TV, the phase modulator and the color burst gate. We know from Chap. 2 that the color reference signal must be supplied to the TV receiver as an 8-cycle burst, superimposed on the horizontal blanking pulse. This is done in the burst gate by using the horizontal sync and blanking pulse of Fig. 3.8. The modulated color subcarrier receives its color information from the line marked "Color Control," which determines the phase of the 3.58-MHz reference. Most electronic games use a limited number of colors, and that means an arrangement of fixed-phase angles. More details on color phase modulation for TV games appear later in this chapter.

3.3 DISPLAY CIRCUITS FOR MOVING PATTERNS

In many respects the motion seen in TV games is similar to that used in the animated cartoons we are familiar with from the movies. A series of different pictures, each having the same stationary background, but with the moving figure slightly displaced, gives the appearance of smooth motion when projected rapidly. The only difference between the jerky motion of early movies and the smooth motion to which we are now accustomed stems from the number of individual changes that appear during a particular time frame. The same principle, sequential images which are only slightly displaced, applies to the moving patterns in electronic games. Again, two different methods, analog and digital, are used.

Analog Method

To move the dot generated in Fig. 3.5 from left to right across the screen, all we need to do is vary the potentiometer A which determines the distance from the left side of the screen. If we want to move the dot from the top to the bottom of the screen, we only have to vary potentiometer C. If we now want to move the dot from the upper left-hand corner diagonally across the screen to the lower right-hand corner, we will have to move potentiometers C and A simultaneously.

In electronic games this motion is accomplished by providing a varying voltage in place of the potentiometers A and C. Figure 3.9a shows the voltage applied at potentiometer A (Fig. 3.5), which provides the motion from left to right and from right to left. Note that the time duration is 10 s. If this voltage is applied in place of potentiometer A, we would expect the dot, the ball in a game of ping-pong or tennis, to move smoothly from left to right in 10 s and back from right to left in the following 10 s.

In Fig. 3.9b, we have shown another triangular voltage, again consisting of two segments of 10 s each. This voltage is applied instead of potentiometer C of Fig. 3.5 and provides vertical motion. The time periods of the voltages applied at A and C of Fig. 3.5 must be the same if we expect the "ball" to travel in a diagonal line.

If the relative voltage between the triangular waveforms shown in Fig. 3.9a and b were different, the ball would not travel completely

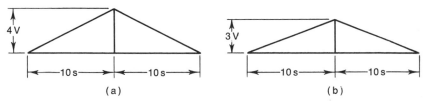

Figure 3.9 Motion signals for dot generator. (*a*) Left-right motion (A); (*b*) up-down motion (C).

diagonally but would have more or less motion in either the horizontal or the vertical direction. If the up-down motion would last only 5 s, the ball would travel in a diagonal direction for the first 5 s and then would continue to travel directly horizontally for the next 5s. If, on the other hand, the up-down motion waveform were not a straight line but a curve, the trajectory of the ball would also be curved. Depending on the waveforms used for the left-right and the up-down motion, complex trajectories can be provided for the ball. The game logic can be designed for different angles, that is, a different ratio of left-right and up-down motions, according to the location where the ball strikes the paddle. To further complicate the game, this ratio between the two triangular waves can be varied at random. A toggle switch at the game controls usually determines whether to speed up or slow down the motion by changing the 10-s duration of Fig. 3.9 to any desired number. Wherever analog motion is used, the waveforms generating this motion will be analogous to the motion itself.

Digital Method

In the digital method of displaying fixed pattern, the location of objects is determined by the instant in time at which pulses are selected by the display control. This implies that any changes in location are determined by changing the display control signals. The detailed digital technique depends on the microprocessor or on specialized logic circuits, but in each type of system motion is generated by sequentially changing the location coordinates of the object to be moved. In the digital method the rate at which the location coordinates are changed determines the speed of the object's motion. Since 60 separate fields are displayed each second, all digital motion-generating sections operate at some submultiple of the 60-Hz vertical sync signal.

   To produce the same motion as described above for the analog method by digital means, we have to decide in how many steps we should move the ball from the upper left-hand corner to the lower right-hand corner within 10 s. If we were to move it in 600 steps, one step for each 60-Hz field, we would have to provide 600 horizontal and 600 vertical changes in coordinates. This is an obvious impossibility since we have only 128 horizontal steps, based on a 2.0-MHz clock, and only 262 vertical steps, one per horizontal line. Allowing for a 6-μs retrace time, we only have 116 0.5-μs steps of locations in the horizontal direction. If we change location in 0.5-μs steps, one step each 100 ms, we will have moved the ball across a 50-μs distance from left to right in 10 s. This does not cover the entire 58-μs horizontal width of this screen, but it is sufficiently close to present an acceptable picture.

Referring back to Fig. 3.7, we have seen that the number of vertical lines that are active ranges from 40 to 234. For purposes of simplification we can assume that 200 lines are active. To traverse that distance in 10 s means that we can change from one horizontal line to the next every 50 ms. If we now look at the overall motion, we see that the ball moves in a diagonal direction but appears to have a smoother movement vertically, one change every 50 ms, than it has horizontally, one change every 100 ms. Fortunately, at this speed the human eye integrates subsequent impressions sufficiently well so that the motion will appear relatively smooth. If we moved the ball across the screen in 100 s by the same digital method, the ball would appear to jump in short steps from left to right, top to bottom.

We have seen how, in the analog method, trajectories other than straight lines or combinations of trajectories can be generated. The same trajectories can, of course, also be generated by the digital method, which merely requires a variation in the rate of change or incrementation of the display control data. As explained in subsequent chapters, for microprocessor games specific logic sections or program portions are designed to provide this kind of motion.

3.4 COLOR DISPLAY CIRCUITS

We know from Chap. 2 that the color information is transmitted by phase and amplitude modulation of the 3.579-MHz color subcarrier. Earlier in this chapter we have seen that the 3.579-MHz crystal provides the basic clock for the digital-display generating circuits in color TV games. At that time we mentioned two special functions essential for adding color to TV games. One of these was the color phase modulator, and the other was the color reference burst circuit. The color reference burst is simply 8 or 10 cycles of the color reference frequency, gated and superimposed on the blanking pedestal of each horizontal blanking pulse, as explained in Chap. 2. This function is usually contained in one of the display ICs.

The second circuit, the color phase modulator, deserves more discussion. As we know from Chap. 2, the phase angle and the amplitude of the color subcarrier determine the hue and saturation of the color on the screen. For broadcast color TV pictures, the phase angle and amplitudes are constantly changing as the three electron beams sweep across the screen of the color picture tube. TV games ordinarily use only a few, fixed colors. As a typical example, the background of a playing field may be green, the ball may be white, and the respective paddles may be red or blue. In some of the games, such as horse racing and tank battles, different players are assigned different colors. The full gamut of colors as used in TV broadcasting is not required in any of the electronic games. Therefore it is possible to provide certain fixed colors by selecting a limited number of phase angles and amplitudes.

Figure 3.10 illustrates the key elements of color display circuits. The simplest way of shifting phase is by means of an *RC* network, illustrated in Fig. 3.10a, which can provide up to 90° of phase shift. By changing the relative values of *R* and *C*, less than 90° of phase shift can be obtained. A single-stage amplifier normally shifts the phase by 180° between input and output. An amplifier with feedback, such as the operational amplifiers available in ICs, can provide different degrees of phase shift, depending on its feedback network. In the circuit of Fig. 3.10b, we illustrate a portion of a commercially available IC, the General Instrument Co. AY-3-8500, which provides the phase angles necessary for most TV games. The 3.579-MHz signal connected to the first amplifier corresponds to cyan. This correspondence is based on tapping the reference signal at the output of the second stage, corresponding to yellow. In the color-converter section of the color display IC, the voltages corresponding to the colors cyan, green, yellow, orange, red, magenta, and blue are gated through according to the color of the objects assigned to various players. For a

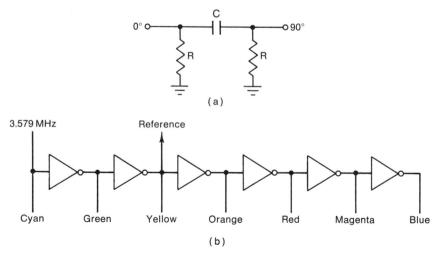

Figure 3.10 IC color phase generator. (*a*) *R-C* phase shifter; (*b*) typical IC phase shifter.

different game, it is only necessary to tap the subcarrier reference signal at a different point, and an entirely different set of colors will now be available. As the viewer switches to a different game, different colors are automatically assigned to different objects.

In order to display the correct color, the control logic or microprocessor must gate the respective 3.579-MHz phase signal onto the composite video signal during the time the particular object is being displayed. ICs are available in which this function is performed automatically. In broadcast TV the color information (hue and saturation) is transmitted over the color subcarrier. The brightness, or luminance, information, however, is transmitted as part of the monochrome signal. In TV games a monochrome signal must also be generated, and this corresponds, as in broadcast TV, to the brightness signal used for monochrome games. It is important that the luminance signal have the correct amplitude to assure that the colors will not appear excessively bright. Excessive brightness on monochrome or color TV could damage the picture tubes because game objects may remain fixed for long periods of time.

Different IC manufacturers use variations of the technique described here, but basically they all generate a limited number of phase vectors, which are then selected to color the desired objects in the display.

3.5 SPECIAL DISPLAY EFFECTS

Random start, location, or motion of an object are important features in many electronic games. Similarly, collisions between ball and bat, racing automobiles, or other competing objects are also important display features. Changes in the size of the objects as they appear to come closer, changes in the appearance of objects as they turn, the display of alphanumerics, and similar features can also be considered as special display effects. In actual practice, however, these special effects are part of the logic control function rather than the display. In microprocessor-controlled games all of the more complex special effects of this type, particularly the detection of collisions of moving objects, size changes, etc., are determined by the program. For this reason these types of special effects are covered in Chap. 8.

One of the most dramatic special display effects, often used in arcade (coin-operated) games, makes use of a partially silvered mirror and allows a fixed "background" display to be superimposed on the TV picture (Fig. 3.11). A good example of this type of special effect is a hunting game in monochrome in which the targets move across the TV screen, with trees and bushes in color optically superimposed on the TV screen. The forest scenery is printed or silk-screened on a piece of glass and illuminated from the back. The viewer, looking at the TV set through the half-silvered mirror, can see the moving TV display and at the same time see the forest as background scenery. The amount of illumination on the TV picture tube and from the forest scene must be properly balanced to give the right effect. To change to another type of game we simply extinguish the light source for the forest display, and only the TV screen will be visible. This type of display requires that the TV tube as well as the background display and the half-silvered mirror all be contained in a lightproof box.

Whether the game is called hunting or target shooting, one of the additional accessories is the rifle. A simple optical system in the rifle barrel focuses a narrow beam of light, from the illuminated target on the TV set, onto a photocell. An amplifier is followed by two logic circuits, one to generate a brief pulse while the light is visible, and the second to generate a brief pulse when the trigger is pressed. When the two pulses coincide, a hit is indicated. When the trigger is pressed without the light-detection pulse occurring, a miss is scored. In some TV games, particularly the more expensive coin-operated ones, the target disappears or appears to "fly apart" as the result of a hit.

A widely used special effect is the flashing of a score or some other part of the game display. In order to generate this effect, the display rate for the item to be flashed is interrupted at a frequency of one to three times per second. Different flashing rates may be provided in some games to indicate different functions.

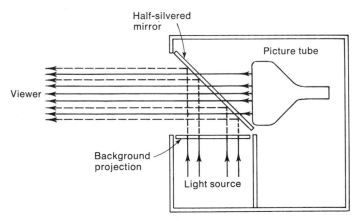

Figure 3.11   Half-silvered mirror for special effects.

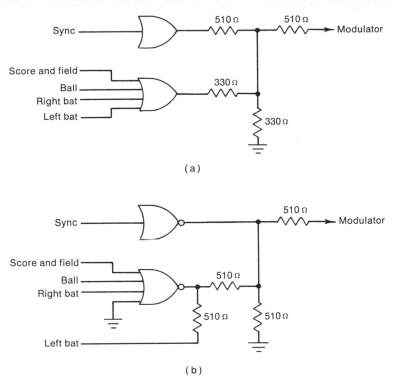

Figure 3.12 Typical special effects circuits. (*a*) Black or white background; (*b*) black and white on grey background.

A special effect that is now available in a variety of games, control-logic- as well as microprocessor-operated, is the ability to reverse the video polarity of selected portions of the display. Figure 3.12 illustrates the circuit for a typical game in which the score, field, ball, and right and left bats or rackets all appear as black on a white screen background. As illustrated in Fig. 3.12*a*, the four video signals are combined through a simple OR gate with the sync signal, which is obtained through another OR gate. The composite video signal is then connected to the modulator. Note the relative amplitudes of the signals as provided by the mixing resistors. By using the combiner circuit of Fig. 3.12*b*, a grey background is obtained instead of a white one, and one of the bats will be bright white and the other bat, as well as the score and field boundary indication and the ball, will appear black. In this circuit NOR gates are used instead of OR gates, and the left bat video signal goes directly to the output of the NOR gate, summing the three video levels. Note also the difference in

mixing resistors for this circuit. This is important in order to estab-
lish the background level of the screen. Again, the output of the
mixing network is supplied to the modulator.

From the circuit of Fig. 3.12 it becomes apparent that, by choosing
the polarity and relative amplitude of different portions of the video
signal, it is possible to arrange a large variety of black, white, grey
combinations for display objects. As was discussed in Sec. 3.4 of this
chapter, a similar variation can be obtained when color is used in a
TV game.

3.6 TYPICAL DISPLAY CIRCUITS

Although the details of individual video display circuits vary with
different electronic games, they can be characterized by either of the
two examples presented here. The first example is typical of the
simpler, logic-controlled games and shows the video portion of the
popular Magnavox Odyssey game. The second example comes from
the RCA Studio II family and is typical of the more sophisticated

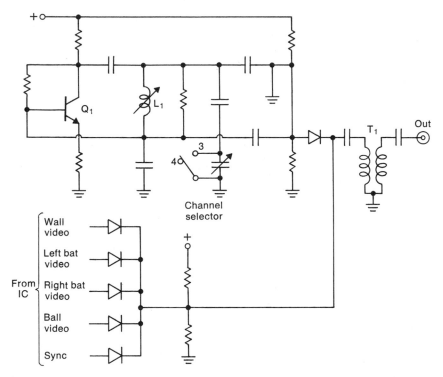

Figure 3.13 Display circuit: Magnavox Odyssey.

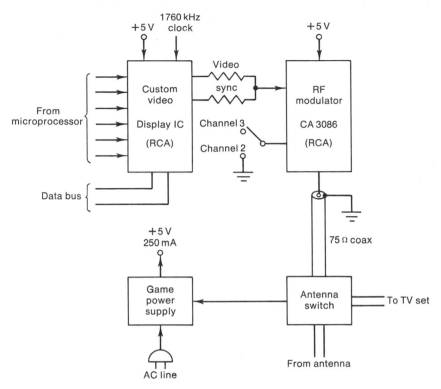

Figure 3.14 Display circuit: RCA Studio II.

microprocessor-controlled games. The entire Magnavox Odyssey game is contained on a single IC, with separate transistors providing the 2.0-MHz clock, voltage regulation, audio amplification, and, most important for this example, the RF oscillator.

As illustrated in Fig. 3.13, four separate video signals, the left and right bats, the ball, and the game pattern (wall), are obtained from the IC and summed together through four diodes. The combined horizontal and vertical sync signal is added, and the total is then applied to a diode modulator. Note that the RF oscillator is tuned by a single coil, L_1, and that either channel 3 or channel 4 can be selected, depending on whether a trimmer capacitor is shorted out or left in the circuit. The output of the RF oscillator is applied to a diode which also acts as the modulator. A filter circuit, consisting of capacitors and the double-tuned transformer, limits the output to the desired frequency band, either channel 3 or channel 4.

The display circuit of RCA's Studio II consists, essentially, of two separate ICs, as illustrated in Fig. 3.14. Six control leads from the microprocessor actuate the custom video display IC, which is also connected to the 8-bit data bus. The video display IC operates on a 1760-kHz clock. All of the different video signals are combined within the IC, and only two external resistors are used to combine the video with the horizontal and vertical sync. The composite video signal goes directly into the RF oscillator and modulator IC, an RCA type CA 3086. Selection of the RF channel is governed by the switches for channel 2 or channel 3. A 75-Ω coax line goes from that IC directly to the antenna switching box. When the switch is set to connect the external antenna directly to the TV set, the game power supply is automatically shut off. The Magnavox Odyssey game, on the other hand, can be either battery-operated or connected to an external power source, but it does not shut off when the antenna switch is set for TV reception.

3.7 TROUBLESHOOTING DISPLAY CIRCUITS

Chapter 12 is devoted to the troubleshooting of all portions of all types of electronic games, but at this time we want to cover trouble-shooting of those specific defects that originate in the display portion.

If you look at the block diagram in Fig. 3.1, it becomes apparent what kind of defects can occur in the antenna switch, the RF generator and modulator, and the display circuits themselves. The trouble-shooting chart of Table 3.1 is intended as a quick reference rather than the ultimate troubleshooting guide. It covers the three most likely symptoms caused by defects in the display portion. The absence of any pattern on the TV screen may be due to the antenna switch, the RF oscillator, the modulator, or the display IC itself. Antenna switch defects are almost always limited to poor contact either in the switching box itself or in its connections. If the antenna switch also controls ac power, a defect in that connection can cause the loss of pattern on the TV screen.

When the RF oscillator itself is either at the wrong frequency or not oscillating, RF signals cannot reach the TV set. To determine whether the RF oscillator is working or not, dc voltage measurements or tests of the oscillator transistor, or IC and its components, will determine where the defect is. If you have a high-gain oscilloscope with an RF-detecting probe, you can see whether there is any RF output at all. Since the normal RF output amplitude is less than 500 μV, considerable gain in the test oscilloscope is required to provide a positive indication. The modulator itself is rarely the source of defects, but it can be either open or shorted. Checking the continuity

TABLE 3.1 DISPLAY CIRCUIT TROUBLESHOOTING CHART

Symptom	Location	Defect	Test
No pattern on TV	Antenna switch	Poor contact	Continuity on switch, leads, connectors, TV terminals
No pattern on TV	Antenna switch	No ac power	Continuity on switch, leads to power supply, ac cord
No pattern on TV	RF oscillator	Wrong frequency	Channel switch, tuning
No pattern on TV	RF oscillator	Not oscillating	DC voltages, transistor, IC, and other components
No pattern on TV	Modulator	Open or shorted	Continuity of modulator, check video with oscilloscope
No pattern on TV	Display IC	No output	DC voltages, check video, and control signals
Pattern not synchronized	Display IC or modulator	Loss of sync pulses	Check sync with oscilloscope, check clock input
Display portions missing or wrong	Display IC or control signals	Partial loss of video	Signal trace video with oscilloscope, move controls and check action with oscilloscope, check control signals

of the modulator circuit and observing the video input with an oscilloscope will help to locate that kind of defect.

If the display IC itself is defective, there will be no output. DC voltages and oscilloscope checks of the video, synchronization, and control signals will help in troubleshooting this type of defect.

When the RF oscillator and the antenna switch operate correctly, but no video signal is available to modulate the output, it is often possible to use the TV set to determine if some RF is received. To do this, connect the TV antenna directly to the TV set, and also connect the antenna switch to the same TV set terminals. With the TV set tuned to a regular broadcast channel and the RF oscillator tuned to the same channel, some interference should be observable when the TV game is turned on and off.

Loss of synchronization can be established when we see some pattern floating or weaving across the TV screen. This symptom is almost always due to a loss of sync pulses in the TV game. Either vertical or horizontal or both sync pulses may be missing or of the wrong polarity. When you observe this symptom, you know that the video and RF portions are working. Checking the appearance of the sync signals with the oscilloscope is the best way to isolate this type of defect.

When some portion of the game display is missing, such as one of the paddles, a ball, or some portion of the boundary marking, the course is likely to be wrong or missing control signals at the display IC. Ordinarily this type of defect originates in the control logic or microprocessor portions. In rare instances the display IC itself or some of the connections to it may be defective.

The troubleshooting chart included in this chapter covers more than 90% of all the problems normally encountered in the RF, modulation, and display circuit portions. For those rare instances where the trouble is more complex, or where it is intermittent, a thorough troubleshooting procedure must be used. Chapter 12 contains suggestions for those hard-to-find troubles.

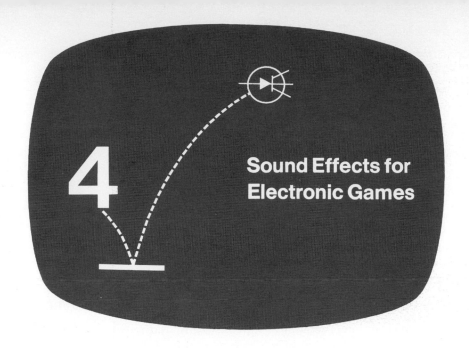

4

Sound Effects for Electronic Games

Picture if you can what it was like to go to the movies in the early 1900s before the advent of "the talkies," and you'll have some idea of the importance of sound effects in today's electronic games. The addition of sound to these games provides excitement, realism, and an additional dimension which greatly helps to maintain player interest and maximize enjoyment of the game.

Most sounds that we hear are complex in nature and contain both harmonic (sinusoidal) and noise components. Thus, in principle at least, it should be possible to synthesize any particular sound, be it a muscial instrument, voice, or special effect, by appropriately combining a sine wave or group of sine waves together with a specific amount of random noise. An overall block diagram for a typical sound synthesizer is given in Fig. 4.1. Note that the relative amplitude of each of the components is adjusted to the proper level by spectrally filtering the individual signals and that the resulting composite waveform is then passed through some type of envelope modulator to provide the needed variations in the temporal characteristic for the particular sound.

In this chapter we will consider the general methods employed in the synthesis of electronically generated sounds. Since most readers have probably had little experience with these techniques, we will

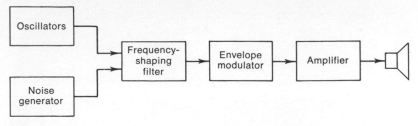

Figure 4.1 General form of a sound synthesizer.

first examine how they have been applied to electronic music generation, an area with which the reader will no doubt be more familiar,
before discussing how these methods are currently being applied in
today's electronic games.

4.1 GENERAL ASPECTS OF THE SOUND SYNTHESIS PROCEDURE

Humans can detect acoustical signals having frequencies in the range
from about 20 Hz to 20 kHz. These signals, when generated, travel
through the air as vibrational waves, and when they strike the
surface of the eardrum they create a corresponding neural signal that
we know as "sound." The periodic sound wave shown in Fig. 4.2a is
a 1-kHz sine wave and is in fact a signal rarely occurring in nature.
As such, this type of sound would be perceived by the ear as being
crisp and clear but somewhat unnatural. Most sounds commonly
encountered are much more complex and contain multiple frequency
components as well as some measure of added random noise.

If the frequency components are integral multiples of one another,
the components are said to be harmonically related. As an example
consider a sound waveform composed of four frequency elements at
$f_0 = 1$ kHz, $f_1 = 2$ kHz, $f_2 = 3$ kHz, and $f_3 = 4$ kHz. Here the element
f_0 is known as the fundamental, f_1 as the first harmonic (or first
overtone), f_2 as the second harmonic (second overtone), etc. When
the frequency components are not integral multiples of one another,
they are called *anharmonic signals.*

Generally, in musical instruments and other acoustical generation
devices, the sound components produced are related in some way to
the size or shape of the sound source. Consider for example the
sound that results from the plucking of a guitar string (Fig. 4.2b). As
might be expected, the frequency of vibration of the string is a direct
function of the string length, thickness, and tension. In addition, the
particular shape of the vibratory pattern generated (and the resulting
amplitude of the acoustical harmonic components produced) is
strongly affected by the position along its length where it is plucked.

However, this does not alter which frequency components will be present, but only how prominent they are.

A similar situation exists for nonmusical sound sources. Consider, for example, the spectral characteristics of the sound produced by a propeller-driven aircraft (Fig. 4.2c). As the reader might expect, the

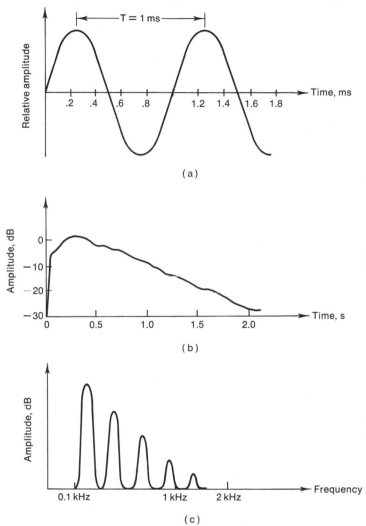

(a)

(b)

(c)

Figure 4.2 Examples of acoustical signal sources. (*a*) A 1-kHz sinusoidal signal. (*b*) Sound produced by a guitar string (released at *t* = 0). (*Adapted from Alan Douglas, Electronic Music Production,* Tab Books, 1973.) (*c*) Spectral characteristics of sound produced by a propeller-driven aircraft. (*Adapted from A. Reigler et al., JASA 25, 1953, p. 395.*)

fundamental frequency of the sound emitted from this type of source is solely determined by the speed of the engine and the number of blades on the propeller. However, the harmonic content of the resulting sound wave produced is dependent on the actual shape of the acoustical pressure wave generated as the propeller cuts through the air, and this of course varies with the pitch and general shape of the blades as well as with the acoustical properties of the air in which the plane is traveling.

From even this brief introduction to sound sources, it is clear that the sounds they emit can be quite complex. Thus, while the design of a circuit to reproduce any specific sound effect could certainly be accomplished, the development of any general-purpose sound synthesis system would appear, at best, to represent a formidable design task. Fortunately, this is not strictly the case.

In order to more fully understand how to proceed with such a design, it will first be necessary to examine the spectral characteristics of complex sound waves and to note that any complex nonsinusoidal waveform may be constructed from a superposition of sine waves. Stated another way, this means that *any* complex periodic waveform may be synthesized by adding a sine wave having the same fundamental frequency as this wave together with an appropriate combination of harmonics of the fundamental frequency. Naturally, each of the signal components must have the proper amplitude and phase relationship to the fundamental to accurately reproduce the original waveform. This group of sinusoidal components is known as the *Fourier series* representation of the original waveform. The spectral characteristics (Fourier series components) of several of the more common waveforms are given in Fig. 4.3. Note that, since the higher-order harmonic terms have rapidly decreasing amplitudes, a fair representation of the original waveform can usually be obtained by combining the fundamental with just the first few harmonics. This waveform construction process is shown in Fig. 4.4 for the case of a square wave.

Thus, in principle, a sound synthesizer (at least for periodic waveforms) could be constructed by simply interconnecting a bank of sine-wave oscillators, phase shifters, and amplitude scalers. However, it is readily apparent that this approach is not all that simple, especially when one considers that it might be necessary to change the pitch of the signal generated. To accomplish this some form of voltage-controlled oscillator (VCO) would be required, with control voltages applied to each of the sine-wave oscillators to shift the pitch of the overall waveform. Clearly there would be a monumental tracking problem associated with the synchronous shifting of the

TIME-COURSE OF WAVEFORM

SPECTRA OF WAVEFORM
(relative harmonic amplitude)

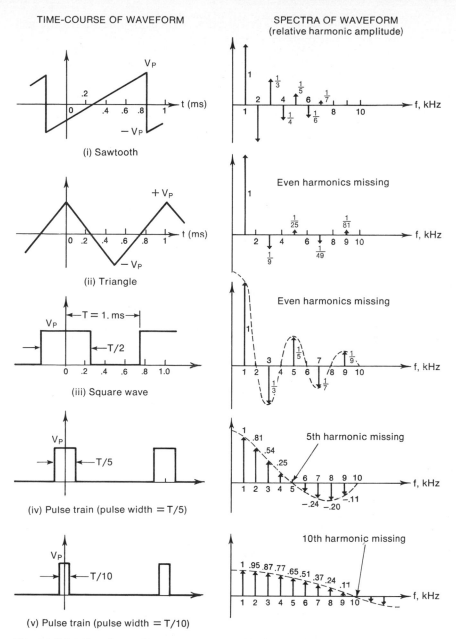

(i) Sawtooth

(ii) Triangle

(iii) Square wave

(iv) Pulse train (pulse width = T/5)

(v) Pulse train (pulse width = T/10)

Figure 4.3 Fourier series components of some of the more common periodic waveforms.

fundamental and each of its harmonics, which, coupled with the fact
that the ear is particularly sensitive to these types of errors, makes
this method wholly unsuitable.

Instead, what is usually done is to make use of a single voltage-
controlled master oscillator, which produces several different types
of output waveforms, with the Fourier series content of these signals
serving as the source for the fundamental component and the various
harmonics needed to create the particular sound. By appropriately
filtering and combining these building-block waveforms together, it
is possible to accurately match the spectral characteristics of nearly
any specific sound (Fig. 4.5). Note too that to change the pitch of the
waveform produced by this system, only a single VCO control voltage needs to be varied and that this variation automatically shifts the

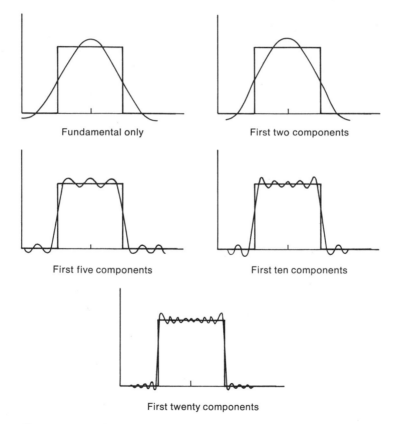

Fundamental only

First two components

First five components

First ten components

First twenty components

Figure 4.4 Waveform construction from the Fourier series
components.

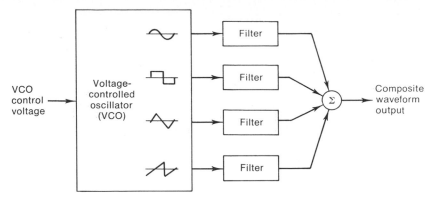

Figure 4.5 Sound synthesizer employing a pure Fourier series approach (a) and a single multiwaveform voltage-controlled oscillator (b).

frequencies of the fundamental and of all harmonics of the waveform. This assures perfect tracking of all the generated frequency components and guarantees that the general shape of the spectral characteristics will be preserved even though the base frequency is shifted.

However, the spectral characteristics of a sound are not its only distinguishing feature. Two acoustical signals can have very similar frequency components and yet can sound very different if the time course of the two waveforms is not the same. In comparing the envelopes of different sounds, it is frequently useful to divide the envelope (at least as an initial approximation) into three distinct regions, known as the waveform's attack, steady-state, and decay times (Fig. 4.6a). Thus, for example, as shown in Fig. 4.6b, the sound emitted when a particular key is struck on a piano is characterized by a rapid attack, zero steady state, and a relatively long decay time. A similar situation exists for the guitar (Fig. 4.2b), except that its attack and decay times are somewhat shorter. However, on comparing these sound waveforms with those produced by the flute or the organ, for example, we would see a marked difference in their envelope characteristics, even though their spectral patterns are similar. Each of the latter instruments is characterized by a long steady-state or sustain time, determined by the breath-holding capability of the player in the case of the flute or by the length of time that the key is depressed in the case of the organ. Clearly the sounds produced in the latter two cases, while possessing certain similarities, are for the most part vastly different. Thus in developing a sound synthesizer, careful attention must be given to both the spectral and temporal

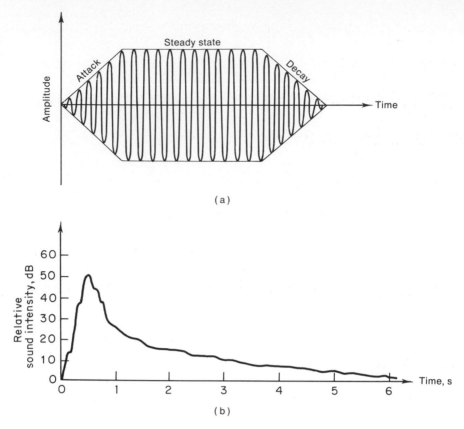

Figure 4.6 (*a*) A simple linear waveform envelope; (*b*) form of the sound produced by a piano.

characteristics of the sound to be duplicated. Along these lines, a general-purpose sound synthesizer system should contain:

1. One or more voltage-controlled oscillators producing a multiplicity of output waveforms (typically sine, triangle, and square are adequate, but the presence of pulse, sawtooth, and ramp waveforms is useful).

2. A white-noise source.

3. Filtering circuits to modify the spectral characteristics of the input waveform.

4. Envelope shaping circuits to modify the temporal characteristics of the waveform.

5. A controller circuit to generate all of the proper electrical control signals in response to a request for the generation of a particular sound.

In Sec. 4.2 we discuss the design of specific circuits for each one of the building blocks needed for constructing this general-purpose sound synthesizer system.

4.2 SPECIFIC CIRCUITS FOR SOUND EFFECTS GENERATION

One of the most important circuits used in nearly every sound effects synthesizer is the VCO waveform generator. A decade ago the construction of this circuit would have represented a formidable engineering task. Today, however, devices performing these functions may be purchased in a single IC package at a cost of under $5 in single quantities. One particular example of this type of IC is the 8038 waveform generator produced by Intersil Corporation. An overall block diagram of the internal circuitry is given in Fig. 4.7.

In order to understand how a typical VCO operates, consider the simpler, three-IC version of this circuit presented in Fig. 4.8a. Here, IC_1 functions as a buffer or voltage follower and IC_3 as a Schmitt trigger or level detector. For the case where $R_3 = 2R_4 = 10$ kΩ, this latter circuit has a hysteresis characteristic of the form given in Fig. 4.8b. When V_2, the input to the Schmitt trigger, is very positive, the output V_3 is fixed at $+10$ V. The output remains at this value until V_2 drops below -5 V. At this point the output snaps to -10 V, where it now remains until the input V_2 again exceeds $+5$ V.

The operational amplifier IC_2, an LM3900 manufactured by National Semiconductor, is a new type of device known as a current differencing amplifier. A conventional op amp amplifies the voltage difference at the two input terminals, while this type of device amplifies the current difference. For our purposes the amplifier's equivalent circuit is essentially that given in Fig. 4.8d. Thus in the function generator circuit given in part a of the figure, IC_2 acts to integrate the difference between the currents I_2 and I_1.

When V_3 is positive, Q_1 is ON, grounding the noninverting input terminal (V_b) on IC_2 and shunting all of the current I_2' to ground, so that $I_2 = 0$. At this point $I_1' = I_2 = 0$, and IC_2 behaves like a conventional integrator to produce a ramp output given by

$$V_2 = \frac{1}{C}\int I_f \, dt = -\frac{1}{C}\int I_1 \, dt = -\frac{1}{C}\int \frac{V_{in}}{R_1} \, dt = -\frac{V_{in}\, t}{R_1 C}$$

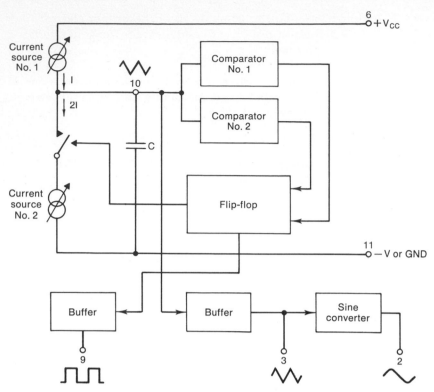

Figure 4.7 Block diagram of the Intersil 8038 waveform generator. (*Intersil Inc.*)

so that the output is linearly decreasing. When V_2 reaches -5 V, the Schmitt trigger changes states, and its output V_3 switches to -10 V. This cuts off transistor Q_1 and allows the current I_2' to enter the noninverting input terminal of the current-differencing op amp. Since $I_2 = I_2' = V_{in}/R_2$ and $I_1' = I_2$, the feedback current I_f through the capacitor is now given by $I_f = I_{1'} - I_1 = I_2 - I_1$, and thus the output voltage V_2 now begins to grow in accordance with the expression

$$V_2 = \frac{1}{C}\int (I_2 - I_1)\, dt = \frac{1}{C}\int \left(\frac{V_{in}}{R_2} - \frac{V_{in}}{R_1}\right) dt = \frac{1}{C}\left(\frac{R_1 - R_2}{R_1 R_2}\right) V_{in} t$$

Figure 4.8 (a) A three-IC voltage-controlled oscillator; (b) hysteresis curve for Schmitt trigger IC_3; (c) waveforms produced by the VCO for case $R_2 = \frac{1}{2}R_1$; (d) equivalent circuit of a current differencing amplifier; (e) ramp and pulse waveforms produced by the VCO for case $R_2 = \frac{5}{6}R_1$.

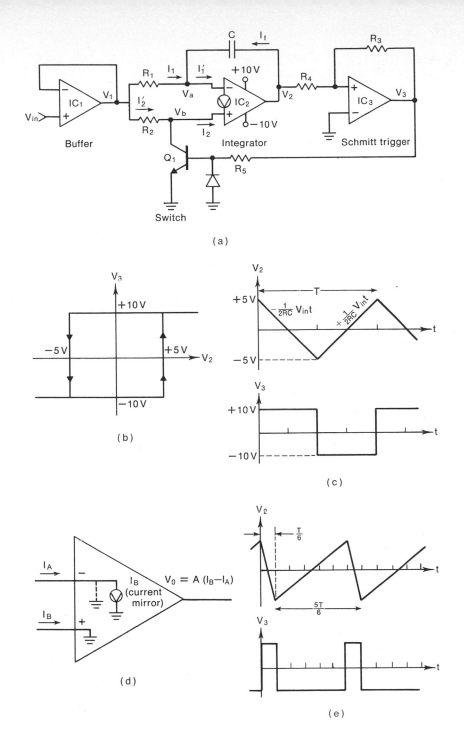

(a)

(b)

(c)

(d)

(e)

63

In particular, if $R_2 = \frac{1}{2}R_1$, then V_2 is a positive-going ramp having the same slope magnitude as before and given by

$$V_2 = \frac{V_{in}t}{2R_2C} = \frac{V_{in}t}{R_1C}$$

Thus for this case the waveform outputs will be symmetrical triangle and square waves having a frequency given by

$$f = \frac{V_{in}}{20R_1C}$$

Note that the output frequency is proportional to the applied input control voltage V_{in} and hence this circuit serves as a VCO. Of course this circuit generates only square and triangle waves, but it could, with the addition of a simple transistor wave-shaping circuit, also be used to produce sine waves. In addition, by altering the $R_1 - R_2$ resistor ratio, it is possible to produce ramps and pulse-type waveforms. A specific example of this, for the case where $R_2 = (\frac{5}{6})R_1$, is shown in Fig. 4.8e.

One other acoustical signal source frequently needed for the generation of special sound effects is the so-called *white-noise* source. This type of signal source contains a uniformly flat output frequency spectrum and gets its name from the fact that, like "white light," it is made up of all frequency components. Broadband white noise produces the familiar hissing sound when amplified and sent to a loudspeaker; properly filtered and controlled in its amplitude characteristics, it may be used to synthesize the sounds of rolling surf, jet planes, thunder, and all types of explosions. Figure 4.9 illustrates two typical circuits used for the generation of random noise signals. The circuit on the left operates by reverse-biasing the base-emitter

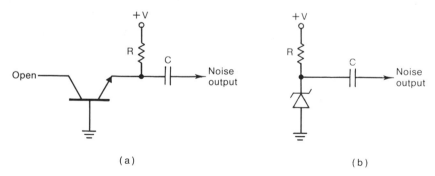

(a)   (b)

Figure 4.9 White noise sources. (a) Transistor; (b) zener diode.

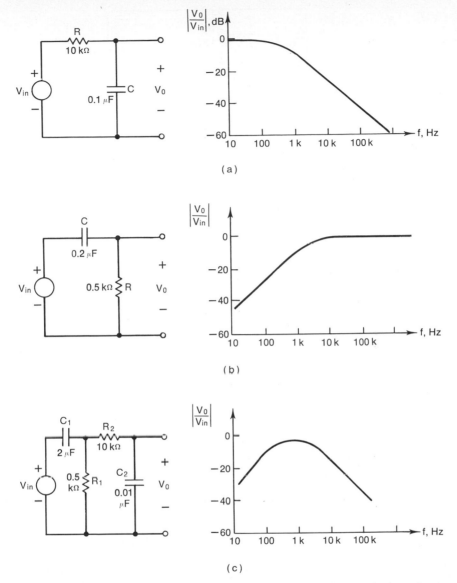

Figure 4.10 Examples of major types of filters used for producing electronic sound effects. (*a*) Low-pass; (*b*) high-pass; (*c*) bandpass.

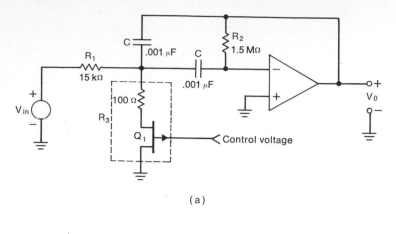

(a)

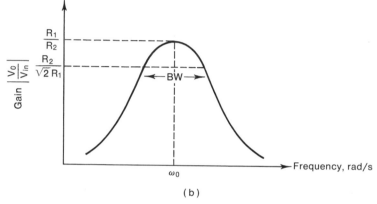

(b)

Figure 4.11 A voltage-controlled bandpass filter. (*a*) Schematic; (*b*) filter frequency response.

junction of the transistor Q in its avalanche breakdown region. Here the current that flows has a shot-noise-like character, and these random current spikes produce the uniformly flat spectral characteristic associated with white-noise sources. A similar random-noise signal may also be obtained by placing the operating point of the zener diode given in Fig. 4.9*b* at the "knee" in its zener characteristic. In both cases the noise level produced is very small, so that significant signal amplification is required.

Once the basic signal has been generated, particular filters are required in order to shape the signal's spectral characteristic into the proper final form. Three main types of filters are of interest for sound-effect applications: these are the low-pass, high-pass, and bandpass filters. For illustrative purposes a simple example of each type along with its corresponding spectral characteristics is given in Fig. 4.10. The filters shown in the figure are examples of passive, fixed-element circuits; that is, they are not capable of amplifying the input signal, nor can their spectral characteristics be altered without replacing the components. Often, however, in generating complex sound effects it is necessary to vary the passband characteristics of the filter as a function of time. Of course this could be done by switching in different filters, but a much more economical solution to the problem is to develop some type of voltage-controlled filter. One example of this type of circuit design is shown in Fig. 4.11.

Specifically this circuit is a bandpass amplifier whose center frequency f_0 is determined by the effective resistance R_3 of the field-effect transistor Q_1. Since the resistance of the FET is a function of the control voltage, this voltage can be used to alter the passband characteristics of the filter. The filter gain for this circuit can be shown to be given by

$$\left| \frac{V_0}{V_{in}} \right| = - \frac{\omega / R_1 C}{\sqrt{(\omega_0^2 - \omega^2)^2 + \left(\dfrac{2\omega}{R_2 C} \right)^2}}$$

where ω = input signal frequency

$$\omega_0 - \text{ center frequency of the filter } = \frac{1}{\sqrt{R_2 R_p \cdot C}}$$

$$R_p = \frac{R_1 R_3}{R_1 R_3}$$

Note that at the center frequency ($\omega = \omega_0$) the filter gain is given by the ratio $-R_2/2R_1 = -50$. In addition, the filter bandwidth is given by the expression

$$BW = \frac{2}{R_2 C}$$

and, since it is independent of R_3, is fixed at 1.33 krad/s or 212 Hz. Depending on the value of R_3, however, the center frequency varies over a large range. When the control voltage is +5 V, Q_1 is assumed to be cut off ($R_3 = \infty$, and $R_p = 15$ kΩ); for this case the filter's center frequency is at 6.66 krad/s or 1.06 kHz. When the control voltage is at zero, the FET is assumed to be on strongly and to have a resistance of 100 Ω; this shifts the filter's center frequency up to about 57.7 krad/s or 9.2 kHz. Thus as the control voltage varies from 0 to 5 V, the filter's center frequency will sweep back and forth between 1 and 9 kHz,

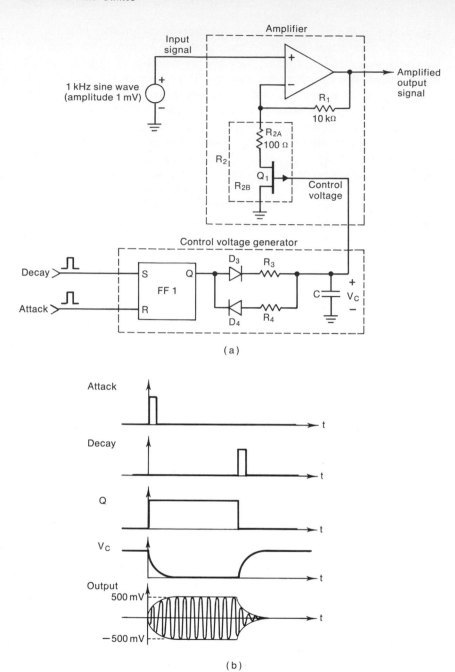

(a)

(b)

Figure 4.12 A voltage-controlled amplifier.

while its amplitude and bandwidth remain fixed at 50 and 200 Hz, respectively.

A similar electronic circuit may also be employed to construct a voltage-controlled amplifier (Fig. 4.12). To understand how this circuit operates, consider that the S-R flip-flop FF_1 is initially set ($Q = 1$) so that the control voltage V_c is high (+5 V), and therefore the P-channel FET Q_1 is cut off. For these conditions the gain of the amplifier, given by the expression $(1 + R_1/R_2)$, is 1, since R_2 is essentially an infinite resistance, and thus a 1-mV amplitude sine wave appears at the amplifier output.

When an "attack pulse" is received (see Fig. 4.12b), the flip-flop is reset, D_4 conducts, and the capacitor C discharges toward zero with a time constant R_4C. During this part of the cycle D_3 is reverse biased. As the control voltage falls to zero, the FET begins to turn on and its resistance falls. When $V_c = 0$ the FET resistance is 100 Ω, and the amplifier gain, $1 + R_1/R_2$, is about 500. At this point the amplifier will "sustain" its amplified 500-mV output signal until the FET is returned to the off state. To initiate the decay portion of the cycle, a master controller circuit (not shown in the figure) generates a decay pulse which is used to set the flip-flop. When Q goes HI, D_3 conducts, causing the control voltage V_c to rise with a time constant R_3C. This of course cuts off the FET and returns the amplifier to the low-gain, or off, condition. The reader should note that since the control-voltage rise- and fall-time constants are not the same, the waveform attack and decay times may be individually controlled by adjusting R_3 and R_4, respectively. In addition, the sustain period is determined by the spacing between the attack and decay pulses.

4.3 GENERATING SPECIFIC SOUND EFFECTS FOR VIDEO GAMES

Interestingly enough, the complex sounds employed in video games seem to be mostly aggressive in nature. Thus, except for the simple "pong"-type paddle and wall noises discussed in Chap. 8, all of the required sounds seem to have something to do with shooting and/or killing an enemy, whether on foot or in a plane, boat, submarine, or spaceship. In this section we will discuss techniques for generating four specific game sound effects:

1. A gunshot

2. A jet plane

3. A flying saucer

4. A propeller-driven aircraft

In each case an attempt will be made to explain the operation of the circuits described in terms of the spectral and temporal characteristics of the sounds being simulated.

Probably one of the most often used video-game sound effects is that associated with the explosive firing of a weapon. With slight tailoring of its spectral characteristics, one basic circuit can be employed to synthesize sounds corresponding to gunshots, machine guns, cannons, and other larger explosive devices.

The sound produced by a gunshot is basically an impulse or high-pressure acoustical signal lasting for a relatively short period of time. As such, it has spectral characteristics similar to those given in Fig. 4.3 for the narrow pulse; that is, it contains a very wide spectrum of frequencies during the time that it is on. A plot of the frequency spectrum associated with a pistol shot is given in Fig. 4.13. In actually synthesizing a gunshot sound, a circuit of the form illustrated in Fig. 4.14 is often employed.

When the gun is fired, the mechanical actuator switch S_1 momentarily closes (a 75-ms closure time appears good), and the power supply voltage builds up exponentially at point A with a time constant approximately given by the $R_1 \cdot C_1$ product. Using the component values given in the figure, this time constant is about 10 ms. As the supply voltage increases, the collector voltage also rises exponentially toward a value of about 8 V, since the steady-state collector current is about 0.2 mA for the circuit components shown.

As the transistor enters the active region, it also begins to amplify

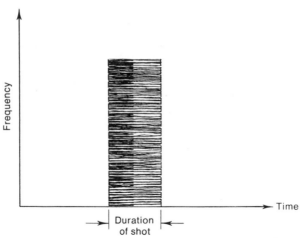

Figure 4.13 Spectral characteristics of a pistol shot. (Darkness indicates relative amplitude.) (*Adapted from W. E. Kock, Seeing Sound, Wiley-Interscience, 1971.*)

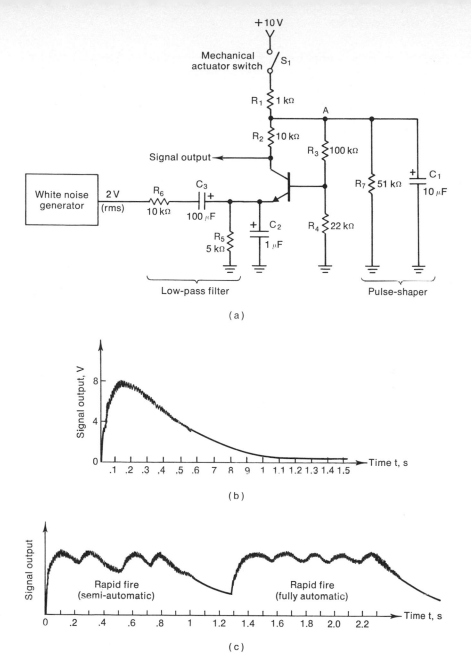

Figure 4.14 (a) Gun-shot sound effect synthesizer circuit. *(Adapted from a similar circuit given in W. E. Olliges et al., Solid State Sound Effect Generating System, U.S. Patent 3,831,172, Aug. 20, 1974.)* (b) Composite collector waveform produced by the gunshot circuit in response to a 75-ms actuator signal. (c) Output produced when simulating automatic weapon firing.

71

the white-noise signal being injected at its emitter. The signal gain from emitter to collector for this specific circuit is about 1. The composite waveform appearing at the collector output is given in Fig. 4.14b. Note that the impulse decays much more slowly than it rises, with a time constant of 200 ms given approximately by $[(R_3 + R_4) \| R_7] \cdot C_1$. This lingering of the gunshot sound creates a realistic reverberation effect.

By simply replacing the one-shot mechanical contact closure with one producing a square-wave-like closure and release pattern, this same circuit can be used to simulate the firing of an automatic or semiautomatic weapon. The collector-signal waveform associated with each of these weapons is illustrated in Fig. 4.14c.

A slight modification of this circuit results in the generation of a sound effect more closely associated with that of an explosion or cannon firing. To accomplish this, a low-pass filter is added at the output of the noise source, as shown in Fig. 4.15, to emphasize the lower-frequency components in the noise signal, and in addition resistor R_7 in the basic circuit given in Fig. 4.14a is removed to increase the decay time. Both of these changes tend to enhance the "booming" effect of the sound and make it more closely simulate that associated with an explosion.

This same circuit can also be used to produce a completely different type of sound effect—that corresponding to a steam locomotive. To achieve this, the mechanical actuator used with the circuit in Fig. 4.14 is simply bypassed, and the power supply voltage provided by a low-frequency square-wave generator. For this case the attack and decay time constants of the waveform are both the same. A 3-Hz square wave produces a "puffing" sound similar to that of a train just pulling out of the station, and an increase in this frequency to about 10 Hz makes the sound emitted resemble that of a train moving at

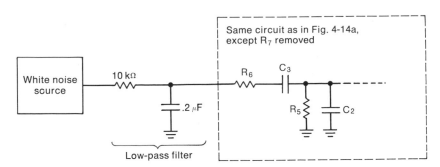

Figure 4.15 Generating an explosive or cannonlike sound. (*Adapted from Kock, Seeing Sound, Fig. 4.14.*)

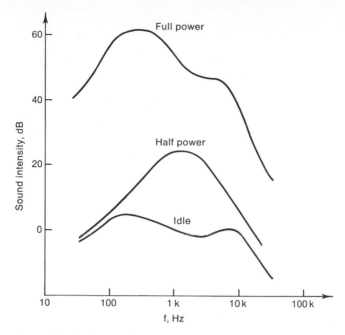

Figure 4.16 Typical jet engine sound spectra.

normal speed. The train can be programmed to accelerate at a given rate by generating the square wave signal in a VCO.

Many video games employ various types of aircraft. Figure 4.16 indicates the spectrum of sounds emitted by a typical turbojet airplane. Notice that as the plane accelerates, the overall loudness of the noise produced increases, with a peak developing in the lower frequency (100 IIz to 1 kIIz) region. The reader should further note that the spectrum is broad-based and contains many frequency components, suggesting that a considerable amount of white noise is present in this signal. One possible circuit for simulating the sound produced by this type of jet plane is indicated in Fig. 4.17.

At the heart of this circuit is a *programmable unijunction transistor*, or PUT as it is more commonly called. The device is basically an SCR (silicon controlled rectifier) which fires when the exponentially rising voltage, V_A, at the anode reaches that at node V_B determined by the $R_1 - R_2$ voltage divider in the circuit. When this occurs, the diode conducts, discharging C_3, and the process repeats again. In the absence of any white-noise signal, the PUT acts as a free running oscillator whose frequency may be varied from about 2 kHz down to about 300 Hz by adjusting the accelerate/decelerate potentiometer R_2. The addition of the white-noise signal at the junction of R_1 and R_2

modulates the PUT's firing voltage and randomizes the signal spikes produced by this oscillator (Fig. 4.17). For small values of R_2 these oscillations are at the high-frequency end of the spectrum, and both they and the white noise from the noise source are strongly attenuated. As the craft accelerates (that is, as R_2 increases), the oscillator frequency decreases, while the amplitude of both the white noise and the oscillator spikes grows considerably. Furthermore, the cutoff frequency of the low-pass filter formed by the $R_1 - R_2 - C_1$ network attenuates the high-frequency components of the white noise in the output so that the sound spectrum created more closely approximates that of a jet operating at full-throttle conditions (uppermost curve in Fig. 4.16).

The sound created by a propeller-driven plane is quite different from that produced by a jet. In the main it consists of a series of

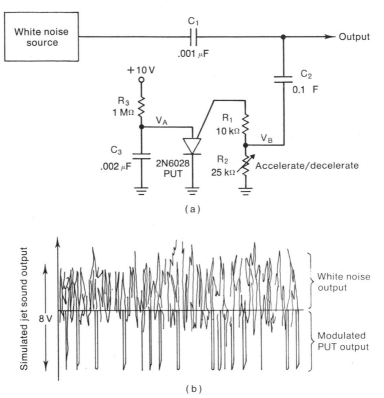

(a)

(b)

Figure 4.17 (a) Circuit for simulating sound of a jet aircraft. *(Adapted from W. E. Olliges et al., Solid State Sound Effect Generating System, U.S. Patent 3,831,172, Aug. 20, 1974.)* (b) Typical output from circuit given in (a).

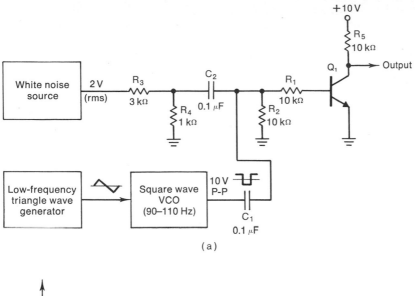

(a)

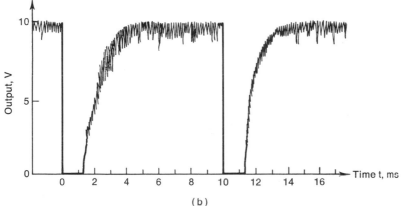

(b)

Figure 4.18 (*a*) Circuit to simulate sound of a propeller-driven aircraft; (*b*) typical output from circuit given in (*a*). (*Adapted from Kock, Seeing Sound, Fig. 4.17a.*)

harmonically related peaks (Fig. 4.2*c*) whose fundamental frequency, as discussed in Sec. 4.1, is determined by the number of times per second that the propeller blade slices through the air. The relative amplitudes of the harmonics depend on the pitch and shape of the blades since this affects the form of the pressure signal generated by the propeller. A simple circuit for generating this type of sound is given in Fig. 4.18*a*.

When the square-wave output of the VCO goes HI (+10 V), Q_1 immediately saturates, causing the output to drop to zero. The transistor remains saturated for about 2 ms, using the circuit components shown, until C_1 charges and the base current drops below that required to saturate the transistor. At this point the collector voltage rises exponentially toward the $+10$-V supply voltage. During the rising portion of the exponential, the transistor is active, and some of the white noise appears in the output, adding a random character to the sound produced and making it seem more realistic (Fig. 4.18*b*). Additional realism may be obtained by slowly modulating the VCO engine speed oscillator with a 2- or 3-Hz triangle-wave signal in response to increases and decreases in the altitude of the aircraft and to throttling of the engine.

As one last sound-effect example, consider the "acoustical image" which one associates with a spaceship. Clearly since most of us have never been on another planet or seen an alien spaceship, the image that the mention of these words suggests has a lot to do with the era in which we grew up. Those of us who can remember some of the early science fiction movie thrillers, such as *The Day the Earth Stood Still* or *The War of the Worlds,* will probably never forget the eerie sounds emitted by the flying saucers as they hovered overhead and as they fired their laserlike weapons. Both of these sounds are easily generated by electronic means. The hovering sound is simply a frequency-modulated sine or triangle wave swept through the 300-Hz to 2-kHz frequency range at a rate of about 8 times per second. This produces a pulsating whistling sound that has somehow become associated with the sound that we think we'll hear when we meet our first flying saucer. To simulate the firing of the ship's "lasers," or "photon-torpedoes" if you're a "Star Trek" fan, the VCO is simply switched over to a square-wave output during the duration of the shot, and this much harsher and louder sound gives the effect of a weapons system being fired.

The sound effects described in this section, of course, just barely scratch the surface of the vast array of acoustical possibilities, and the reader may well wonder just where video games are heading, and, more specifically in relation to this chapter, just what types of sound effects will be found in tomorrow's games. To be sure, as these games become more intelligent, so too will the level of acoustical responses they produce. In fact, it is highly likely that these machines will soon be talking back to the player in English. Voice synthesizer read-only memories and other support ICs are already available in talking calculators for the blind as well as in special-purpose digital voltmeters. Therefore, as their prices continue to fall, it is likely that these devices will find their way into electronic games, and that soon it may become commonplace to find a machine verbally consoling a player about a recent loss to it in a game of blackjack. What is even more eerie is that, as electronic speech-recognition techniques continue to improve, the day may come when the machine listens to the player and then responds appropriately to the player's comments.

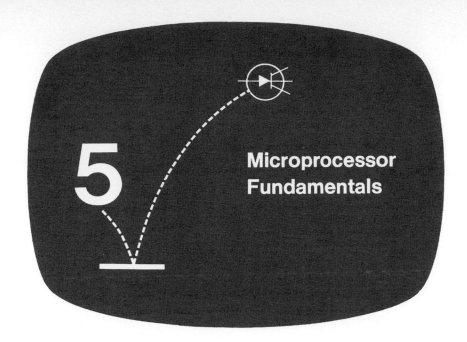

5

Microprocessor Fundamentals

5.1 INTRODUCTION

In its simplest form a *computer* may be thought of as a general-purpose piece of electronic hardware that is programmed by the user to carry out a specific task. By changing the *program,* or list of instructions given to the computer, the user is able to reconfigure the machine in a near-infinite number of ways. It is precisely this characteristic, along with the "innate intelligence" of the computer, that has made it so attractive for incorporation into electronic games.

A general-purpose computer is composed of five major building blocks (Fig. 5.1): memory, control, arithmetic/logic unit (ALU), and input and output sections. As a carry-over from the early days of computers, the combination of the control and ALU sections is often referred to as the central processing unit (CPU) of the machine. The memory is used for storing both the data and the program to be executed, while the ALU is the area in the computer where all of the mathematical operations are performed. Modern computers are parallel devices, and therefore several *bits* (binary digits) of data are processed simultaneously within the ALU. The number of bits handled by the computer as a group is known as the computer's *word size,* and a group of 8 bits is often referred to as a *byte.* Most computers are fixed-word-length machines.

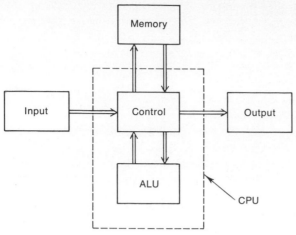

Figure 5.1 Basic computer building blocks. (*Adapted from Electronic Buyers' Handbook and Directory, vol. 8., CMP Publications Inc., 1977.*)

Data enters and leaves the computer through the input-output (I/O) sections. Typical I/O devices include keyboards, teletypes, switches, displays, tape and disk units, and video terminals. The last section of the computer, the control unit, ensures the proper flow of data throughout the machine. Specifically, it is responsible for all system timing and for routing of both instructions and data within the CPU, between the CPU and memory, and into and out of the processor.

As a result of significant technological developments, it has become possible to construct large-scale integrated circuits (*LSIs*) containing a computer's entire control and ALU sections in a single IC package. These devices are known as *microprocessors*. Since, as shown in Fig. 5.1, they contain two of the five basic computer building blocks, it is possible to think of a microprocessor as being two-fifths of a computer. Furthermore, recent technological advances have allowed the addition of memory as well as I/O hardware onto the processor chip, so that these newer devices may be truly classified as (micro)computers.

The microcomputer offers the manufacturer of electronic games many important advantages over conventional digital or relay logic. To begin with, system modifications are much easier to make since "bugs" can usually be removed by altering the software rather than the hardware of the machine. To do this the user need only replace that portion of the program containing the error. Since the program is usually stored in IC read-only memories (ROMs), these changes can be easily accomplished. In the same way, the manufacturer can economically bring out "new, improved" versions of older games to maintain player interest. To appreciate this new development, one only has to compare this "chip switching" method with the updating procedure required for a purely hardware-oriented machine. More often than not, when considerable modifications are required in the latter case, the older system is simply scrapped and a new design begun.

Designers particularly favor the use of microprocessors for the newer, more sophisticated electronic games, where their versatility and "programmable intelligence" have been found to offer significant advantages over conventional digital design techniques. Add to these factors the high reliability, low parts count, reduced inventory, and lower cost of microprocessors, and it is not too difficult to see why many of the newer higher-level electronic games are relying heavily on microprocessor-based designs.

5.2 GENERAL MICROPROCESSOR ARCHITECTURE

A typical microprocessor architecture, or internal structure, consists of a control section, an ALU, and an array of interconnected data storage registers. The processor illustrated in Fig. 5.2 contains one general-purpose register known as the accumulator (A) and three special-purpose registers: the instruction register (IR), program counter (PC), and memory address register (MAR).

The accumulator is the most important register in the CPU and is used in all data-manipulation operations. Generally the ALU has two data inputs, one of which comes from the accumulator (A), and the other from either memory, an input device, or one of the other registers in the processor. In addition, the ALU has one data output path leading back into the accumulator. In this way, for all arithmetic and logical operations performed by this ALU, the initial contents of the accumulator always serve as one of the inputs to the ALU, and the final answer obtained when the instruction is executed and placed back in the accumulator.

In order to execute a program, the computer basically performs the same operations over and over again. It "fetches" an instruction from memory, figures out its meaning, and executes it. The program counter (PC) keeps track of which instruction the computer is currently processing, and during each fetch operation the number currently in the PC determines the address in memory from which the next instruction will be selected. At the end of each regular instruction cycle, the PC is incremented by one so that the subsequent instruction fetched will be from the next location in memory. When a jump instruction is executed, the contents of the PC are replaced by

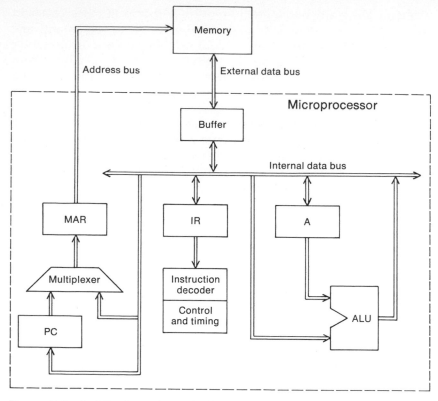

Figure 5.2 Architecture of a typical computer.

the address of the location to be jumped to; then, the next fetch will occur from that address.

As its name implies, the memory address register (MAR) is used to address the memory for both memory "read" and "write" operations. For an ordinary instruction fetch, the MAR is simply loaded with the current contents of the PC, while for special memory reference operations, multiple fetches are required. The first word fetched from memory is placed in the instruction register (IR) as usual, while the second word fetched is sent to the MAR to address the memory prior to executing the instruction. This concept is explicitly described in Sec. 5.4.

Instructions fetched from memory are placed in the IR, where they are decoded (interpreted) by the control unit. The total number of instructions that a machine is capable of executing is known as its *instruction set*. The versatility and power of a particular microprocessor are determined, to a large extent, by the quality and quantity of instructions contained in its particular instruction set. Most microprocessors have fixed instruction sets, but a few, termed *micropro-grammable,* allow the user to develop special instructions. These machines, while certainly more difficult to apply, offer the designer a near-optimal way to implement a specific application problem.

In order to solve problems by using a computer, the user must express the problem in an ordered sequence of instructions that can be understood by the machine. This list of instructions is known as a *computer program.* In preparing a specific program, the operator would probably prefer to write it in a familiar language, e.g., English. Unfortunately, the computer can only understand binary coding. Therefore some type of translation is required, and depending on the sophistication and cost of the machine, the translation burden rests either with the computer or with the operator.

In the most primitive machines the program is entered in pure binary notation (*machine language*); however, binary words contain long strings of ones and zeros and are extremely difficult to work with for all but the shortest programs. One improvement on this approach is to group several bits together and replace them by an equivalent symbol. This results in shorter expressions which are easier to remember, view, and enter on a keyboard. The *hexadecimal number sytem* makes use of 4-bit groups and is listed in Table 5.1 along with its binary and decimal equivalents for comparison.

TABLE 5.1   COMPARISON OF DECIMAL, BINARY, AND HEXADECIMAL NUMBERS

Decimal (Base 10)	Binary (Base 2)	Hexadecimal (Base 16)
0	0000	0
1	0001	1
2	0010	2
3	0011	3
4	0100	4
5	0101	5
6	0110	6
7	0111	7
8	1000	8
9	1001	9
10	1010	A
11	1011	B
12	1100	C
13	1101	D
14	1110	E
15	1111	F
16	10000	10

TABLE 5.2   COMPARISON OF MACHINE LANGUAGE AND ASSEMBLY
LANGUAGE INSTRUCTIONS

| Machine language | | Assembly | |
Binary code	Hexadecimal code	language mnemonic	Meaning
1101 0101	B5	CLA	Clear accumulator.
0100 1101	4D	STOP	Stop further program execution.
0111 0011	73	STO 51	Store accumulator in memory location 51.
0101 0001	51		
1111 0010	F2	ADD 25	Add contents of memory location 25 to A.
0010 0101	25		

SOURCE: Kock, *Seeing Sound*, Wiley, Fig. 5.1.

While the hexadecimal system offers a significant improvement over binary coding, it too is still a foreign language to the operator and becomes tedious when long programs must be written. For such cases, some type of mnemonic or symbolic shorthand notation more representative of the type of operation to be performed is preferred. A list of several typical instructions, along with their binary, hexadecimal, and mnemonic equivalents, is given in Table 5.2. It seems clear that it would be much easier for the programmer who wants to clear the accumulator to remember the instruction CLA rather than its hexadecimal equivalent B5 (or, worse yet, 1011 0101).

Programs using mnemonics instead of machine language statements are known as *assembly language programs* and require a special program known as an *assembler* to translate them into machine language for eventual use by the computer.

5.3   SUBROUTINES, NESTING, AND THE STACK

In writing programs, it is often found that certain groups of instructions are repeated over and over again. For example, in a specific application program it might be necessary to multiply two numbers together at several different points in the program. The group of instructions required to multiply these two numbers is shown by the box labeled "MULT" in Fig. 5.3*a*.

One alternative to this approach, which is usually more efficient in terms of memory size required, is to set up this group of instructions as a small program of its own known as a *subroutine*. Thereafter, whenever it is necessary to multiply two numbers together in the program, the MULT subroutine is "called," the multiplication is performed, and the answer is "returned" to the main program.

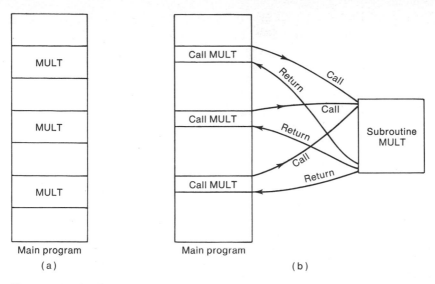

MULT	
MULT	
MULT	
Main program	Main program
(a)	(b)

Figure 5.3 Utilization of subroutines in program design.

As can be seen from Fig. 5.3*b*, a problem can arise concerning where to return when the subroutine is called from several different points in the main program. To find its way back to the point in the main program which initiated the original subroutine call, the computer saves the return address in a temporary storage area known as a *stack*. The stack gets its name from the method used for storing dishes in cafeterias (Fig. 5.4). Here the last dish "pushed" onto the stack will be the first one "popped" off. The subroutine address stack operates in a similar fashion. When the subroutine is *called*, the caller's address is pushed onto the top of the stack, and when the *return* instruction is executed, it is popped off the stack and placed in the PC, so that the program execution resumes in the main program at the location following the original call instruction. Note that the computer can also "nest" subroutines, that is, have one subroutine call another, etc., and still be able to find its way back to the main program.

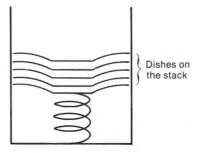

Dishes on the stack

Figure 5.4 The stack. (*Adapted from Kock, Seeing Sound, Fig. 5.1.*)

Often as part of the execution of a subroutine, the contents of certain registers in the CPU may be altered. If these quantities are needed by the main program, they may be saved by pushing them onto the stack prior to calling the subroutine and popping them back on returning to the main program.

Two different types of stacks are found in microcomputers. The first is known as a *hardware stack* and uses a special group of registers within the CPU for storing these return addresses. These registers are useful in that external memory need not be allocated, but the hardware stack has limited nesting capability owing to its small size. The second type, called a *software stack*, uses RAM locations for address storage. Although more difficult to set up, this type of stack provides virtually unlimited storage for return addresses and register contents which must be saved. In a software stack the current top of the stack is "pointed to" by the stack pointer register internal to the CPU.

5.4 MICROPROCESSOR EXECUTION OF A SAMPLE PROGRAM

In order to illustrate how a microcomputer, or for that matter how any computer, operates, it is useful to trace through the execution of a sample program such as that in Fig. 5.5. This illustrative program involves the solution of the equation

$$Z = X + Y$$

for the case where $X = 5$ and $Y = 4$. To formulate this problem for solution by the computer, the data (i.e., the values of 5 and 4 for X and Y) will be stored in memory along with the program (Fig. 5.5*b*), and the final answer Z will be placed at a specific location in memory. Memory locations 00 to 07 are reserved for the program, 20 to 21 for the data, and 25 for the answer Z. It should be noted that some of the instructions, specifically those which refer to memory (*memory reference instructions*), are multiword instructions, where the first word identifies the type of operation to be performed and the second word the location of the data to be used.

The flowchart in Fig. 5.5*a* shows diagrammatically how the program will proceed when it is executed, and the specific program execution sequence is given in Fig. 5.5*c*.

To fetch an instruction from memory, the contents of the PC are placed in the MAR, a memory-read operation is performed, and the contents of the addressed word placed in the instruction register. If the instruction is of the multiword type previously discussed, then additional fetches will be required. This information will be placed in the MAR and used to address memory in order to provide the additional information needed during the execution phase of the instruction cycle.

Referring to the sample program in question, consider that program execution begins with the PC contents initially equal to zero. Thus, the first fetch will occur from memory location 00 and will be the clear accumulator (CLA) instruction. When this instruction is executed, the accumulator will be cleared to zero (see Fig. 5.5c). The next fetch (from memory location 01) will be the ADD instruction, which is a multiword instruction and will therefore require two fetches before execution. During the second fetch (from location 02), the address of the variable X (the number 20) will be placed in the MAR. In this way, during the execute phase of this instruction, the data contained at location 20 (the number 5) will be added to that already in the accumulator (the number 0) and the result placed in the accumulator. Program execution will continue along sequentially

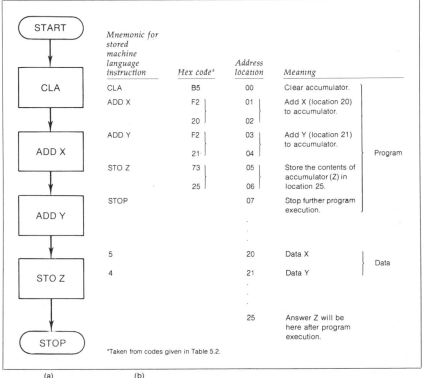

(a)   (b)

Figure 5.5 (a) Flowchart for execution of the sample program; (b) memory organization for the sample program. (*Adapted from Kock, Seeing Sound, Fig. 5.1.*)

PC	MAR	IR	A	Memory location Z	Operations performed
0	?	?	?	?	Initial register contents
0	0	CLA	?	?	a) Place PC in MAR, fetch 1st instruction and place in IR.
1	0	CLA	0	?	b) Execute 1st instruction and increment PC.
1	1	ADD	0	?	a) Place PC in MAR and fetch 2d instruction.
2	2	ADD	0	?	b) Increment PC, place in MAR.
2	21	ADD	0	?	c) Fetch 2d word and place in MAR.
3	21	ADD	4	?	d) Execute 2d instruction and increment PC.
3	3	ADD	5	?	a) Place PC in MAR and fetch 3d instruction.
4	4	ADD	5	?	b) Increment PC, place in MAR.
4	22	ADD	5	?	c) Fetch 2d word to place in MAR.
5	22	ADD	9	?	d) Execute 3d instruction and increment PC.
5	5	STO	9	?	a) Place PC in MAR and fetch 4th instruction.
6	6	STO	9	?	b) Increment PC, place in MAR.
6	25	STO	9	?	c) Fetch 2d instruction word and place in MAR.
7	25	STO	9	9	d) Execute 4th instruction and increment PC.
7	7	STOP	9	9	a) Place PC in MAR and fetch 5th instruction.
7	7	STOP	9	9	b) Execute 5th instruction.
				MACHINE STOPS	

Figure 5.5 (*c*) Program execution sequence.

in this fashion until the stop instruction is executed, terminating the program. If at this point the contents of location 25 are examined, the answer to the problem, the number 9, will be found.

At this point the reader may well wonder why the stop instruction is needed. After all, it would seem that the program is essentially finished after the STO Z instruction is completed. However, consider for a moment what would happen if no stop instruction were employed and the program simply ended at location 07. On completion of this last instruction in the program, the computer would keep right on going and, therefore, the PC would be incremented as usual, a fetch would be made from the next memory location (address 08), and the "instruction" found at that location would be executed by the machine. Just what "instruction" this would be, and what would happen when it was executed, would depend entirely on what specific numbers happened to be at that memory location. Furthermore, this process would continue throughout the memory, with the computer indiscriminantly fetching and executing everything in its path. During this process it is highly likely that the computer would modify or destroy the original program, and therefore some type of programming technique is required to prevent the computer from drifting into "forbidden" memory regions.

One method of achieving this, besides using the stop instruction previously discussed, is to employ a jump instruction. A jump is a multiword instruction; the first word informs the computer that the current instruction is to be a jump, and the second word tells it what address to jump to. To execute this instruction, the computer simply places the second word directly into the PC so that the next instruc-

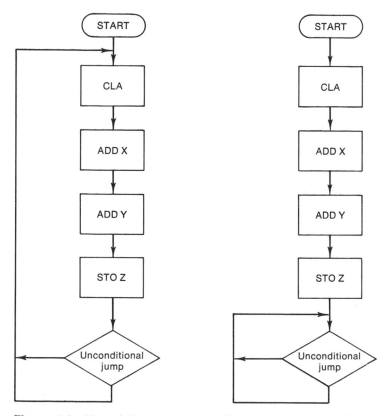

Figure 5.6 Use of the jump instruction to prevent entry into forbidden memory regions.

tion fetched will be from that location. Two possible program implementation schemes using unconditional jumps are illustrated in the flowcharts given in Fig. 5.6. When executing the program illustrated in Fig. 5.6a, the computer will continuously loop through the entire program, while with that given in Fig. 5.6b the machine will execute the program once and then "hang itself up" in a tight loop at the bottom of the program. With either approach, however, during program execution the computer will always remain in the "allowed" sections of memory.

5.5   INTERFACING MICROPROCESSORS TO I/O DEVICES

The microprocessor's I/O channels are its link to the outside world. Data generally leaves from the processor's accumulator and is "written" into selected output ports or is "read" into the accumulator from a specific input port. The simplest input and output ports contain tristate logic, and latches, respectively (Fig. 5.7). *Tristate* (or three-state) devices essentially behave like electronically controlled switches, and thus many of these may be simultaneously "hung" onto the data bus as long as only one is active at a time. *Latches,* on the other hand, are simply multibit storage devices which can "memorize" the contents of the data bus on command.

Information on the data bus is continually changing, and therefore when the processor wishes to read data from an input port into the accumulator, it sends out an IN pulse, which tells the device when to place its data on the bus. Conversely, to write data from the accumulator into an output port, the processor generates an OUT pulse to inform this port when the data on the bus is stable and may be latched.

For systems containing more than one I/O port, some mechanism must also be provided for distinguishing between them. This is accomplished by assigning different addresses to each port. The address information is then combined with the appropriate IN or OUT pulse to activate the selected device. Consider, for example, the design of a single output port for a processor capable of addressing 2^8, or 256, different output channels. To select one specific port, the processor will need to generate an 8-bit address, and therefore each of the system's I/O ports will require an 8-bit (1 out of 256) address decoder. For the circuit shown in Fig. 5.7, the port has been assigned the number 3, and therefore if a 03 (00000011) address is present at the same time that the OUT pulse occurs, then the information on the processor data bus at that time will be latched into this output port.

For systems requiring significant numbers of I/O ports, the logic-

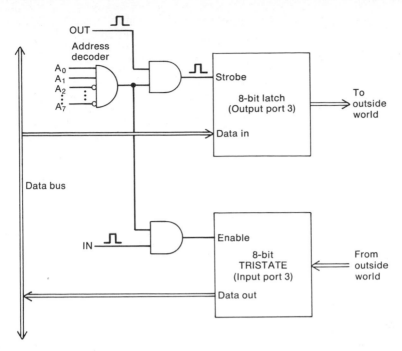

Figure 5.7 Connecting an I/O port to a microprocessor.

gate decoder approach discussed above soon becomes unwieldy, and some form of medium-scale integration (MSI) decoder circuit is preferred. One example of this port-expansion technique is shown in Fig. 5.8. Here the outputs are normally high. However, when a specific line is addressed and the proper enable signals occur, the selected output line goes LO, and the proper port is activated. By connecting the four least significant bits of the address lines to the decoder inputs, and the remaining address lines and OUT pulse signal to the enable inputs shown in the figure, up to 16 output ports may be controlled.

In some microprocessors special instructions are not employed for I/O operations. Instead, I/O devices are treated as though they were memory locations. This approach is advantageous because then many special memory-reference instructions can be used with the I/O devices. These include register-to-memory data transfers, as well as instructions to increment, decrement, and test the contents of memory locations. However, this increase in versatility is not without cost. Memory address busses are usually much larger than special-purpose I/O busses, and therefore systems employing this type of memory-based I/O will require larger and more complex port-

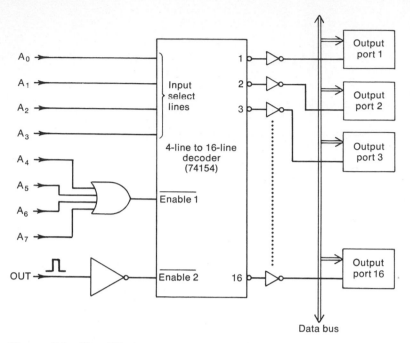

Figure 5.8 Simplified port expansion technique.

select decoder logic. In addition, the instructions needed to address memory are usually longer, and hence programs written using this approach will generally require more memory space and will take longer to execute.

5.6 SPECIAL MICROPROCESSOR CONTROL SIGNALS AND OPERATIONS

The circuit shown in Fig. 5.9 is that of a typical 8-bit microprocessor. Most of the device terminal functions are self-evident, with the exception perhaps of the RESET, WAIT, READY, interrupt request (INT REQ), interrupt acknowledge (INTA), hold (HLD), and hold acknowledge (HLDA) lines.

The RESET input initializes the processor either on initial power-up or on operation of the front panel "reset" switch. In most processors, activating the RESET line clears the program counter, so that on release of this control signal, program execution begins from memory location zero. The remaining control and status signals are associated with the transfer of data in and about the microcomputer system.

The READY control input and the WAIT status signal are employed together to permit the microprocessor to operate with "slow" memories. Whenever the CPU addresses this particular memory, special circuits within this section of memory send back a control signal which pulls down the processor's READY line. This causes the CPU to enter a WAIT state, suspending further program execution and allowing the memory extra time to respond. After a predetermined length of time, the memory-logic releases the READY line, and the CPU resumes its normal activity. Additional electronics may also be added onto the WAIT and READY lines to single-step the processor, a feature particularly useful when debugging programs.

The remaining device lines control the transfer of data to and from external I/O devices. In Sec. 5.5 we discussed one specific method of data I/O, in which the CPU completely controls the data transfer operation. When using this technique, the CPU either transfers data to the I/O ports whenever it gets around to it or else "polls" each port and generates a data transfer when requested. While this approach is valid for certain types of I/O data transfers, it is wholly inadequate when immediate processor attention to a particular device is required or when large blocks of data must be rapidly transferred. For these cases *interrupt* and *direct memory access* (DMA), respectively, are the indicated choices.

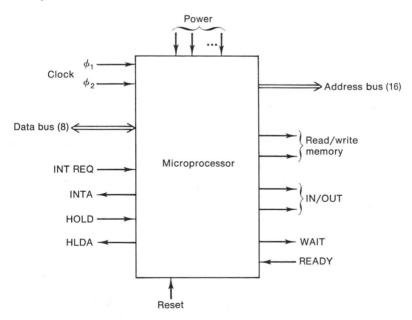

Figure 5.9 Typical microprocessor pinout.

The use of an interrupt I/O scheme allows an external device to get the attention of the CPU immediately by interrupting it. Once interrupted, the processor suspends its current activity, "services the interrupt," and then returns to its original task. As an example of the utility of this approach, consider the interfacing of a keyboard to a microprocessor as shown in Fig. 5.10. If a polling approach is used, the processor has to spend all of its time checking bit D7 on the input port in order to determine if a key has been struck. If, instead, the strobe output of the keyboard is connected to the interrupt line on the processor, the CPU can usefully accomplish other tasks, completely ignoring the keyboard except when it needs service. In this way, when a key is struck, an interrupt will occur, and the processor will enter its service routine, read the keystroke data from the input port into the accumulator, properly store it, and then return to the main program. Most microprocessors also have a *vectored interrupt* capability, which permits them to respond to several different types of interrupt instructions, branching to specific service routines appropriate to each.

The hold (HLD) and hold-acknowledge (HLDA) lines on the processor are utilized during direct memory access (DMA) data trans-

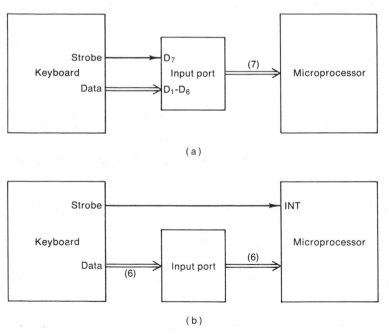

(a)

(b)

Figure 5.10 Keyboard interfacing techniques. (a) Polling approach; (b) interrupt approach.

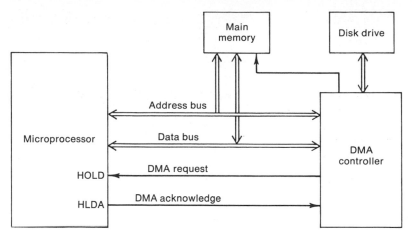

Figure 5.11 Direct memory access (DMA) for I/O devices.

fers. DMA is particularly useful for transferring large blocks of data between, say, a disk drive or magnetic tape and main memory. Here, proceeding by the usual route of reading data from an input port into the accumulator and then writing it into main memory is just too slow. With a DMA approach the accumulator, and in fact the entire processor, is bypassed, and the transfer operation is controlled by external hardware (see Fig. 5.11).

To initiate this process on receipt of a DMA request, the processor is placed in a HOLD state. This tristates the address and data buses and effectively disconnects the microprocessor from the circuit. In addition it generates a HLDA signal, activating the DMA controller. The controller now takes over the data and address buses and directly supervises the data transmission between the main memory and the selected I/O device. When the data transfer is completed, the controller interrupts the processor, releasing it from the hold state, and normal program execution resumes.

5.7 A SAMPLE MICROPROCESSOR—THE 8080

The 8080 microprocessor is a powerful single-chip 8-bit CPU containing a highly versatile set of 78 instructions. It has a 16-bit address bus and an 8-bit data bus, which are brought out to separate pins on the processor, reducing the need for external multiplexing of data. In addition to supporting up to 65 kilobytes of RAM and ROM, the 8080 can directly address 256 input and output ports.

The internal architecture of the 8080 may be divided into four major sections (Fig. 5.12): the register array and address logic, the

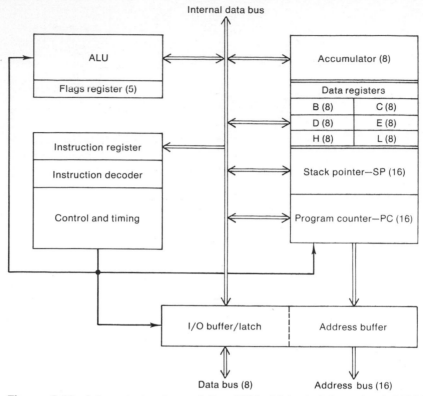

Figure 5.12 Internal structure of the 8080. (*Adapted from Intel 8080 Microcomputer System User's Manual, 1975.*)

arithmetic/logic unit, the IR and control unit, and the bidirectional (3-state) data bus buffers. The CPU contains an 8-bit accumulator, six 8-bit scratchpad data registers, a 16-bit program counter, a 16-bit stack pointer, an 8-bit instruction register, and a testable flags register. Depending on the results of the specific instructions executed by the CPU, different bits (C, P, AC, Z, S) in the flags register will be affected. The C flag bit is set when a carry is produced, P when the parity is even, AC when an auxiliary carry is produced, Z when the result is zero, and S when the sign of the result is negative.

The 8080 instruction set includes decimal as well as binary arithmetic, conditional branching, logical operations, and many types of register-to-register and memory-reference instructions. A full instruction cycle, that is, the time required to fetch and execute a single instruction, requires anywhere from 4 to 17 clock cycles for completion, depending upon the type of instruction. Instructions such as "ADD B REGISTER TO ACCUMULATOR" need only a few clock cycles because they are carried out entirely within the CPU, while the call instruction, for example, requires many more clock cycles, since the return address must first be pushed onto the stack, and then a jump executed to the selected area in memory. The 8080A microprocessor has a maximum clock speed of 2 MHz, and thus instruction execution times on this processor can vary anywhere from 2 to 8.5 μs. The number of clock cycles associated with each of the 8080 instructions is given in the rightmost column of Table 5.3. For some instructions (the conditional call and return) two cycle times are given; conditional calls (returns) require fewer clock cycles if the test being made fails, since then no call (return) is executed.

Let's examine the instruction set a bit more closely. Each of the 8-bit data registers (A, B, C, D, E, H, L) may be individually loaded, incremented, decremented, and tested. In addition, they may also be grouped together as 16-bit register pairs (B and C, D and E, H and L), with similar operations possible. The HL register pair can also be used as a pointer to memory; that is, it is possible to store or retrieve data from a memory location whose address is given (pointed to) by the contents of the HL pair. This addressing technique is particularly useful for rapidly accessing sequential lists of data in memory. Several types of higher-accuracy double-word-length arithmetic instructions are also available for use with these register pairs.

The 8080 has a 16-bit stack pointer register which permits any portion of external RAM to be used as a last-in–first-out stack, allowing for nearly unlimited subroutine nesting. A special instruction (LXI SP) is used to initialize the location of the stack. In addition to saving addresses, it is also possible to save the contents of all the data registers as well as those of the accumulator and flags registers by employing the PUSH and POP instructions. These are especially useful for servicing interrupts since the status of the various registers can be PUSHed onto the stack before servicing the interrupt and POPed back when the processor returns to the main program.

A complete discussion of these instructions will be given in Chap. 6. However, for reference, a listing of the entire 8080 instruction set is given in Table 5.3, which contains information on what each instruction does, the mnemonic symbol used to represent it, the number of memory bytes needed to store it, the number of clock cycles required to execute it, and the flags affected by it. The entries in the flags column indicate the effect produced on each of the flag bits when the instruction is executed. The symbols used have the following meanings:

—	No effect
↕	Set or reset depending on result
0	Reset to 0
1	Set to 1

TABLE 5.3 8080 INSTRUCTION SET

Mnemonic	Description	Number of bytes	Number of clock cycles	Flags affected			
				C	Z	S	P
MOV r_1, r_2	Move register to register	1	5	—	—	—	—
MOVE M,r	Move register to memory	1	7	—	—	—	—
MOV r,M	Move memory to register	1	7	—	—	—	—
MVI r	Move immediate to register	2	7	—	—	—	—
MVI M	Move immediate to memory	2	10	—	—	—	—
HLT	Halt	1	7	—	—	—	—
INR r	Increment register	1	5	—	↔	↔	↔
DCR r	Decrement register	1	5	—	↔	↔	↔
INR M	Increment memory	1	10	—	↔	↔	↔
DCR M	Decrement memory	1	10	—	↔	↔	↔
ADD r	Add register to A	1	4	↔	↔	↔	↔
ADC r	Add register to A with carry	1	4	↔	↔	↔	↔
SUB r	Subtract register from A	1	4	↔	↔	↔	↔
SBB r	Subtract register from A with borrow	1	4	↔	↔	↔	↔
ANA r	AND register with A	1	4	0	↔	↔	↔
XRA r	Exclusive-OR register with A	1	4	0	↔	↔	↔
ORA r	OR register with A	1	4	0	↔	↔	↔
CMP r	Compare register with A	1	4	↔	↔	↔	↔
ADD M	Add memory to A	1	7	↔	↔	↔	↔
ADC M	Add memory to A with carry	1	7	↔	↔	↔	↔
SUB M	Subtract memory from A	1	7	↔	↔	↔	↔
SBB M	Subtract memory from A with borrow	1	7	↔	↔	↔	↔
ANA M	AND memory with A	1	7	0	↔	↔	↔
XRA M	Exclusive-OR memory with A	1	7	0	↔	↔	↔
ORA M	OR memory with A	1	7	0	↔	↔	↔

Mnemonic	Operation	Bytes	States	Z	S	P	CY	AC
CMP M	Compare memory with A	1	7	↔	↔	↔	↔	↔
ADI	Add immediate with A	2	7	↔	↔	↔	↔	↔
ACI	Add immediate with A with carry	2	7	↔	↔	↔	↔	↔
SUI	Subtract immediate from A	2	7	↔	↔	↔	↔	↔
SBI	Subtract immediate from A with borrow	2	7	↔	↔	↔	↔	↔
ANI	And immediate with A	2	7	↔	↔	↔	0	↔
XRI	Exclusive-OR immediate with A	2	7	↔	↔	↔	0	0
ORI	OR immediate with A	2	7	↔	↔	↔	0	0
CPI	Compare immediate with A	2	7	↔	↔	↔	↔	↔
RLC	Rotate A left (shift)	1	4	—	—	—	↔	—
RRC	Rotate A right (shift)	1	4	—	—	—	↔	—
RAL	Rotate A left through carry (shift)	1	4	—	—	—	↔	—
RAR	Rotate A right through carry (shift)	1	4	—	—	—	↔	—
JMP	Jump unconditional	3	10	—	—	—	—	—
JC	Jump on carry	3	10	—	—	—	—	—
JNC	Jump on no carry	3	10	—	—	—	—	—
JZ	Jump on zero	3	10	—	—	—	—	—
JNZ	Jump on nonzero	3	10	—	—	—	—	—
JP	Jump on positive	3	10	—	—	—	—	—
JM	Jump on minus	3	10	—	—	—	—	—
JPE	Jump on parity even	3	10	—	—	—	—	—
JPO	Jump on parity odd	3	10	—	—	—	—	—
CALL	Call unconditional	3	17	—	—	—	—	—
CC	Call on carry	3	11/17	—	—	—	—	—
CNC	Call on no carry	3	11/17	—	—	—	—	—
CZ	Call on zero	3	11/17	—	—	—	—	—
CNZ	Call on nonzero	3	11/17	—	—	—	—	—
CP	Call on positive	3	11/17	—	—	—	—	—
CM	Call on minus	3	11/17	—	—	—	—	—
CPE	Call on parity even	3	11/17	—	—	—	—	—
CPO	Call on parity odd	3	11/17	—	—	—	—	—

TABLE 5.3 8080 INSTRUCTION SET (Continued)

Mnemonic	Description	Number of bytes	Number of clock cycles	Flags affected			
				C	Z	S	P
RET	Return	1	10	—	—	—	—
RC	Return on carry	1	5/11	—	—	—	—
RNC	Return on no carry	1	5/11	—	—	—	—
RZ	Return on zero	1	5/11	—	—	—	—
RNZ	Return on nonzero	1	5/11	—	—	—	—
RP	Return on positive	1	5/11	—	—	—	—
RM	Return on minus	1	5/11	—	—	—	—
RPE	Return on parity even	1	5/11	—	—	—	—
RPO	Return on parity odd	1	5/11	—	—	—	—
RST	Restart	1	11	—	—	—	—
IN	Input	2	10	—	—	—	—
OUT	Output	2	10	—	—	—	—
EI	Enable interrupt	1	4	—	—	—	—
DI	Disable interrupt	1	4	—	—	—	—
NOP	No operation	1	4	—	—	—	—
LXI B	Load immediate register pair B & C	3	10	—	—	—	—
LXI D	Load immediate register pair D & E	3	10	—	—	—	—
LXI H	Load immediate register pair H & L	3	10	—	—	—	—
LXI SP	Load immediate stack pointer	3	10	—	—	—	—
PUSH B	Push register pair B & C on stack	1	11	—	—	—	—
PUSH D	Push register pair D & E on stack	1	11	—	—	—	—
PUSH H	Push register pair H & L on stack	1	11	—	—	—	—
PUSH PSW	Push A and flags on stack	1	11	—	—	—	—
POP B	Pop register pair B & C off stack	1	10	—	—	—	—

Mnemonic	Description							
POP D	Pop register pair D & E off stack	1	10	—	—	—	—	—
POP H	Pop register pair H & L off stack	1	10	—	—	—	—	—
POP PSW	Pop A and flags off stack	1	10	↔	↔	↔	↔	↔
STA	Store A direct	3	13	—	—	—	—	—
LDA	Load A direct	3	13	—	—	—	—	—
XCHG	Exchange D & E, H & L registers	1	4	—	—	—	—	—
XTHL	Exchange top of stack, H & L	1	18	—	—	—	—	—
SPHL	H & L to stack pointer	1	5	—	—	—	—	—
PCHL	H & L to program counter	1	5	—	—	—	—	—
DAD B	Add B & C to H & L	1	10	—	—	↔	—	—
DAD D	Add D & E to H & L	1	10	—	—	↔	—	—
DAD H	Add H & L to H & L	1	10	—	—	↔	—	—
DAD SP	Add stack pointer to H & L	1	10	—	—	↔	—	—
STAX B	Store A indirect	1	7	—	—	—	—	—
STAX D	Store A indirect	1	7	—	—	—	—	—
LDAX B	Load A indirect	1	7	—	—	—	—	—
LDAX D	Load A indirect	1	7	—	—	—	—	—
INX B	Increment B & C registers	1	5	—	—	—	—	—
INX D	Increment D & E registers	1	5	—	—	—	—	—
INX H	Increment H & L registers	1	5	—	—	—	—	—
INX SP	Increment stack pointer	1	5	—	—	—	—	—
DCX B	Decrement B & C	1	5	—	—	—	—	—
DCX D	Decrement D & E	1	5	—	—	—	—	—
DCX H	Decrement H & L	1	5	—	—	—	—	—
DCX SP	Decrement stack pointer	1	5	—	—	—	—	—
CMA	Complement A	1	4	—	—	—	—	—
STC	Set carry	1	4	—	—	↔	—	—
CMC	Complement carry	1	4	—	—	↔	—	—
DAA	Decimal adjust A	1	4	↔	↔	↔	↔	↔
SHLD	Store H & L direct	3	16	—	—	—	—	—
LHLD	Load H & L direct	3	16	—	—	—	—	—

SOURCE: Adapted from INTEL 8080 Microcomputer System User's Manual, September 1975. (Copyright 1975.)

TABLE 5.4 SYSTEM STATUS INFORMATION DEFINITIONS

Symbol	Data bus bit	Definition
INTA	D0	Interrupt acknowledge signal.
WO	D1	Current operation will be either a memory write or output function.
STACK	D2	Contents of stack pointer register are now on address bus.
HLTA	D3	Halt acknowledge signal.
OUT	D4	Address bus will contain address of an output port (OUT = 1) when $\overline{WR}$ goes LO.
M1	D5	CPU is in the fetch cycle of the first byte of the instruction.
INP	D6	Address bus contains address of an input port device, and its data should be placed on the data bus when DBIN goes HI.
MEMR	D7	Current instruction subcycle will be a memory read, and memory data should be placed on the bus when DBIN goes HI.

SOURCE: Kock, *Seeing Sound*, Wiley, Table 5.3.

A minimum 8080 microcomputer system may be configured with relatively few IC packages. Basically all that is needed besides the CPU chip itself is a 2-phase clock generator, a system status latch, ROM and/or RAM, the appropriate I/O ports, and a handful of logic gates.

The system status outputs, defined in Table 5.4, are latched from the data bus at the beginning of each instruction subcycle and used to tell the world outside the CPU what's coming up during each portion of the instruction execution. The DBIN control signal informs the external input devices when the data bus is free to accept data, while the $\overline{WR}$ control signal is used to indicate to output devices that the data on the bus has stabilized and may be taken by them.

It is interesting to note that a system of the sort described above containing about 1 kilobyte of RAM, 16 kilobytes of ROM, and a few I/O ports would probably be adequate for all but the most sophisticated video games, and could probably be built for less than $100.

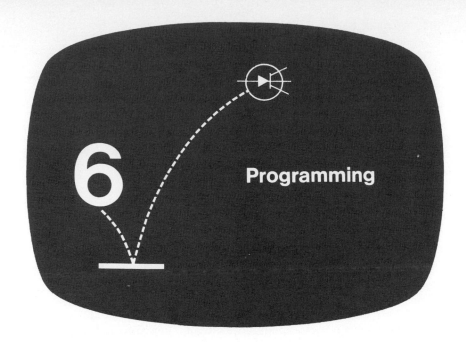

6.1 INTRODUCTION TO PROGRAMMING

This chapter introduces programming concepts. A brief discussion of general programming topics is followed by the presentation of seven fundamental programming rules which are basic to any microprocessor software design. Flowcharts are introduced, and a detailed explanation is provided of the instruction set for the 8080 microprocessor, which was discussed in Chap. 5. Typical examples of programs for generating random numbers and for playing card and dice games give the reader a first glimpse at the application of microcomputers to electronic games. The chapter concludes with a discussion of debugging methods as they apply to microprocessor programs.

A computer is a piece of general-purpose electronic hardware which when programmed converts into a specialized piece of equipment capable of solving the particular problem that the programmer has in mind. The program itself consists of instructions and data. The instructions tell the machine what to do, and the data is the information to be operated upon by the computer. Both instructions and data are stored in the memory of the computer.

In formulating a program for a particular application (an *application program*), it is possible to write it in machine language, assembly language, or some other high-level language, such as BASIC or

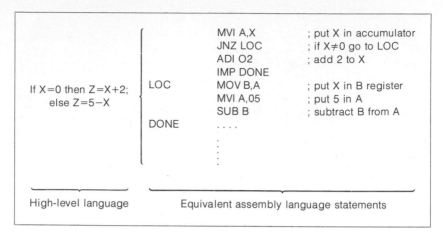

If X=0 then Z=X+2; else Z=5−X		MVI A,X	; put X in accumulator
		JNZ LOC	; if X≠0 go to LOC
		ADI O2	; add 2 to X
		IMP DONE	
	LOC	MOV B,A	; put X in B register
		MVI A,05	; put 5 in A
		SUB B	; subtract B from A
	DONE	. . . .	

High-level language   Equivalent assembly language statements

Figure 6.1 Comparison of high-level language and assembly language statements.

FORTRAN. With less expensive systems, machine language programming in either binary or hexadecimal is usually required. This procedure, while tolerable for small-program development, soon becomes unwieldy in larger designs.

An *assembler* greatly eases the programming task and is probably one of the most commonly used programming tools. An assembler is nothing more than a special-purpose program which translates the assembly language mnemonics into their equivalent machine language statements. In addition most assemblers also permit the use of symbolic addresses, as well as symbolic names for data, registers, and variables. Generally, one line of assembly language code translates into one line of machine code.

Many readers may be familiar with special high-level languages such as FORTRAN and BASIC. These languages, along with several specifically designed for use with microprocessors, are also available for microcomputer program development work. Their greatest attributes are their similarity to English and ordinary algebra and the compact nature of their program statements, since one high-level language statement usually translates into many machine language statements (Fig. 6.1). For these reasons programs written using these high-level languages are often shorter, easier to debug, and generally less tedious for the designer to develop.

However, high-level languages have their drawbacks. In order to perform the program translation into machine language, a large, sophisticated program known as a *compiler* is required. This program occupies a good deal of memory, and in fact a minicomputer or an even larger machine is usually required to run it. Furthermore, the generally compact nature of most high-level language statements means that program translation into machine code is not optimal; in fact, the designer of the program, given enough time, could undoubtedly write a much more compact program, one whose execution time would be well below that created by any compiler. Therefore, when developing programs for use with mass-produced micro-processor-based electronic games, where every extra byte of memory used may translate into extra dollars of ROM required, compilers should be used with caution. One way to partially circumvent this problem is to first write the program using a compiler and then "tweak" the resulting machine code produced in order to obtain a near-optimal result.

Regardless of the programming language you ultimately decide to work with, the rules for good microprocessor-based software design remain the same:

1. Carefully define and understand the application problem. This will prevent your having to redo the software as each new "exception" to the program you've written is discovered.

2. Design the program from the top down; that is, attempt to understand and block out the overall design problem first, and then continually subdivide it into smaller, more readily solved, programming problems. While it is tempting to dig into the specifics of a small portion of the problem to start programming immediately, avoid this until you have a clear understanding of how all the parts will fit together.

3. Design the software so that it can be easily updated and changed. Along these lines, good documentation is important both to the next person who will work with the program and to the designer. Often, when returning to an old program after several days on another project, it's hard to believe that you ever wrote it. Good documentation helps to get you back on the right track with minimal effort.

4. Make ample use of flowcharting in all phases of program design; it helps you to rapidly understand and review how the overall program fits together.

5. Investigate whether or not there are any prewritten (canned) routines available that can be utilized in your specific application program. For those portions of the

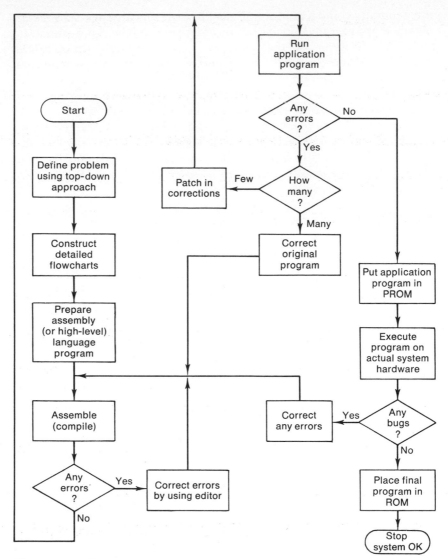

Figure 6.2 Developing the application software. (*Adapted from Kock, Seeing Sound, Fig. 5.1.*)

program where prewritten software is unavailable, design your own *algorithms* (procedures) and translate the problem into machine language using either an assembler or compiler program. Make use of an *editor program*[1] in developing your program.

[1]An editor is a program which allows the designer to construct, edit, store, retrieve, and combine programs together by making use of a few simple commands.

6. Run the application program on some type of development system, and, depending on the number of errors encountered, either patch in the corrections or go back to the original program and make the changes.

7. Execute the program on the actual system hardware, and remove any remaining bugs. When all errors have been eliminated and final changes made, commit the program to ROM.

These steps are summarized in the flowchart given in Fig. 6.2. The remainder of this chapter is devoted to helping the reader develop basic microprocessor programming skills with particular emphasis on their application to electronic games.

6.2 FLOWCHARTS

Computers have proved to be extremely powerful tools for solving a wide variety of problems; however, in some ways they aren't very smart. They do exactly what they're told. Thus, if even a single program statement is out of place, the entire program may "bomb out" when it's run. When this happens, novices inevitably think that there's something wrong with the machine, but they soon come to realize that the computer itself is rarely at fault and that in fact most such errors are created by organizational problems on the part of the programmer.

Therefore it is important to carefully formulate and document all programming problems—first in order to have any chance of success on the initial run of the program, and second to be able to diagnose its ills should it fail to run on the first try. Flowcharts provide a particularly good way to accomplish these tasks and help you to visualize the overall structure of the program. Basically a *flowchart* is a graphic representation of what the final program will look like. All major program functions are represented by separate boxes interconnected by arrows to indicate the flow direction of the program. A list of the most important flowchart symbols is given in Fig. 6.3.

The oval-shaped symbol is used to indicate the beginning or end of a particular program or subroutine. The two most commonly used symbols in flowcharting are the rectangular *computational box* and the diamond-shaped *decision-making* or *branching box*. Note that the decision box has a single entry point and two exit points. If a previously written program is used as a part of a newer program, it is simply indicated by the barred rectangular box shown in the figure without duplication of its flowchart. The same rectangular symbol is also used for the subroutine call statement.

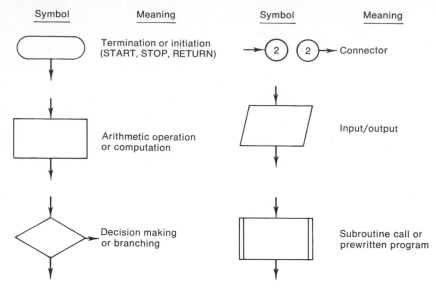

Symbol	Meaning	Symbol	Meaning

Termination or initiation (START, STOP, RETURN)

Connector

Arithmetic operation or computation

Input/output

Decision making or branching

Subroutine call or prewritten program

Figure 6.3 Flowchart symbols.

In order to illustrate how to employ flowcharts for program development, several examples, of increasing complexity, will be given. As a first example we will develop a program to determine which of three numbers A, B, or C is the largest. This example involves the use of the decision box, and to simplify the problem solution it is helpful to define the following mathematical operations.

Symbol	Meaning
$A = B$	A equals B
$A \neq B$	A not equal to B
$A > B$	A greater than B
$A < B$	A less than B
$A \geq B$	A greater than or equal to B
$A \leq B$	A less than or equal to B

For now let's assume that in any single decision box any one of these mathematical operations may be tested for. The flowchart solution for the problem is given in Fig. 6.4.

On program initiation the data for the numbers A, B, and C is entered into the machine. This input box could, for example, represent a keyboard input device. In the first decision-making box the numbers A and B are compared; if A is greater than B, it is next compared with C, and if it is larger than both B and C, the number A is exhibited in some form of visual display. Should the number A fail in either of these tests, then either B or C is the largest, and a similar test must be performed comparing their relative sizes. On completion the program stops, and the output display will indicate which of the three numbers A, B, or C is the largest.

In some cases it is useful to be able to execute a certain group of instructions within a program more than once. This operation is readily accomplished by a technique known as *looping*. A specific partial program flowchart illustrating this concept is given in Fig. 6.5. Before entering the loop the "index" I is initialized, and this index keeps track of the number of passes made through the loop. At some point within the loop the index value is changed. It may be incremented or decremented, usually by one, but also if desired by any number. At the bottom of the loop there is a a decision box which monitors the value of the index and causes the loop to be executed over and over again until a decision is made to exit. In the example shown, the loop, and hence all computations within the loop, will be repeated 10 times.

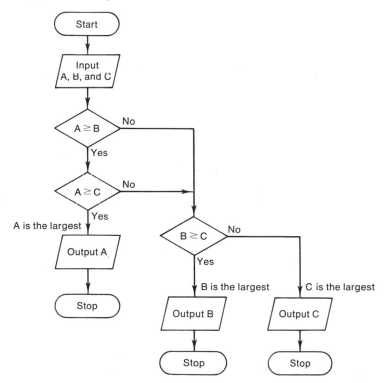

Figure 6.4 Flowchart for program to determine the largest of three numbers *A*, *B*, and *C*.

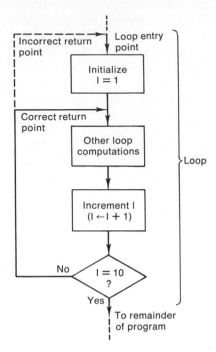

Figure 6.5 Program looping.

One common programming error is shown by the dotted return path from the decision box. Here, the program will get "hung up" in the loop forever, since each time the return occurs the index *I* will be reinitialized to one so that an exit from the loop will never occur.

In the previous example the exit from the loop occurred after a predetermined number of passes through the loop. However, in

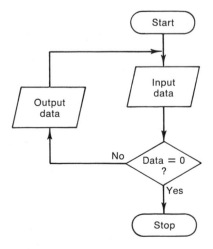

Figure 6.6 Flowchart illustrating looping without the use of an index.

some cases, the loop doesn't have an index, and loop exiting is determined by the generation of a particular result or the input of a specific piece of data. Consider, for example, the problem illustrated in Fig. 6.6. Here the computer continually inputs data and then displays it on a particular output device. The program continues looping forever until it encounters a specific piece of data, in this case a zero, and then terminates. Note that this type of program

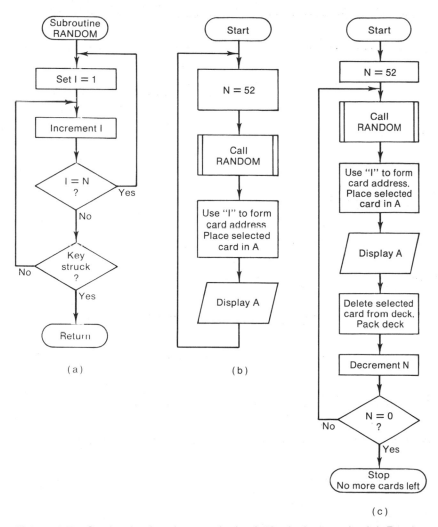

Figure 6.7 Card selection from a deck of 52 playing cards. (*a*) Random number generator; (*b*) card selection from a deck with replacement; (*c*) card selection from a deck without replacement.

allows a list of undetermined length to be read into the machine as long as the last piece of actual data is followed by a zero data. To accomplish the same task using the index counter approach would require an accurate tabulation of the total amount of data to be used and a program modification each time this number is changed.

In the last flowchart example of this section, we will formulate a problem of considerable interest in video card games: simulating card selection from a deck of 52 playing cards. The flowchart will be developed for two different cases, the first for card selection with replacement back in the deck, and the second, as is the case in most card games, for selection without replacement. In order to develop these programs, some type of random-number generation routine will be required. One possible subroutine to accomplish this is illustrated in the flowchart of Fig. 6.7*a*. Here the index just keeps incrementing from 1 up to 52 and then back again until a key is hit on the keyboard simulating player selection of a card from the deck. At this point, the incrementing stops, the program exits the subroutine, and control is returned to the main program.

In the case of card selection with replacement, the random number program is used to generate the address containing the name of the selected card, and the size of the card list always remains the same (Fig. 6.7*b*). If the cards are drawn without replacement, then the size of the random number list generated must be reduced by one each time a card is drawn, the card drawn deleted from the "deck," and the card list remaining packed together. This procedure is illustrated in Fig. 6.7*c*.

6.3 THE 8080 MICROPROCESSOR INSTRUCTION SET

The 8080 instruction set consists of 78 basic instructions, which may be divided into five major categories:

1. Data transfer group

2. Arithmetic group

3. Logical group

4. Branch group

5. Stack, I/O, and machine control group

Instructions classified within the data transfer group involve the movement of data between the microcomputer registers and memory, as well as between individual registers. Instructions in the arithmetic group focus on the standard operations of addition and subtraction, while those in the logical group permit AND, OR, EXOR, complement, and rotate operations to be performed on data in registers or memory. The decision-making capability of the processor resides in its branch group instructions, which allow the execution sequence of a program to be altered based on the results of tests performed on the contents of registers or memory. The last group of instructions, the stack, I/O, and machine control group, govern the machine's control over interrupt, I/O operations, and the software stack. In addition this group affects the overall operation of the processor.

The basic data word size in the 8080 is the 8-bit byte, with D0 representing the least significant bit (LSB) and D7 the most significant bit (MSB):

Single-byte data word

D7	D6	D5	D4	D3	D2	D1	D0

Each word in memory is specified by a 16-bit, or 2-byte, address and thus the 8080 can directly address up to 2^{16}, or 65,536, bytes of RAM or ROM.

Instructions used with the 8080 vary in length from 1 to 3 bytes. For single-byte instructions, INR A (increment the accumulator), for example, all of the information necessary to execute the instruction is contained in that byte.

Single-Byte Instruction

D7	D0	Op code

In the 2- and 3-byte instructions, however, additional information besides the operation code (op code) is required. This information, in the form of an address or data, is contained in byte 2 or bytes 2 and 3 of the instruction.

Double-Byte Instruction

Byte 1	D7 — D0	Op code
Byte 2	D7 — D0	Data or address

Triple-Byte Instruction

Byte 1	D7 D0	Op code
Byte 2	D7 D0	
Byte 3	D7 D0	Data or address

The 8080 employs four major addressing modes: immediate, direct, register, and register indirect. In the immediate addressing mode, depending on the type of instruction, either the second byte or the second and third bytes of the instruction contain the actual data to be utilized. With direct addressing, bytes 2 and 3 specify the address of the memory location where the data will be found. It should be noted that the higher-order part of the address is contained in byte 3 of the instruction and the lower-order portion in byte 2.

The 8080 also permits data to be moved directly from one specific register to other points in the microcomputer. This is known as *pure register addressing.* In the last addressing technique, the register indirect mode, the register pair specified in the instruction contains the address of the memory location where the data will be found.

Data Transfer Group

In the 8080 instruction repetoire it is possible to transfer data between any two of the general-purpose data registers with a single-byte instruction, the MOV. In its most general form this instruction may be written as:

Mnemonic	Meaning
MOV r_1, r_2	Move contents of r_2 into r_1.

where r_2 represents the data source register and r_1 the destination register for the data. For example, to transfer the contents of the H register to the accumulator, the programmer need only write:

Mnemonic	Hex code	Meaning
MOV A, H	7C	A ← H

It should be noted that the execution of this instruction does not alter the contents of the source, in this case the H register. The hexadecimal coding for this instruction was obtained from Table 6.1.

By using the immediate instructions, it is possible to load a specific register with data which comes directly from the second byte of the instruction. Illustrated below is one such move immediate instruction (MVI), in which the contents of the C register are being loaded with the hexadecimal number 57 (written for clarity as 57_H).

Mnemonic	Hex code	Description
MVI C	0E	Load C register with 57_H.
57H	57	

As we have mentioned previously, words in memory may be addressed by two techniques—direct addressing and indirect addressing. With direct addressing, the 2 bytes following the instruction provide the address information, with byte 2 representing the lower-order and byte 3 the higher-order portion of the address. As an example, suppose that we wish to place the contents of memory location 53A6 into the accumulator. The 3-byte instruction to accomplish this would be:

Mnemonic	Hex code	Meaning
LDA	3A	Load accumulator with contents of memory location 53A6.
A6	A6	
53	53	

The corresponding instruction to store the contents of the accumulator at the same location would be:

Mnemonic	Hex code	Meaning
STA	32	Store contents of accumulator in memory location 53A6.
A6	A6	
53	53	

Besides using the direct addressing scheme employed above, it is also possible to use the contents of specific register pairs as memory reference addresses. This indirect addressing technique is extremely powerful for processing data lists and for calculating addresses from program execution results.

TABLE 6.1 MACHINE LANGUAGE CODES FOR THE 8080 INSTRUCTION SETS

Data transfer group

MOVE IMMEDIATE

06	MVI	B,	⎫
0E	MVI	C,	
16	MVI	D,	
1E	MVI	E,	⎬ D8
26	MVI	H,	
2E	MVI	L,	
36	MVI	M,	
3E	MVI	A,	⎭

MOVE

40	MOV	B,B
41	MOV	B,C
42	MOV	B,D
43	MOV	B,E
44	MOV	B,H
45	MOV	B,L
46	MOV	B,M
47	MOV	B,A
48	MOV	C,B
49	MOV	C,C
4A	MOV	C,D
4B	MOV	C,E
4C	MOV	C,H
4D	MOV	C,L
4E	MOV	C,M

4F	MOV	C,A
50	MOV	D,B
51	MOV	D,C
52	MOV	D,D
53	MOV	D,E
54	MOV	D,H
55	MOV	D,L
56	MOV	D,M
57	MOV	D,A
58	MOV	E,B
59	MOV	E,C
5A	MOV	E,D
5B	MOV	E,E
5C	MOV	E,H
5D	MOV	E,L
5E	MOV	E,M
5F	MOV	E,A
60	MOV	H,B
61	MOV	H,C
62	MOV	H,D
63	MOV	H,E
64	MOV	H,H
65	MOV	H,L
66	MOV	H,M
67	MOV	H,A

68	MOV	L,B
69	MOV	L,C
6A	MOV	L,D
6B	MOV	L,E
6C	MOV	L,H
6D	MOV	L,L
6E	MOV	L,M
6F	MOV	L,A
70	MOV	M,B
71	MOV	M,C
72	MOV	M,D
73	MOV	M,E
74	MOV	M,H
75	MOV	M,L
77	MOV	M,A
78	MOV	A,B
79	MOV	A,C
7A	MOV	A,D
7B	MOV	A,E
7C	MOV	A,H
7D	MOV	A,L
7E	MOV	A,M
7F	MOV	A,A

LOAD/STORE

0A	LDAX	B
1A	LDAX	D
2A	LHLD	Adr
3A	LDA	Adr
02	STAX	B
12	STAX	D
22	SHLD	Adr
32	STA	Adr

LOAD IMMEDIATE

01	LXI	B,	⎫
11	LXI	D,	⎬ D16
21	LXI	H,	
31	LXI	SP,	⎭

Arithmetic group

ACCUMULATOR*

80	ADD	B
81	ADD	C
82	ADD	D
83	ADD	E
84	ADD	H
85	ADD	L
86	ADD	M
87	ADD	A
88	ADC	B
89	ADC	C
8A	ADC	D
8B	ADC	E
8C	ADC	H
8D	ADC	L
8E	ADC	M
8F	ADC	A

90	SUB	B
91	SUB	C
92	SUB	D
93	SUB	E
94	SUB	H
95	SUB	L
96	SUB	M
97	SUB	A
98	SBB	B
99	SBB	C
9A	SBB	D
9B	SBB	E
9C	SBB	H
9D	SBB	L
9E	SBB	M
9F	SBB	A

DOUBLE ADD†

09	DAD	B
19	DAD	D
29	DAD	H
39	DAD	SP

INCREMENT‡

04	INR	B
0C	INR	C
14	INR	D
1C	INR	E
24	INR	H
2C	INR	L
34	INR	M
3C	INR	A
03	INX	B
13	INX	D
23	INX	H
33	INX	SP

DECREMENT‡

05	DCR	B
0D	DCR	C
15	DCR	D
1D	DCR	E
25	DCR	H
2D	DCR	L
35	DCR	M
3D	DCR	A
0B	DCX	B
1B	DCX	D
2B	DCX	H
3B	DCX	SP

Acc IMMEDIATE*

C6	ADI	⎫
CE	ACI	⎬ D8
D6	SUI	
DE	SBI	⎭

27	DAA*

TABLE 6.1 MACHINE LANGUAGE CODES FOR THE 8080
INSTRUCTION SETS (Continued)

Logical group					*Stack, I/O, and Machine Control Group*					
A8	XRA	B	A0	ANA	B	**STACK OPS**			**CONTROL**	
A9	XRA	C	A1	ANA	C					
AA	XRA	D	A2	ANA	D	C5	PUSH	B	00	NOP
AB	XRA	E	A3	ANA	E	D5	PUSH	D	76	HLT
AC	XRA	H	A4	ANA	H	E5	PUSH	H	F3	DI
AD	XRA	L	A5	ANA	L	F5	PUSH	PSW	FB	EI
AE	XRA	M	A6	ANA	M					
AF	XRA	A	A7	ANA	A	C1	POP	B	**INPUT/OUTPUT**	
						D1	POP	D		
B0	ORA'	B	E6	ANI		E1	POP	H	D3	OUT	D8
B1	ORA	C	EE	XRI		F1	POP	PSW*	DB	IN	D8
B2	ORA	D	F6	ORI	D8					
B3	ORA	E	FE	CPI		E3	XTHL			
B4	ORA	H				F9	SPHL			
B5	ORA	L	**ROTATE†**							
B6	ORA	M								
B7	ORA	A	07	RLC						
			0F	RRC						
B8	CMP	B	17	RAL						
B9	CMP	C	1F	RAR						
BA	CMP	D								
BB	CMP	E	2F	CMA						
BC	CMP	H	37	STC†						
BD	CMP	L	3F	CMC†						
BE	CMP	M								
BF	CMP	A								

Branch group

JUMP			**CALL**			**RETURN**		**RESTART**		
C3	JMP		CD	CALL		C9	RET	C7	RST	0
C2	JNZ		C4	CNZ		C0	RNZ	CF	RST	1
CA	JZ		CC	CZ		C8	RZ	D7	RST	2
D2	JNC		D4	CNC		D0	RNC	DF	RST	3
DA	JC	Adr	DC	CC	Adr	D8	RC	E7	RST	4
E2	JPO		E4	CPO		E0	RPO	EF	RST	5
EA	JPE		EC	CPE		E8	RPE	F7	RST	6
F2	JP		F4	CP		F0	RP	FF	RST	7
FA	JM		FC	CM		F8	RM			
E9	PCHL									

D8 = constant, or logical/arithmetic expression that evaluates to an 8-bit data quantity.
D16 = constant, or logical/arithmetic expression that evaluates to an 16-bit data quantity.
Adr = 16-bit address
*All flags (C, Z, S, P) affected.
†Only CARRY affected.
‡All flags except CARRY affected (exception: INX and DXC affect no flags).
SOURCE: Adapted from a table published by Processor Technology Corp. The 8080 Mnemonics are copyrighted by Intel Corp.

In the 8080 processor, the HL register pair is most often used for this type of addressing, since most of the indirect addressing instructions specifically refer to this register pair. For example, to transfer data from a specific memory location, address 0053, to the accumulator, the HL register pair is first loaded with the data 0053, and then the following indirect MOV instruction executed.

Mnemonic	Hex code	Meaning
MOV M, A	77	Move contents of accumulator into the memory location addressed by HL.

Note that this is a single-byte instruction in which the contents of A are stored in the memory location "pointed to" by the contents of the HL register pair. At first this approach may seem cumbersome, since it looks as if we have to load the HL pair each time before this kind of instruction can be executed. However, to really appreciate the power of this instruction, consider the following sample program:

	Mnemonic	Meaning
	MVI A	Set A = 0.
	00	
	LXI H	Initialize HL pair to 00FF.
	FF	
	00	
LOOP	MOV M, A	Fill selected section of memory with 0s.
	DCR L	
	JNZ LOOP	

Here the MOV M,A instruction has been placed inside a repetitive loop. On each pass through the loop, 0s are placed in the memory location pointed to by the HL register pair, and the pointer is then moved to the next memory location; this continues until the loop is exited when L goes to 0. In this way, this small six-step program has been employed to clear the entire section of memory from address 00FF to address 0000.

By using a similar instruction, MOV A,M, data may be transferred from a specific memory location to the accumulator. Similar transfers are also possible between memory and any of the other general-purpose data registers (B, C, D, E, H, L) through use of the instructions MOVr,M and MOV M,r, where r represents the register under consideration. These instructions are listed in Table 6.2, and the specific hexadecimal machine codes associated with each are given in Table 6.1.

It is also possible to move data between memory and the accumulator by using the BC and DE register pairs in conjunction with appropriate load (LDAX) and store (STAX) instructions. Thus, for example, to use the DE register pair as a pointer to memory to store the contents of the accumulator, the programmer need only write the single-byte instruction:

Mnemonic	*Hex code*	*Meaning*
STAX D	1A	Store contents of accumulator in the memory location pointed to by the content of the DE pair.

Note, however, that with these instructions data transfer is possible only between M and A, and not between memory and any of the other registers.

Within the data transfer group several register-pair load/store instructions are also available. These instructions make it possible to move data to and from these register pairs more efficiently than by the equivalent single-register MOV instructions. For example, to

TABLE 6.2   DATA TRANSFER GROUP INSTRUCTIONS

	Number of bytes
1. Move: destination, source	
Reg. 1, Reg. 2 MOV B,E	1
Reg. 1, Mem. Ref. MOV C,M	1
Mem. Ref., Reg. 2 MOV M,D	1
Reg. 1, immediate byte MVI E,20	2
NOTE. M = indirect memory reference using H,L register pair.	
2. Load/store accumulator	
Direct LDA addr	3
STA addr	3
Indirect LDAX reg pair	1
STAX reg pair	1
3. Load/store register pairs	
Direct (H,L pair only) LHLD addr	3
SHLD addr	3
Immediate LXI reg pair,	
pairs (B,C; D,E; H,L; S,P) 2 date bytes	3
4. Exchange pairs (H,L with D,E) XCHG	1

load the HL register pair with the contents of two successive memory locations, 4350 in L and 4351 in H, the programmer could write:

Mnemonic	Hex code	Meaning
LDA		Load A with contents of memory location 4350.
50		
43		
MOV L, A		Load L with A.
LDA		
51		Load A with contents of memory location 4351.
43		
MOV H, A		Load H with A.

However, the same task could also be accomplished with the following single instruction:

Mnemonic	Hex code	Meaning
LHLD	2A	Load L register with contents of memory location 4350 and H with contents of 4351.
50	50	
43	43	

Unfortunately, this instruction is available only for the HL register pair. However, there are LOAD IMMEDIATE instructions which permit any of the register pairs to be loaded with the data given in bytes 2 and 3 of the instruction. In this way, to load the BC register pair with the data A83C the programmer simply writes:

Mnemonic	Hex code	Meaning
LXI B	01	Place the data 3C (byte 2) in the C register and the data A8 (byte 3) in the B register.
3C	3C	
A8	A8	

Note that here too byte 2 is placed in the low-order register and byte 3 in the higher-order register.

The last instruction in the data transfer group, the exchange (XCHG), is used to interchange the contents of the HL and DE register pairs. This operation is frequently useful in programs involving the simultaneous employment of several indirect addressing schemes.

Arithmetic Group

In order to fully understand the instructions contained in this group, a knowledge of binary numbers as well as addition and subtraction procedures in binary and binary-coded-decimal (BCD) arithmetic is necessary. Those readers needing a review in these subjects should consult one of the references given at the end of the chapter.

The first four sets of instructions in this group are self-explanatory (Table 6.3) except to note that the ADD WITH CARRY, and SUBTRACT WITH BORROW instructions are employed when performing multibyte arithmetic. Examples of these operations will be given below. Consider first a simpler program involving the addition of two single-byte numbers, 36_H and $4C_H$. The following are two possible techniques for performing this addition:

Mnemonic	Hex code	Mnemonic	Hex code
MVI A	3E	MVI A	3E
36	36	36	36
MVI B	06	ADI	C6
4C	46	4C	4C
ADD B	80		

In the example given on the left, the A and B registers are first loaded with a 36_H and $4C_H$ respectively, and the contents of the B register are added to A. In the example on the right, A is again loaded with a 36, but then an ADD IMMEDIATE instruction is employed in which the second byte of the instruction is itself the data to be added to the accumulator. For both cases the final answer in the accumulator, the result of the hexadecimal addition of 36_H and $4C_H$, will be 82_H.

For large numbers an 8-bit data word size may not be sufficient. In such cases multibyte arithmetic will be required. Consider for example the development of a routine to perform the following hexadecimal subtraction:

$$\begin{aligned} &8AB3_H \\ -&2586_H \\ \hline &652D_H \end{aligned}$$

To accomplish this with our 8-bit processor, the two least significant hexadecimal characters, or lower-order bytes, are first subtracted (with no borrow), and then after this is done the higher-order bytes are subtracted. For the latter case, however, a SUBTRACT WITH BORROW is required to take into account the possibility that the previous lower-order subtraction generated a borrow. One possible program to perform this task may be given as:

Mnemonic	Hex code	Meaning
LXI B	01	Place minuend in BC pair and subtrahend in DE pair.
B3	B3	
8A	8A	
LXI D	11	
86	86	
25	25	
MOV A, C	79	Subtract lower-order bytes store lower-order portion of result in C.
SUB E	93	
MOV C, A	4F	
MOV A, B	78	Subtract higher-order bytes with borrow.
SBB D	9A	
MOV B, A	47	Store higher-order result in B.

The final answer, $652D_H$, is stored in the BC register pair. A complete listing of the instructions found in the arithmetic group is given in Table 6.3 and their equivalent hexadecimal machine code listings in Table 6.1.

A similar program could also be written to perform multibyte addition: however, the double-byte addition of two numbers can be directly accomplished by making use of the special register-pair double ADD instructions. Here the register pair specified in the instruction (HL, BC, DE, SP) is added to the HL pair, and the result stored in the HL registers. One interesting application of this instruction is obtained when the HL register pair is added to itself, that is, when a DAD H instruction is executed. Whenever a number is added to itself, twice the original answer is obtained. Therefore, this instruction may be used to multiply the contents of the HL register pair by 2 and is particularly useful as part of a general multiplication subroutine. One additional feature of this instruction is that, since multiplication by 2 in binary systems is the same as a shift left, the execution of a DAD H instruction produces a single-bit shift left in the HL register pair.

The meanings of the increment and decrement register, memory, and register-pair instructions are apparent. These types of instructions are often used for loop counting, where, for example, a register is decremented and continuously tested for 0. When the register reaches 0, the looping operation is terminated and the remainder of the program executed. One note of caution, however; the INX and DCX register-pair instructions do not affect the flags (see Table 5.3), and hence they cannot be easily used as loop index counters.

The decimal-adjust-the-accumulator (DAA) instruction is employed when working with BCD arithmetic. As an example of the application of this instruction, consider the addition of the two BCD numbers 43_D and 38_D.[2] If these numbers were just added by ordinary binary addition, the result would be 8B, which is not the correct decimal answer. By applying the DAA instruction to this intermediate result, the correct answer, 81, is obtained. A partial program listing to perform this decimal addition would be written as:

Mnemonic	Hex code	Meaning
MVI A	3E	Load the data to be added into the A and B registers.
43	43	
MVI B	06	
37	37	
ADD B	80	Perform binary addition of *A* and *B*.
DAA	27	Decimal adjust the result.

Logical Group

These instructions allow for logical AND, OR, XOR, and bit-shifting operations to be performed on the accumulator. The additional data for implementing these instructions is found either in the second byte of the instruction (immediate data) or in one of the general-purpose registers. All logical operations are performed on a bit-by-bit basis, so that, for example, when the A and B registers are "ANDed" together, bit D7 of A is "ANDed" with D7 of B, etc. Those readers unfamiliar with these logical operations should refer to any of the references at the end of the chapter for a complete description of these terms.

Besides their obvious logical functions, these instructions may be employed for masking, clearing, and setting of specific bits in the accumulator. Suppose, for example, that the programmer wishes to clear the accumulator, that is, set it equal to 0. A quick glance at the 8080 instruction listing given in Table 6.4 reveals that while it is possible to set and complement the carry as well as to complement the accumulator, no specific instruction exists to clear it. However,

---

[2]The subscript D following each number means that it is to be considered as a decimal (or BCD) number.

TABLE 6.3 ARITHMETIC GROUP INSTRUCTIONS

			Number of bytes
1.	Add to accumulator		
	ADD	reg. or mem. ref.	1
	ADI	data	2
2.	Add with carry to accumulator		
	ADC	reg.for mem. ref.	1
	ACI	data	2
3.	Subtract from accumulator		
	SUB	reg. or mem. ref.	1
	SUI	data	2
4.	Subtract with borrow from accumulator		
	SBB	reg. or mem. ref.	1
	SBI	data	2
5.	Double byte add register pair to H,L		
	DAD	reg. pair (B,C; D,E; H,L; S,P)	1
6.	Decrement register or pair		
	INR	reg. or mem. ref.	1
	INX	reg. pair (B,C; D,E; H,L; S,P)	1
7.	Increment register or pair		
	DCR	reg. or mem. ref.	1
	DCX	reg. pair (B,C; D,E; H,L; S,P)	1
8.	Decimal adjust accumulator		
	DAA		1

this can still be accomplished using either of the two following methods:

Mnemonic	*Hex code*
MVI A	3E
00	00

This method requires a 2-byte instruction; however, the same result can be accomplished in a single byte by writing:

Mnemonic	*Hex code*
XRA A	AF

Here the accumulator is simply "exclusive-ORed" with itself. Recall that in an exclusive-OR (XOR) operation, a nonzero result is obtained only when the input bits are different. However, since each bit in the accumulator will be XORed with itself, these input bits will always be the same, and therefore the result in each case will be 0, clearing the accumulator.

TABLE 6.4   LOGICAL GROUP INSTRUCTIONS

		Number of bytes
1.	Logical AND with accumulator	
	ANA reg. or mem. ref.	1
	ANI data	2
2.	Exclusive OR with accumulator	
	XRA reg. or mem. ref.	1
	XRI data	2
3.	Logical OR with accumulator	
	ORA reg. or mem. ref.	1
	ORI data	2
4.	Compare with accumulator	
	CMP reg. or mem. ref.	1
	CPI data	2
	NOTE: No changes are made to the accumulator only the flags are set.	
5.	Rotate accumulator 1 bit	
	Left RLC	1
	Right RRC	1
	Left through carry RAL	1
	Right through carry RAR	1
6.	Complement accumulator CMA	1
7.	Set carry bit STC	1
8.	Complement carry bit CMC	1

In some applications it is necessary to "mask off" or strip away a particular part of a data word and replace it with either 1s or 0s. For example, suppose the data in the accumulator were a 9B, and further suppose that it was desired to remove from the word its most significant hex character, the 9, and replace it by a 0. A programmer formulating this procedure would plan to mask off the four most significant bits in the accumulator. One method of achieving this is illustrated in Fig. 6.8. Each bit in the accumulator is "ANDed" with

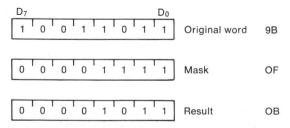

Figure 6.8 AND masking of a word in the accumulator.

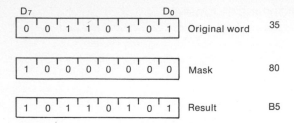

Figure 6.9 OR masking of a word in the accumulator.

its corresponding mask bit, effectively stripping away bits D4 to D7 from the original accumulator word and replacing them by 0s.

At times an effect opposite to that previously discussed is required; that is, it is necessary to set bits to one at specific locations in the word. For example, let's suppose that it is necessary to set bit D7 in the accumulator to one. To do this the accumulator is simply "ORed" with a data word having a one in the D7 location and zeros at all other positions. This operation guarantees that the selected bits will be set to one, while the remaining bit locations in the word will be unaffected (Fig. 6.9).

The rotate instructions in the logical group allow the data contained in the accumulator to be shifted one bit to the left or right. The rotate is of the end-around type and, as shown in Fig. 6.10, may either include or not include the carry bit. When a ROTATE WITHOUT CARRY instruction is executed, for example, a rotate accumulator right (RRC), each bit moves down one position to the right, that is, D7 to D6, D6 to D5, etc. In addition the least significant bit D0 rotates into both D7 and the carry flag bit. In a rotate including the carry, for example, an RAR instruction, the bit shifting is the same as before within the accumulator. However, for this case D0 is shifted into the carry bit, and the carry into accumulator bit D7 (Fig. 6.10*b*).

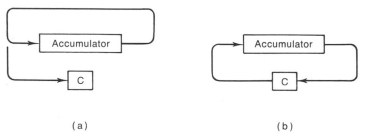

(a)   (b)

Figure 6.10 Rotate accumulator operations. (*a*) Rotate right without carry (RRC); (*b*) rotate right with carry (RAR).

These rotate instructions are especially useful for implementing multiply and divide functions, for serial data transmission, and for individual bit testing on a given word. For example, suppose that one wished to test the status of bit D2 in the accumulator. This could be accomplished by rotating D2 into the carry bit position and then testing the carry to determine its value. The three rotate instructions shown in the example below move accumulator bit D2 into the carry flag position.

Mnemonic

```
         .
         .
         .
       RAR
       RAR
       RAR
       JNC X
       JMP Y
```

If the flag is 0, the program will branch to address X, and if it is 1, it will be directed to address Y.

One additional note: for the carry bit to be cleared, it must first be set to 1 and then complemented, since no clear carry instruction is available.

Branch Group

No computer instruction set is complete unless it includes some type of branching operations. Otherwise the processor is doomed to execute the same list of instructions in one specific sequence forever. The *branch group instructions* allow the microcomputer to alter the program execution sequence in response to specific types of data, data processing results, or input conditions. The various subcategories within the branch group are listed in Table 6.5.

A *jump* is an instruction which permits the program execution sequence to be altered. In the 8080 all jumps are 3-byte instructions in which the first byte indicates the type of jump instruction being implemented, and the remaining bytes the address to be jumped to. The 8080 instruction set includes both conditional and unconditional jumps.

Whenever an unconditional jump is executed, the program counter (PC) is loaded with bytes 2 and 3 of the instruction, and program execution continues from the "jumped to" address. For the case of conditional jumps, however, the jump is executed only when the condition specified by the instruction is satisfied. Otherwise, the instruction is ignored, and the execution sequence continues at the location following the jump. In the 8080, conditional jumps are available which test the zero, carry, parity, and sign flag bits (see Table 5.3). As an application of the conditional jump consider the following partial program listing:

Mnemonic	*Hex code*
.	.
.	.
.	.
DCR E	ID
JZ	CA
47	47
3C	3C
.	.
.	.

Here when the decrement E (DCR E) instruction is executed, it affects all of the flag bits, and therefore if the E register is 0, the zero flag bit will be set to 1. When the jump on zero (JZ) instruction is executed next, it tests the condition of the zero flag bit, and if it is found to be set to 1, will cause a branch to memory location $3C47_H$. If this flag bit

TABLE 6.5 BRANCH GROUP INSTRUCTIONS

			Number of bytes
1.	Jump instructions		
	Unconditional		
	Direct	JMP addr	3
	Indirect	PCHL	1
	Conditional		
	Zero flag	JZ addr	3
		JNZ addr	3
	Carry flag	JC addr	3
		JNC addr	3
	Parity flag	JPE addr	3
		JPO addr	3
	Sign flag	JP addr	3
		JM addr	3
2.	Call instructions		
3.	Restart instructions		
4.	Return instructions		

is 0, then program execution will simply continue at the location following the jump instruction. The point to note here is that the flag conditions tested for are determined by the last instruction immediately preceding the conditional jump which affected them. The following example illustrates one common 8080 programming error:

```
        .
        .
        .
    ADI A
    35
    DCX B
    JP
    47
    3C
```

Here the programmer expected to continue jumping to location 3C47 as long as the BC register pair was greater than or equal to 0, when in fact what was actually tested for in the jump instruction was the sign of the accumulator contents after the data word 35 was added to them. This situation arose because, as shown in Table 5.3, the register increment (INX) and decrement (DCX) instructions don't affect the flag's register, and therefore the conditional jump branch direction will be determined by the last instruction which affected the sign flag bit, in this case the add immediate (ADI) instruction.

In addition to those branch instructions in the jump category, similar sets of instructions are available to call a subroutine, and to return from it. In the sample subroutine given below, the program checks to see if the number currently in the accumulator is divisible by 3. It does this by performing successive subtractions of 3 from the A register.

Hex address	Symbolic address	Mnemonic	Meaning
4000	Start	SUB I	Subtract 3 from A.
4001		03	
4002		RM	If return here, number is not divisible by 3.
4003		CZ YES	If this routine called, number is divisible by 3.
4004		73	
4005		D5	
4006		JMP START	
4007		00	
4008		40	

Eventually, if the original number is not divisible by 3, a negative result will be produced in A, and the routine will execute the return on minus (RM) instruction. If, however, the A register initially contains a multiple of 3, then eventually as it is continually decremented by 3, it will reach zero. When this happens, the call on zero (CZ) instruction will cause a jump to the subroutine YES starting at memory location D573, which will indicate to the operator, perhaps

D_7	D_6	D_5	D_4	D_3	D_2	D_1	D_0
1	1	N_3	N_2	N_1	1	1	1

Figure 6.11 Basic structure of the restart instructions.

on some type of display, that the original number in A was in fact divisible by 3.

The restart (RST r) instruction is actually a special single-byte CALL instruction which is only permitted to jump to one of eight different points near the beginning of memory. When this instruction, like all CALL instructions, is executed, the current contents of the PC are saved on the top of the stack, and the program counter is loaded with an address whose value is eight times $N_3N_2N_1$ given in Fig. 6.11. The hex code for each of the eight possible restart instructions is obtained by placing the restart address in bits D3, D4, and D5, and ones in all other bit locations. For example, the binary code for an RST 0 instruction would be 11000111, or C7 in hex code. When executed it would initiate a CALL instruction to memory location 0000H. A summary of all possible RST instructions, along with their respective restart points in memory, is given in Table 6.6.

It should be noted that this is also the method employed by the 8080 to execute interrupts. When an interrupt is recognized by the machine and the interrupt acknowledge signal is sent out by the processor, the latter is requesting that the interrupting device jam a restart address onto the data bus by appropriately pulling down bit

TABLE 6.6   THE RESTART INSTRUCTION

Mnemonic	Binary code								Hex code	Address "called"
	D7	D6	D5	D4	D3	D2	D1	D0		
RST. 0	1	1	0	0	0	1	1	1	C7	0000
RST. 1	1	1	0	0	1	1	1	1	CF	0008
RST. 2	1	1	0	1	0	1	1	1	D7	0010
RST. 3	1	1	0	1	1	1	1	1	DF	0018
RST. 4	1	1	1	0	0	1	1	1	E7	0020
RST. 5	1	1	1	0	1	1	1	1	EF	0028
RST. 6	1	1	1	1	0	1	1	1	F7	0030
RST. 7	1	1	1	1	1	1	1	1	FF	0038

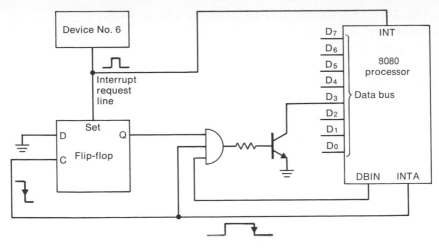

Figure 6.12 Simplified vectored interrupt circuit.

lines D3, D4, and/or D5. The processor then inputs this data bus information to the instruction register and executes it as the next instruction. If none of the data bus lines were pulled down, they would all float high (FF), and an RST7 instruction would be input to the IR and executed by the processor in response to the interrupt.

To achieve "vectoring" to other memory locations, the proper bit values must be created in D3, D4, and D5 in response to the INTA signal. Shown in Fig. 6.12 is a simplified vectored interrupt circuit. This circuit generates an RST6 whenever an interrupt from device 6 occurs. Therefore, the SERVICE routine associated with this particular interrupt would begin at memory location 0030.

Stack, I/O, and Machine Control Group

This group of instructions (Table 6.7) manipulates data on the stack, controls the flow of data to the outside world, operates the interrupt system, and governs the status of the machine.

The input and output instructions are 2-byte commands, with the first byte indicating whether it is an input or output instruction, and the second byte which of the 256 distinct I/O ports is being addressed. Thus to read data from input port 38 into the accumulator, the programmer writes:

Mnemonic	*Hex code*	*Meaning*
IN	DB	Read data currently at input port 38 into A.
38	38	

TABLE 6.7 I/O, STACK, AND MACHINE CONTROL GROUP
INSTRUCTIONS

		Number of boxes
1.	Input to accumulator from input port	
	IN port number	2
2.	Output to output port from accumulator	
	OUT port number	2
3.	Enable interrupts	
	EI	1
4.	Disable interrupts	
	DI	1
5.	Push/pop register pair	
	(BC, DE, HL, PSW)	1
6.	Exchange top of stack with HL XTHL	1
7.	Move HL to SP	
	SPHL	1
8.	Halt HLT	1
9.	No operation NOP	1

To output data to port FF from the accumulator, the corresponding
instruction is:

Mnemonic	*Hex code*	*Meaning*
OUT	D3	Write contents of A into output port FF.
FF	FF	

In addition to communicating with the processor by means of the
I/O ports, the 8080 also provides the user with an external interrupt
control line. By employing the interrupt enable and disable instructions, the processor may choose to either recognize or ignore interrupts during a specific portion of the program. When the 8080 is
RESET, interrupts are automatically disabled by resetting the internal enable interrupt flip-flop, and therefore, if it is necessary that
interrupts be processed, it is first necessary to execute an enable
interrupt (EI) instruction on coming out of reset. In addition, once an
interrupt is recognized by the processor, the interrupt flip-flop is
reset to prevent the occurrence of multiple interrupts.

As mentioned in Sec. 5.6, in servicing interrupts and in executing
subroutines, the contents of the processor's internal data registers
are frequently altered, and it is therefore convenient to have a
temporary storage area for this information while executing these
routines. In the 8080 this data may be stored in the stack by making

use of the PUSH and POP instructions. For example, to store the contents of the BC register pair on the stack, only a single-byte PUSH B instruction is required. When this instruction is executed, the contents of the B register are stored on the current top of the stack, the stack pointer (SP) register decremented, and the C register contents then pushed into the next lower byte of memory. To execute the POP B instruction, the processor reverses the procedure, and the data on the top of the stack is placed back in the BC register pair (Fig. 6.13). It is interesting to observe that after executing a PUSH B instruction, the microprocessor has no way of knowing that the data currently on the top of the stack belongs to the BC register pair, and therefore, if this instruction were followed by a POP D, the data in the BC pair would effectively be transferred to the DE registers.

As shown in Fig. 6.13, the SP register always points to the last data entered on the stack, the so-called top of the stack, although, since the 8080 loads the stack from the top down, the location pointed to might more appropriately be called the "bottom of the stack." The SP register may be initialized by using the LXI instruction previously discussed, or by means of the SPHL instruction, which places the contents of the HL pair into the stack pointer register. The XTHL instruction is used to exchange the contents of the HL register pair with the data currently on the top of the stack.

The last two instructions in this group, the HALT and the NOP, are particulary interesting. When a HALT instruction is executed, the processor stops dead in its tracks and enters a HALT state, thus

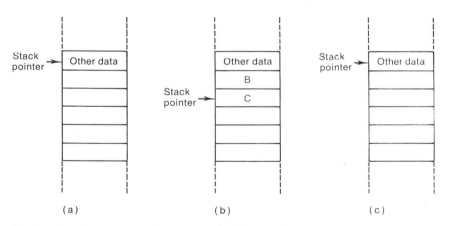

(a)   (b)   (c)

Figure 6.13 Implementation of the PUSH and POP instructions. (a) Original status of the stack; (b) stack contents after PUSH B is executed; (c) stack contents after POP B executed.

becoming idle. To release the computer from this state, it must either be reset or interrupted. The NOP (no operation) is an instruction which does nothing; that is, it requires 4 clock cycles to execute, and yet when it's done the condition of the processor is the same as it was before the instruction was operated upon. Why then is it used? It has two principal applications. The first is to waste time, i.e., to provide a time delay. With a 2-MHz clock, each NOP executed requires 2 μs of the computer's time—put five of them in a row, and you've generated a 10-μs delay. Clearly, when the long time delays are needed, this method is unsuitable because a huge number of NOPs would be required. For generating these longer delays, a more efficient algorithm of the form discussed in Sec. 6.5 is needed.

The NOP is also used to provide the program with blank spaces which may later be filled with actual instructions. All computer novices think that the programs they have just written are perfect and will never need any modifications, but experienced programmers know that this is rarely the case. Anticipating changes and later additions, they leave space for modifications in the form of NOPs scattered throughout the program. The novice, on the other hand, has made the program "as compact as possible" right from the beginning and therefore, when that extra single-byte instruction needs to be added, has to make room for it by pushing all the instructions below it down by 1 byte. A development system may have built-in software to take care of this "insertion" for you, but if you're assembling the program by hand, inserting this additional instruction is at best a very tedious job.

6.4 PROGRAMMING EXAMPLES

In programming, believe it or not, "neatness counts." The care with which you lay out the problem before you start programming, the quality of the flowcharts you construct, and, most important of all, the way you write out the coding of the actual program, all go a long way toward increasing the probability that your program will run properly on the first shot. The basic concepts of program organization and flowcharting have already been discussed. In this section we will introduce the program coding sheet and will demonstrate, through the use of several examples, how to organize and write computer programs using the 8080 microprocessor's instruction set.

The coding sheet shown in Fig. 6.14 may be divided into two main areas—the right-hand side, where the mnemonics are entered, and the area on the left, where the hexadecimal codes for the addresses

Hexadecimal code		Mnemonic		
Address	*Instruction*	*Label*	*Instruction*	*Comments*
0000	C605		ADI #05	Add 05 (hexadecimal) to A.
02	80	LOOP:	ADD B	Add B to A.
03	00		NOP	
04	2F		CMA	Complement A.
05	47		MOV B, A	Move A into B.
06	C20200		JNZ LOOP	LOOP is a symbolic address.
09	76		HLT	Stops processor.

Figure 6.14a The program coding sheet.

and instructions are placed. Each instruction mnemonic generally contains two parts—the *operation* (op code) and the *operand*. The operation portion of the instruction describes the action to be performed, and the operand the data to be used in performing it.

Typical examples of specific 8080 instruction mnemonics are given in the figure. Note that several of them, such as the HLT and NOP, do not require any operands. The reader should further observe that some of the operands, such as ADI 05, MOV M,A, or ADD B, refer to registers or data, while others, specifically the operands used with the branching instructions, indicate the branch address. These symbolic addresses refer to specific instruction addresses listed in the "Labels" column and are used to symbolically specify the branching action of the program.

The "Comments" column is the place on the coding sheet where all documentation information should be placed. Again, programs devoid of entries in this column are

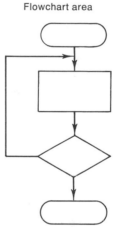

Flowchart area

Figure 6.14b The program coding sheet.

really incomplete and will, in the long run, be of limited utility. In addition to the documentation of the program, a space should be provided on the coding sheet for entering the flowchart, or portion of it, currently being developed (see Fig. 6.14*b*). Like the comments section, the flowchart makes reading and understanding the program easier, and it should therefore be utilized whenever possible.

The left-hand side of the coding sheet is used for entering the hexadecimal equivalents of the instruction codes as well as their corresponding addresses. For simplicity, think of the 65,536 words in the 8080 memory space as being composed of 256 pages of 256 lines (or bytes) per page. In hexadecimal notation the first page is 00 and the last FF, with similar notation utilized for the line numbers. The instruction code entries follow those given in Table 6.1, and, depending on the systems you have available, the translation process from mnemonics into hex code can be done either with an assembler program or by hand. With a little practice you should find, at least for small programs, that hand assembly is not all that difficult.

In the remainder of this section we will trace through the development of four sample programs from flowchart to mnemonic (source code) listing to actual hexadecimal coding. In each case the examples chosen were selected for their demonstration of particular programming techniques as well as for their relevance to electronic games.

Example 1: A Random-Number Generator

In developing electronic versions of various games of chance, some type of program is needed to simulate "lady luck" and assist in rolling the dice, in selecting cards from a deck, or in turning a roulette wheel. The routine flowcharted in Fig. 6.15 is used to produce "programmed luck" and is in fact a pseudo-random number generator. Depending on the number N initially loaded into the B register, the program will generate random numbers having values between 0 to N and will continue to do so until the player alters this sequence by hitting a key on the control panel, creating an interrupt.

The program operates by initially loading the number N into the B register and then successively decrementing it. As long as B is not equal to 0, the program keeps jumping back to LOOP and repeating this process. When B is finally reduced to 0, the program falls through to the JMP RANDOM instruction, and the B register is again initialized. Note that as part of this routine, interrupts are continuously enabled.

If, while executing this program, the player initiates an interrupt by striking the console key, the processor will stop what it's doing and jump to the INTERRUPT SERVICE routine, saving the return address on the stack. Once in the interrupt routine, the number in the B register at the time the interrupt occurred is visually displayed for the player in output port FF. After the number has been displayed, the processor *returns* to the main program. This process can be repeated over and over by the player, and the odds of obtaining a particular number will always remain the same—one out of $(N + 1)$.

Hexadecimal code		Mnemonic		
Address	Instruction	Label	Instruction	Comments
1000	0633	RANDOM:	MVI B, #33	Generates random numbers
	FB	LOOP:	EI	from 0 to *N* (for this
	05		DCR B	case N = 33H = 51D).
	C20210		JNZ LOOP	
	C30010		JMP RANDOM	
0038	78	INTERRUPT:	MVI A, B	Displays number in B
	D3FF		OUT #FF	register at the time
	C9		RET	of the interrupt.

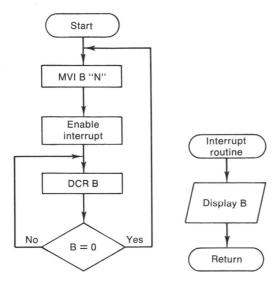

Figure 6.15   A random-number generator.

Fixed odds of this sort are useful for games involving the throwing of dice or selection of cards from a deck with replacement after drawing and for games like roulette where the probability of the ball falling into a particular slot remains the same throughout the game.

In most card games, however, cards are drawn without replacement, and therefore as each card is selected, the odds for getting one specific remaining card continue to change and in fact increase as the pack gets smaller. One possible program for generating these types of variable odds is shown in Fig. 6.16. Here the number initially placed in the C register represents the original size of the deck. At the start of the game this number is loaded into the B register, and thereafter the program is essentially the same as that for fixed odds,

Hexadecimal code		Mnemonic		
Address	Instruction	Label	Instruction	Comments
1000	OE33	VAR BEGIN:	MVI C, #33	C contains deck size.
02	41	VAR ODDS	MOV B, C	
03	FB	LOOP:	EI	
04	05		DCR B	
05	C20310		JNZ LOOP	
08	C30210		JMP VAR ODDS	
0038	78	INTERRUPT:	MOV A, B	
39	D3FF		OUT #FF	
3B	OD		DCR C	
3C	FO		RP	Return to random-number routine if C > 0. Otherwise go to GAME OVER routine
3D	C38010		JMP GAME OVER	(see Fig. 6.17)

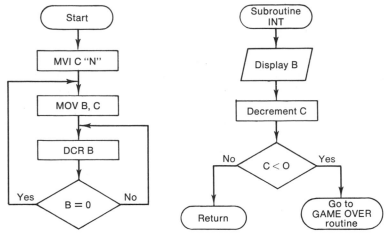

Figure 6.16 A random-number generator with variable odds.

except that each time the program is interrupted, simulating withdrawal of a card, the number in the C register is decremented, and the odds are changed. This process continues until the deck has been exhausted and C goes negative, at which time the GAME OVER subroutine (Fig. 6.17) is called.

Example 2: Packing the Deck

In order to see how the VARIABLE ODDS subroutine may be employed in an actual card game, it will first be necessary to develop one other important program—a PACK DECK subroutine (Fig. 6.17). This subroutine will be used to compact and relist the cards remain-

Hexadecimal code		Mnemonic			
Address	*Instruction*	*Label*		*Instruction*	*Comments*
1F20	46	PACK DECK:	MOV	B, M	Save selected card.
21	23	PACK MORE:	INX	H	
22	5E		MOV	E, M	Push card beneath it
23	2B		DCX	H	into vacated space.
24	73		MOV	M, E	
25	23		INX	H	
26	79		MOV	A, C	
27	BD		CMP	L	Any more cards to pack?
28	C2211F		JNZ	PACK MORE	
2B	0D		DCR	C	Any more cards in deck?
2C	FC301F		CM	GAME OVER	
2F	C9		RET		
1F30	3EFF	GAME OVER:	MVI	A, #FF	Displays an FF in output
32	D3FF		OUT	#FF	part FF to indicate game
34	C3341F	SELF:	JMP	SELF	over and then stops.

Figure 6.17   The PACK DECK subroutine.

ing in the deck after one card is drawn without replacement. For use with this routine, the data corresponding to the cards in the deck (1 byte per card) is stored as a list at the 52 memory locations 1000_H to 1033_H (Fig. 6.18). In this listing, the least significant byte of the data is used to represent the card's suit, with a 0 standing for hearts, a 1 for diamonds, a 2 for spades, and a 3 for clubs. The most significant

Memory location	Data stored	Card represented
1000	10	Ace of hearts
1001	20	Two of hearts
1002	30	Three of hearts
.	.	.
.	.	.
.	.	.
100C	D0	King of hearts
100D	11	Ace of diamonds
100E	21	Two of diamonds
.	.	.
.	.	.
.	.	.
1032	C3	Queen of clubs
1033	D3	King of clubs

Figure 6.18   Original deck of cards list in memory.

byte is used to represent the face value of the card, with 1 to 9 used for the corresponding cards and A for a ten, B for a jack, C for a queen, and D for a king. Thus, for example, a C3 would represent a queen of clubs and a 40 a four of hearts. To use this type of program in an actual video card game (see Chap. 10), an additional routine would be required to convert these codes to actual pictures of the cards on a screen, but for now we'll consider this program complete when a card has been selected from the deck, its hexadecimal code displayed, and that card deleted from the card list.

The operation of the PACK DECK routine may be best understood by carefully examining both the program listing and the comments given in Fig. 6.17. Note that the HL register pair initially contains the address of the card to be removed from the deck, the B register holds the selected card, the C register contains the current deck size, and E acts as a temporary storage register. When a specific card is selected by loading the HL pair with its address, it is placed in the B register

Memory listing		Number of cards	Card selected	Selected card address (HL register	
Address	Contents	(C register)	(B register)	pair)	Comments
1000	12	3	?	10 ? ?	
1001	30				Initial
1002	B3				values
1003	71				
1000	12	2	30	1001	After 1st interrupt
1001	B3				with random
1002	71 End of deck				number
1003	00				01 selected
1000	B3	1	12	1000	After 2d interrupt
1001	71 End of deck				with random
1002	00				number
1003	00				00 selected
1000	B3 End of deck	0	71	1001	After 3d interrupt
1001	00				with random
1002	00				number
1003	00				01 selected
1000	00	−1	B3	1000	After fourth interrupt
1001	00				with random
1002	00				number
1003	00				00 selected

"Game Over"—All cards dealt out

Figure 6.19 Operation of the PACK DECK subroutine.

Hexadecimal code		Mnemonic		
Address	Instruction	Label	Instruction	Comments
0038	68	INTERRUPT:	MOV L, B	Main routine same as that
	2610		MVI H, #10	given in Fig. 6.16.
	CD201F		CALL PACK DECK	See Fig. 6-17 (pulls card
	78		MOV A, B	from HL address and places in B)
	D3FF		OUT #FF	Displays number currently in B.
	C9		RET	

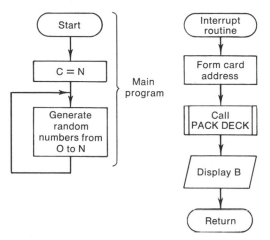

Figure 6.20 Interrupt routine for card selection without replacement program.

with the MOV B, M instruction, and then all cards remaining on the list are moved up one space in memory. This movement is accomplished by means of the PACK MORE loop in the program, and the reader is advised to trace through the loop one time using a specific address to demonstrate how this packing is achieved. The overall operation of this routine is best illustrated by an example such as that given in Fig. 6.19. Here it has been assumed that the deck initially contained four cards: an ace of spades (12), a three of hearts (30), a jack of clubs (B3), and a seven of diamonds (71). The complete program for this card selection game makes use of the entire PACK DECK subroutine (Fig. 6.17) and also the Variable Odds Number Generation package (Fig. 6.16), with the interrupt routine modified as shown in Fig. 6.20.

In actual operation the random-number routine continuously loops, producing numbers that vary from 0 to N, where N is the number currently stored in the C register. On interrupt, that is, when the player requests a card, the current contents of the B register are used to form the playing card's address. The PACK DECK routine places the selected card in the B register, and the remainder of the interrupt routine outputs the selected card onto the visual display.

Let's now look at the specific program shown in the example. On the first pass, random numbers between 0 and 3 are generated; when the player interrupts the processor, one of these, a 01 in the example, is placed in the L register, and the PACK DECK subroutine executed. The card addressed by the HL pair, the three of hearts (30) at location 1001, is stored in the B register and then deleted from the card list. In addition, those cards beneath the three of hearts on the list are then moved up one position, and the deck size decreased by one. This process continues, as shown, with the four cards drawn in the following order: three of hearts, ace of spades, seven of diamonds, and jack of clubs. After the jack has been dealt, the game is automatically terminated, since, as shown by the fact that the C register contents are negative, all the cards have been dealt out.

Hexadecimal code		Mnemonic		
Address	Instruction	Label	Instruction	Comments
1000	1E05	START:	MVI E, #05	
02	1606	LOOP 1:	MVI D, #06	
04	FB	LOOP 2:	EI	
05	15		DCR D	
06	CD1010		CALL PACK	
09	C20410		JNZ LOOP 2	
0C	1D		DCR E	
0D	CD1610		CALL PACK	
10	C20210		CALL LOOP 1	
13	C30010		JMP START	
16	F5	PACK:	PUSH PSW	Save flags.
17	43		MOV B, E	
18	04		INR B	
19	14		INR D	
1A	7A		MOV A, D	
1B	07		RLC	Shift D to most
1C	07		RLC	significant byte.
1D	07		RLC	
1E	07		RLC	Pack in E.
1F	80		ADD B	Place result in B.
20	47		MOV B, A	
21	15		DCR D	
22	D3FF		OUT #FF	Display rolling dice.
24	F1		POP PSW	Recover flags.
25	C9		RET	
0038	F5	INTERRUPT:	PUSH PSW	Save A.
39	CDE600	CHECK:	CALL KEYBD	Check for ASC II key
3C	FED3		CPI #D3	"S" (Start roll key)
3E	C23900		JNZ CHECK	depressed.
41	F1		POP PSW	Recover A.
42	C9		RET	

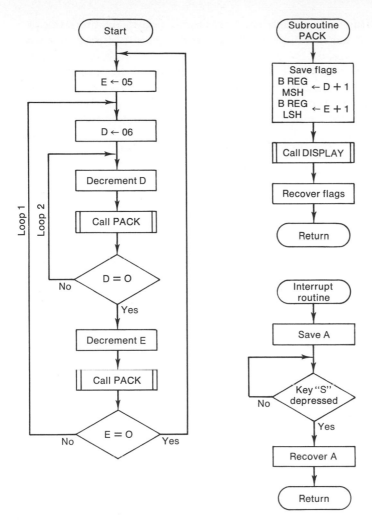

Figure 6.21 Electronic craps.

Example 3: Electronic Craps[3]

As another example of the utility of the random number generation techniques previously discussed, let's consider the design of an electronically operated crap game. The overall program strategy is illustrated in the flowcharts and program listings given in Fig. 6.21. The main program continuously "rolls the dice" in the D and E registers; that is, it produces random numbers in these registers

[3]Based on an original idea submitted to the authors by G. Foulkes, White Plains, New York.

corresponding to the numbers 1 through 6 found on the faces of a die. On each pass through the loops in the main program, the least significant bytes in the D and E registers are combined together, using the PACK subroutine, and the resulting word placed in the B register. In the actual program, the numbers in D and E vary from 0 to 5 and are incremented before being packed into B. Thus, for example, a 05 in D and a 03 in E would be packed as follows:

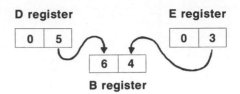

When the program is running, these numbers are continuously changing (rolling) in the display. To stop the dice from rolling, the player hits the STOP key, which creates an interrupt causing the processor to enter the INTERRUPT SERVICE routine. In this routine the dice no longer roll, and the last number in the B register remains on the display. To determine when to exit this routine, the processor continually checks to see whether or not key S, labeled "Start Roll," has been struck. To do this the processor monitors the keyboard input port by using the KEYBOARD IN subroutine, which will be discussed later. When the S key is struck, producing a hex code D3 in the A register, the processor leaves the interrupt routine and returns to the main program, and again the dice start rolling.

Perhaps, as a review of programming principles, it might be worthwhile to discuss the fine details of this program. Let's begin with the PACK subroutine and examine the register contents after each instruction is executed, assuming that D and E initially contain an 02 and an 04, respectively (Fig. 6.22). On entering this routine, the contents of the flags register are saved by being pushed onto the stack. The next sequence of instructions, 1017 to 1021, increments and packs the DE register contents into the B register for display. Note that on return to the main program the DE register contents are unaltered (Fig. 6.22). In addition, since the status word (A and Flags registers) is popped off the stack just prior to returning to the main program, the zero flag bit value is determined by the decrement instruction which was executed prior to entering the subroutine. Thus, for example, when the PACK subroutine returns control to the main program at location 1009, the branching of the JNZ instruction at that location will be determined by the value to which the zero flag bit was set by the previous DCR D instruction at address 1005.

Instruction address	Register contents after instruction addressed at left is executed			
	A	B	D	E
—Initial values	?	?	02	04
10 17	?	04	02	04
18	?	05	02	04
19	?	05	03	04
1A	03	05	03	04
.	.	.	.	.
.	.	.	.	.
.	.	.	.	.
1E	30	05	03	04
1F	35	05	03	04
20	35	35	03	04
21	35	35	02	04

Figure 6.22 Operation of the DICE PACK subroutine.

In the interrupt routine, the accumulator contents are saved by use of the PSW instruction prior to entering this routine because this data could be needed later by the PACK subroutine. The details of the KEYBOARD INPUT subroutine will not be discussed at this point, except to note that when the processor enters this routine it will stay there until a key is struck on the player's keyboard. When the processor returns from this routine (after a key has been hit), the equivalent ASCII entry[4] for the particular key struck will have been placed in the accumulator. Through the action of the compare immediate (CPI) instruction, the value of the data contained in A is compared with the ASCII entry for the key S (a D3). The program will remain "hung up" in this loop until an S key is eventually hit. When this occurs, the CPI instruction will set the zero flag bit, the JNZ instruction will not branch back to location 0039, the A register will be reloaded with its original data, and control will be returned to the main program.

The main program contains two nested loops (loops within loops). In LOOP 2 the D register contents are continuously decremented until D becomes 0, and then the program drops into LOOP 1. Here, E is decremented by 1, D is reinitialized by 06, and the program reenters LOOP 2. As long as the program remains within these loops, the changing DE register contents are continuously packed

[4]ASCII (American Standard Code for Information Interchange) is an internationally recognized code often used with electronic keyboards and telecommunication equipment.

into the B register and displayed, giving the appearance of rolling dice. Eventually, as shown below, both D and E are simultaneously 0, and at this point the JMP START instruction is executed, and the process begins anew.

D register contents	E register contents	Comments
06	05	Initialized values
05	05	
04	05	
03	05	
02	05	
01	05	
00	05	
00	04	
06	04	One complete cycle
.	.	
.	.	
.	.	
00	04	
00	03	
.	.	
.	.	
.	.	
03	01	
02	01	
01	01	
00	01	
00	00	
06	05	New cycle begins

It should be apparent from a careful examination of the listing above that even though all combinations come up, these dice are "loaded." If you understand the direction in which the bias exists, you can probably make yourself some extra money by playing this game with friends and relatives. Better still, as a test of your programming skill, can you fix this dice game so that all combinations are equally likely?

Example 4: A General-Purpose Time Delay

For many electronic game applications, the microprocessor's speed is just too great. Nobody playing against a machine wants it to hit the ball back in 15 ms or to have it deal out all the cards in a poker game in 3 ms. Instead we prefer some type of "human" behavior in which these chores are carried out more slowly by the machine. This slowing down of the processor's apparent speed is accomplished by making use of time-delay routines.

In Sec. 6.3 we discussed how the NOP can be used to generate short time delays but soon becomes inadequate when large delays are required. The program illustrated in Fig. 6.23 is more widely applicable than the NOP and is suitable for creating delays ranging from a few microseconds to nearly a second. Basically, it involves hanging the program up in a loop for a specific number of passes dependent on the delay required.

The total delay produced depends on the numbers initially loaded into the D and E registers and on the number of clock cycles required for each instruction. If we examine the loop portion of the program, we see that each pass through the loop requires 24 clock cycles:

	Initialize D and E registers	
LOOP	DCX D	(5) ⎫
	MOV A, E	(5) ⎬ 24 clock cycles per pass
	ORA D	(4) ⎪
	JNZ LOOP	(10) ⎭

The loop is exited when both D and E are 0. Unfortunately, the DCX instruction does not affect any flags, so the zero condition is tested for by placing E in the accumulator and "ORing" it with D. This operation affects the flags and produces a zero result (that is, sets the zero flag bit) only when *both* D and E are 0. The total number of clock cycles that the loop will execute may be expressed in terms of the initial contents of the D and E registers as:

$$\text{Total cycles} = D \cdot (256 \times 24) + E \cdot 24$$
$$= D \cdot 6144 + E \cdot 24$$

Hexadecimal code		Mnemonic			
Address	Instruction	Label	Instruction		Comments
0000	31FF00	START:	LXI	SP, #00FF	Initialize the stack pointer.
03	AF		XRA	A	⎫
04	D320		OUT	#20	⎬ Clean output port 20.
06	CD1000		CALL	DELAY	
09	3D		CMA		⎫ Output an FF to signal
0A	D310		OUT	#20	⎬ timeout completed.
0C	76		HLT		Stop.
0010	11C2A2	DELAY:	LXI	D, #A2 C2	Load delay number.
13	18	LOOP:	DCX	D	(D = A2, E = C2).
14	7B		MOV	A, E	
15	B2		ORA	D	
16	C21300		JNZ	LOOP	
19	C9		RET		

Figure 6.23 A general-purpose time delay subroutine.

If D and E are both initially loaded with FF, the maximum delay = 1,572,864 cycles is produced. With a 2-MHz clock this corresponds to a 0.786-s time delay.

To obtain a specific delay, 500 ms, for example, let's again assume a 2-MHz clock, and note that for this case a total of 0.5 s/ (0.5 μs per clock cycle) or 1,000,000 clock cycles are required. Solving for specific values of D and E in the equation above, we find that this delay can be achieved with an A2 in D and a C2 in E. When the program given in the figure is actually run, output port 20 will contain a 00 for 500 ms, and thereafter it will have an FF. Note that to obtain a delay which is some multiple of 500 ms, this routine may simply be called more than once.

6.5   SOFTWARE DEBUGGING METHODS

In order to troubleshoot computer software, you can generally use some type of *signal-tracing* procedure in which PRINT statements are inserted at various points in the program and replace the more conventional troubleshooting instrument—the oscilloscope. Probably you would start tracing at a point near the system input (beginning of the program) and work your way through the various sybsystems (program branches and subroutines), probing all important test points. In some cases several different input signals (initial register, memory, and input port data values) will be required to completely troubleshoot the system.

Program debugging may also be accomplished by making use of *signal-injection* rather than signal-tracing procedures. For this case the various data registers are preset to specific values, and execution of the application program is begun at some point other than the start of the program, in order to isolate the defective stage.

To assist in performing these troubleshooting operations, both hardware and software design aids are available; however, we will save the hardware approaches for Chap. 12, on video game troubleshooting techniques, and will utilize this section to take a close look at three specific software debugging routines—breakpoints, tracing, and patching.

A *breakpoint* is a form of jump instruction inserted at various points in the application program which when executed terminates the application program and transfers control to the breakpoint routine. Insertion of a breakpoint at a specific point in a program is a good way to tell if that point is ever reached during execution of the main program or whether the computer is hung up at some earlier step in the program.

Hexadecimal code		Mnemonic		
Address	Instruction	Label	Instruction	Comments
1000	AF		XRA A	⎫
01	C601		ADI #01	⎪
03	C602		ADI #02	Sample application
05	C605		ADI #05	program.
07	00		NOP	⎪
08	C30810	LOOP:	JMP LOOP	⎭
				Breakpoint routine.
0038			OUT #FF	Display A.
3A			RET	

Figure 6.24 Sample program for illustrating breakpoint usage.

One way to implement a breakpoint in a program is to insert a restart instruction at the point in the program where a break is desired. For example, if an RST 7 instruction were placed at location 0007 in the sample program given in Fig. 6.24, all instructions preceding the breakpoint would first be executed by the processor, so that a 08 would be in A at the time the breakpoint is encountered. When the RST 7 instruction is executed, the processor will jump to the routine located at 0038, and will display all data of interest, in this case the 08 contained in the A register. One problem with this program as it is shown in this figure is that program locations at which breakpoints have been previously inserted must be restored

Hexadecimal code		Mnemonic		
Address	Instruction	Label	Instruction	Comments
1040	F1	FIX BKPT:	POP PSW	⎫
41	E1		POP H	Repair old breakpoint.
42	77		MOV M, A	⎭
43	2A2010	START:	LHLD #1020	
46	E5		PUSH H	⎫
47	7E		MOV A, M	Save location and
48	F5		PUSH PSW	contents of break point.
49	3EFF		MVI A, #FF	⎫ Put in a restart.
4B	77		MOV M, A	⎭
4C	C30010		JMP BACK	Return to application program.

NOTES:
1. Desired breakpoint location is entered in memory locations 1020 and 1021 for lower and higher order address bytes respectively.
2. Start program at location 1043 for first breakpoint inserted.
3. Start program execution at location 1040 for all subsequent breakpoints.
4. Breakpoint routine is same at that given in Figure 6-24.

Figure 6.25 Program for automatic breakpoint insertion and removal.

to their old values before new breakpoints can be inserted. The program listed in Fig. 6.25 illustrates a technique for automatically accomplishing this task. Here the address and contents of the current breakpoint are saved on the stack and then restored to their original condition when a new breakpoint is selected.

In troubleshooting some application programs, the selective type of information provided by a breakpoint routine may not be sufficient; for these cases a special routine, known as a *trace program*, which essentially breakpoints every instruction in the program, may prove to be more useful. Basically this program, in conjunction with the hardware shown in Fig. 6.26, is used to interrupt the processor after each instruction in the application program. In this way if the interrupt routine contains a program to display all of the register contents, it is possible to use this routine to trace through the application program, monitoring all pertinent data points in the processor as the program progresses.

As shown in Fig. 6.27, the software requirements for this trace routine are minimal; however, in order to initiate the first interrupt sequence it is necessary to place a restart instruction (in this case an RST 7) in front of the application program. When this instruction is executed, the processor will immediately jump to the service routine,

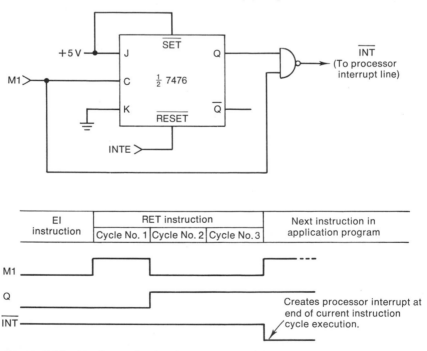

Figure 6.26 Hardware for implementation of a trace program.

Hexadecimal code		Mnemonic		
Address	Instruction	Label	Instruction	Comments
1000	AF		XRA A	
01	FF		RST 7	
02	3C		INR A.	
03	00		NOP	Application program
04	3C		INR A	
05	76		HLT	Start of trace interrupt
0038	D320	TRACE:	OUT #20	routine to display A
3A	CD9000		CALL DELAY	See Fig. 8.20a.
3D	FB		EI	
3E	C9		RET	

Figure 6.27 Software for a simple trace program.

which for the particular example given will cause the initial number in A (00) to be displayed. After a 1-s time delay (see lower part of Fig. 6.27), interrupts will be enabled, releasing the trace flip-flop from the reset mode. At this point, when the return instruction begins and the M1 (fetch) pulse is generated, the flip-flop will be set. However, as shown in the figure, an interrupt will not be generated until the next M1 cycle in the application (main) program. In this way, the interrupt will be processed, and the appropriate register contents displayed at the end of each instruction cycle in the main program.

When the specific application program given in Fig. 6.27 is executed, successive display outputs of 00, 01, 01, and 02 will be obtained. The 00 output is caused by the 0 in A during the initial RST 7 pass through the interrupt routine. The two 01 outputs are the results of interrupt instructions during the INR A and NOP instructions at locations 0002 and 0003, and the last output, the 02, is caused

Hexadecimal code		Mnemonic		
Address	Instruction	Label	Instruction	Comments
1000	AF		XRA A	
01	FF		RST 7	
02	C32010		JMP PATCH	
05	76	PRET:	HLT	
1020	3C	PATCH:	INR A	Instructions deleted from
21	00		NOP	main program.
22	3C		INR A	
23	04		INR B	
24	80		ADD B	Patched program.
25	BF		CMP A	
26	C30510		JMP PRET	

Figure 6.28 Patching a program.

by interrupting the main program at the last INR A instruction just before the processor halts. It should again be mentioned that by a relatively simple modification of the trace software it would be possible to display the contents of all of the CPU's registers or any other data of interest at the conclusion of each instruction in the main program.

Often, after a bug has been detected by one of the methods previously discussed, some modification of the original program will be required. Consider, for example, what you would do if you found that the program given in Fig. 6.27 contained an error and in fact you needed to insert the following instructions between lines 0004 and 0005:

INR B

ADD B

CMP A

For this specific program, since it's so short, the simplest method of making this modification would probably be to insert these instructions directly in memory and move down all codes following them by the appropriate number of spaces. If, however, the program were much longer, this would certainly not be a viable approach, and in that case reassembly of the entire program would seem to be required.

However, there is a third alternative, known as *patching,* which is illustrated in Fig. 6.28 for the previous example. Here all that is done is to insert a jump to the patch routine and then another back to the main program when that patch routine is done. This method is especially useful if you're trying out a particular idea in the application program and might even be used as a part of the final version of the program even though it does waste a few bytes of memory.

REFERENCES

Barna, Arpad, and Dan I. Porat: *Introduction to Microcomputers and Microprocessors,* Wiley, New York, 1976.

Bartee, Thomas C.: *Digital Computer Fundamentals.* McGraw-Hill, New York, 1977.

Nagle, H. Troy, Jr., B. D. Carroll, and J. David Erwin, *An Introduction to Computer Logic,* Prentice-Hall, Englewood Cliffs, N.J., 1975.

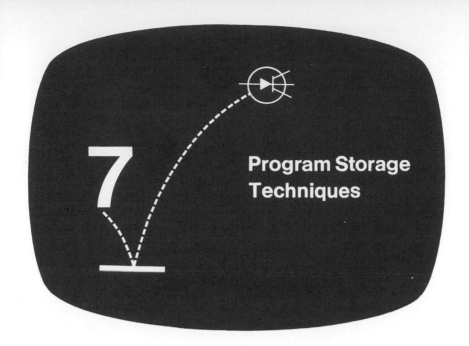

Program Storage Techniques

7.1 INTRODUCTION

The last two chapters introduced the microprocessor and gave specific examples of how these computerlike devices could be programmed to carry out the sophisticated tasks associated with today's electronic games. Little mention was made of the program storage requirements for implementing these games.

In this chapter we will examine the various forms of digital storage and carefully investigate their advantages, disadvantages, and, more important, their applicability to programmable electronic games. As shown in Fig. 7.1, many forms of digital storage exist, and depending on the particular application one or the other may prove more useful.

Generally speaking, memory may be divided into two major categories read-only memory (ROM) and read-write memory (RWM). With ROM devices the digital information is permanently stored so that even the removal of power will not cause this information to be lost. This feature, known as *nonvolatility*, makes ROMs particularly useful for storing fixed programs and subroutines as well as for table-look-up and character-generation applications. Some ROMs, specifically erasable programmable ROMs (EPROMs) and electrically alterable ROMs (EAROMs) do permit the internally

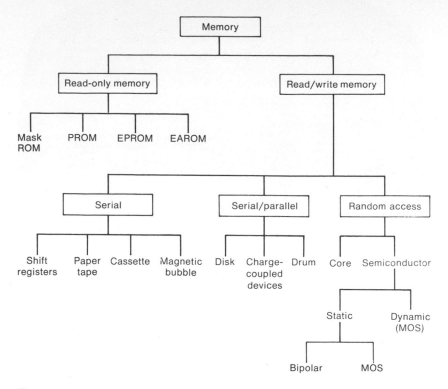

Figure 7.1 The memory spectrum. (*From Kock, Seeing Sound, Fig. 5.1.*)

stored information to be altered, though only with considerable difficulty. In fact, a new term, read mostly memory (RMM), has been proposed for these devices, but for now the term ROM, although not strictly correct, appears to have stuck to them.

With RWM devices, memory may be both examined (read from) and altered (written into) with equal ease. Serial devices, such as shift registers, magnetic tape, and the newer magnetic bubble memories, store data serially 1 bit behind the next. Therefore the amount of time that it takes to locate a particular piece of data in this type of memory (known as its *access time*) depends on where the data is located in the memory. For example, if you're using magnetic-tape storage, and the tape is currently at the beginning of the reel while the data you're interested in is located somewhere near the end, it could take several minutes to locate this specific block of data. In spite of this rather serious drawback, these types of serial devices are still quite popular because they provide a very inexpensive way to store large quantities of data. Furthermore although it may take quite a while to find the start of a particular data block, once it is located, the actual data transfer rates can be extremely high if the remaining data is all stored in sequence. As a result of these attributes, it is quite likely that many of the newer programmable and multifunction electronic games will employ some type of cassette, magnetic bubble, or magnetic card as mass storage for entering specific game programs into the processor's main memory and for storing user-written games.

In direct contrast to these serial memory devices, we have random-access memory (RAM). In this type of memory all storage locations have equal access time; that is, the time to read or write information into this type of storage is independent of the word's location in the memory. Core memory with the digital 1 and 0 information stored in tiny doughnut-shaped magnetic structures was the first type of RAM storage available. To store a 1 the core was magnetized in one direction, and the magnetization direction was simply reversed to store a 0. However, core memory is costly, power-hungry, and not amenable to IC fabrication techniques, and as a result it has finally yielded to semiconductor IC memory in most new designs. These all-solid-state RAM units are truly marvels of modern technology and offer low cost, high density, low power consumption, and high speed. They do, however, have one major drawback: unlike core memories they are volatile; that is, if power to them is lost, so is the information stored in them. In some computer designs where this information loss would be critical, battery backup for the memory is provided. For electronic game usage, however, this would at best be impractical, and therefore in electronic game designs the game program is usually placed in some type of nonvolatile storage, for example, a ROM. However, in the newer, more sophisticated general-purpose electronic games that operate with microprocessors, it is very possible that serial mass storage devices will be employed to hold a large number of different games, and that when a particular game is played, the program for it will be transferred from the serial device into the RAM area of the machine. In addition, RAM storage will be needed to hold user-written game programs.

Two major types of semiconductor RAM are in use today: static and dynamic. In *static memory devices* the digital information is stored in conventional flip-flops made from cross-coupled gates of the form shown in Fig. 7.2. Here as a result of the feedback, if the output of N_1 is HI that of N_2 is LO and vice versa. The flip-flop thus has two stable states: when Q is HI, it is said to be in the Logic 1 state; and when Q is LO, it is in the Logic 0 state. A momentary LO applied to the $\overline{\text{SET}}$ input guarantees that Q will be set to 1, and a LO

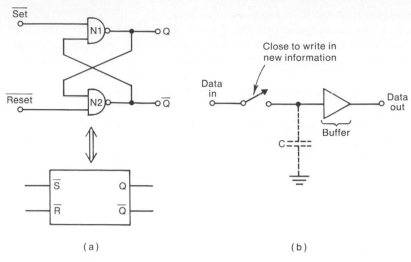

Figure 7.2 Two types of data storage. (*a*) Basic static memory element—the flip-flop; (*b*) basic dynamic memory cell.

on $\overline{\text{RESET}}$ that it will be reset to 0. If no external inputs occur, the flip-flop will remain in its current state as long as power is applied.

Dynamic memory elements operate on an entirely different principle—that of charge storage on a capacitor. When the switch *S* in Fig. 7.2*b* is closed, the incoming HI or LO data is applied to the capacitor *C*. When the switch is opened, the information remains in the memory cell in the form of charge stored on the capacitor. However, in order to prevent this information from "leaking away," the data stored in dynamic memory cells must be periodically "refreshed," typically once every few milliseconds. Given that dynamic memory devices have all of these refresh problems, the reader will probably be surprised to learn that their sales are well beyond those of equivalent static devices. This results from the fact that dynamic memory cells occupy much less chip area than static flip-flops, offer higher packing densities, and in addition are faster and consume less power.

From this brief introduction to the spectrum of current memory technology one fact stands out—no single storage method will satisfy all of the requirements of today's microprocessor-based electronic games. ROM will probably be needed to store the basic game program and will be used to provide the tabular information required to display the various objects and characters in the video field. RAM will be utilized to store the current frame of video information being displayed and will be continuously updated by the processor as objects in the scene move about.

In current multigame, processor-based systems, the game format is changed by replacing plug-in cartridges containing ROMs. However as manufacturers continually search for lower costs, future games will probably employ some form of magnetic mass storage such as tape cassettes or magnetic cards. Regardless of its final form, for the processor to make use of any type of serial mass storage input medium, the data must first be transferred into some type of RAM. Therefore in these games additional RAM will be needed for program storage.

7.2 SEMICONDUCTOR MEMORY: ROM AND RAM

Read-only memories have long been used as code converters, mathematical function look-up tables, and character generators; however, their more recent program storage application in microprocessor-based systems has skyrocketed their sales and given them an importance in overall memory design comparable to that of RAMs. Paralleling this growth, there have been significant improvements in ROM density, speed, and power reduction. In fact, 32-kilobit ROMs which consume less than 500 mW of power and have access times under 500 ns are available today for under $20.

Figure 7.3 illustrates a typical ROM application—a keyboard encoder circuit which has been constructed from conventional diodes and resistors. This particular circuit is a decimal keyboard encoder. It is designed so that when a specific key is pressed, the binary code equivalent of that key is produced at the output. In addition, the circuit produces a "key press" signal to indicate that one of the keys has been struck. In designing this circuit, a diode is placed on each bit line where a "one" output is desired when a particular key is depressed. Thus, for example, to generate a 0011 output when the key numbered 3 is hit, diodes are required on the b_1, b_0, and KP (keypress) lines. At first it might appear that these diodes aren't necessary and could in fact be replaced by short circuits. However, if this were done, "sneak paths" for current flow would exist and would create erroneous outputs. The use of diodes at nodes where one outputs are required prevents the formation of these sneak paths.

Although useful for illustrative purposes, the diode-resistor network is actually uncommon in today's ROMs. Instead, in order to make maximum use of current IC fabrication techniques, ROMs are

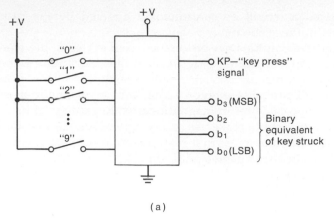

(a)

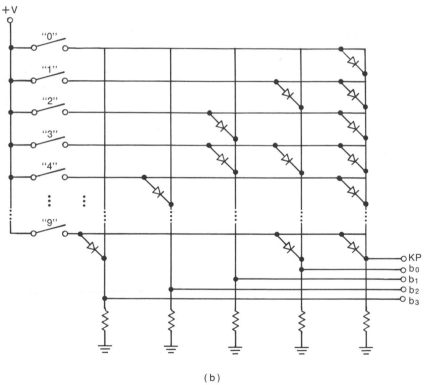

(b)

Figure 7.3 A keyboard encoder ROM.

usually constructed with either bipolar or MOS transistors. In mask programmed ROMs the manufacturer constructs a general-purpose array of transistors for the ROM and, as the last step in its manufacturer, connects the gates (or emitters in the case of bipolar devices) on those transistors where a one output is desired.

Note that it is possible to view this keyboard encoder circuit as being a look-up table in which the input key information addresses the ROM and thereby "looks up" the binary code corresponding to the key depressed.

The ROM discussed in the previous example contained 10 inputs and 5 outputs; i.e., it was a 10 × 5 or 10-word × 5 bits per word ROM. Because of the small number of inputs and outputs, no address decoding was required since the ROM could be encapsulated in a package containing only 17 pins (10 input, 5 output, and 2 power leads). Consider next the case of a keyboard encoder ROM for a conventional typewriter. This type of input device contains about 48 different keys. Therefore, to construct a ROM encoder circuit for such a keyboard would require a package containing about 60 leads. For this design problem it would be much more efficient to use some type of address decoder. With this approach a ROM containing 2^N words may be addressed with only N binary input leads. When the number of decoded signals is relatively small (generally less than 32), the linear address decoding technique shown in Fig. 7.4a is reasonable. However, as the size of the ROM increases much beyond this point, a pure linear addressing scheme becomes impractical.

Consider, for example, the design of a 2^{10}, or 1024, word single-bit ROM. This type of ROM would have 10 input address lines and a single-bit output line. If constructed by a linear addressing technique, the ROM would require a 1-out-of-1024 decoder (Fig. 7.4a). Such a decoder would be extremely difficult to construct and would have a geometry inconsistent with good IC design. A better technique is to use the coincident addressing scheme shown in Fig. 7.4b, which, while maintaining the same number of external address leads, greatly reduces the complexity of the required decoder circuits. Sometimes the X decoder outputs are called the row-select lines and the Y decoder outputs the column-select lines. In this example, the 1-kilobyte ROM is constructed by making use of two 5-line address decoders. Thus, to address cell $9Y - 29X$, the X address decoder selects line 29 (input 11101) and the Y address decoder line 9 (input address 01001). This coincident addressing approach is similar to the technique employed to find a particular building on a street map by specifying the names of the intersecting horizontal and vertical streets.

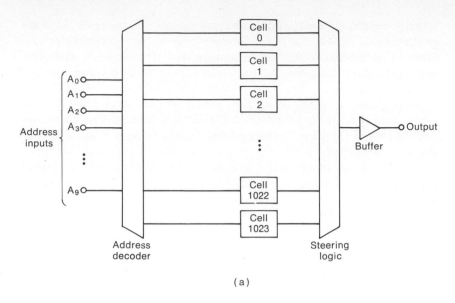

(a)

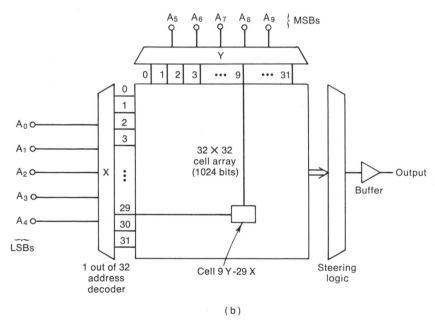

(b)

Figure 7.4 Memory addressing schemes. (*a*) Linear addressing; (*b*) coincident.

Also contained in the ROM and shown in Fig. 7.4 is steering logic which routes the selected cell information to the output buffer. If the ROM contains multibit words, the address decoders simultaneously select all of the bits in the word, with each directed to the appropriate output buffer (Fig. 7.5). A similar addressing scheme is also employed with RAMs.

Mask programmed ROMs are inexpensive and are generally used in well-defined applications where no further bit changes will be required. However, during the system development stage, it is often convenient to have a field programmable ROM (PROM). These devices permit the user to program the ROMs and remove any program bugs, and ensure correct system operation prior to committing the final program to mask-type ROM. Generally these PROMs contain fusible links which are blown or transistor base-emitter junctions which may be electrically shorted in order to enter the appropriate data into the memory. Besides being useful during product development, PROMs can also be viable production compo-

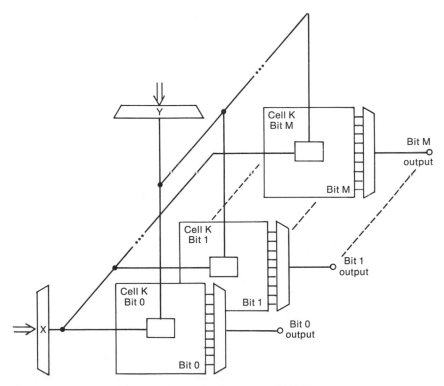

Figure 7.5 Organization of a multibit-per-word ROM.

nents. The use of PROMs instead of mask programmed ROMs avoids mask preparation charges, which are typically on the order of $1000, and also eliminates the long turnaround time associated with ROM production. Furthermore, if many different types of ROMs are needed in relatively small production volumes, it may in the long run be much less expensive to stock one type of PROM and program it as it's needed.

During the early stages of product development, the large number of program changes required can even make the use of fusible PROMs expensive since once an incorrect link is blown the PROM is useless and must be discarded. At this time in the product development cycle the erasable programmable read-only memory (EPROM) finds its greatest application. Two types of EPROM are currently available. The first of these, which is far and away the most popular, makes use of isolated-gate MOS transistors. The device is programmed by applying large voltages to the drain of the transistor, which causes avalanche breakdown to occur and charges the buried gate. When this voltage is removed, the gate is again isolated and essentially remains charged forever, inducing a permanent conduction channel between the drain and source of the transistor. Actual lifetimes projected for these types of PROMs are from 10 to 100 years. To be erased the PROM is simply exposed to ultraviolet light, with the resulting photon stimulation providing a leakage path for discharging the transistor gates and returning all transistors to their off condition. Ten minutes of exposure time under the UV light source is usually all that's required to completely erase the chip's memory.

Also available is a second type of EPROM, known as an electrically alterable ROM (EAROM), which permits particular bits in the memory to be erased by application of a suitable voltage. Although these devices are extremely useful, at present their high cost has prevented them from finding widespread application.

Depending on the particular system requirements, either bipolar or MOS-type ROMs may be employed. Bipolar units are generally used where access times under 100 ns are needed, while MOS-type ROMs, being slower and not quite as expensive, are employed in less critical applications. For use with conventional microprocessors the speed of MOS-type ROMs is usually more than adequate.

The RWMs used with microprocessor systems are generally semiconductor devices. For smaller designs static RAM chips are usually employed since they are available in multibit single package arrays and are easily interfaced to the processor. When memory requirements exceed several thousand bytes, the use of dynamic RAMs becomes practical. Here, although extra refresh electronics are required, their cost is more than compensated for by the smaller size, higher speed, and lower power consumption of these dynamic memories. Static memories are available in both bipolar and MOS forms, while dynamic memory devices are constructed using only MOS transistors since their high input impedance prevents the rapid discharge of the information from the storage capacitors. At the time of the writing of this text, 4K static and 16K dynamic RAMs are already available, with 64K devices due to appear shortly.

7.3 MICROPROCESSOR MEMORY INTERFACING AND ADDRESSING TECHNIQUES

In the previous sections we examined the innards of RAM and ROM semiconductor devices. In this section we're going to take a look at these devices at the chip level and investigate how these IC packages may be assembled into memory arrays and, more important, how they may be efficiently interfaced to microprocessors.

The ROM illustrated in Fig. 7.6 is typical of those devices currently available and is an 8192-bit device internally organized as an array of 1024 eight-bit words. The 10 input address leads A_0 to A_9 select the word in the ROM to be examined, and the data located at that address appears at the output terminals O_1 to O_8. The ROM output buffer is a tristate device and is enabled when both chip select lines ($\overline{CS_1}$ and $\overline{CS_2}$) are connected to a LO. The reader will recall that a

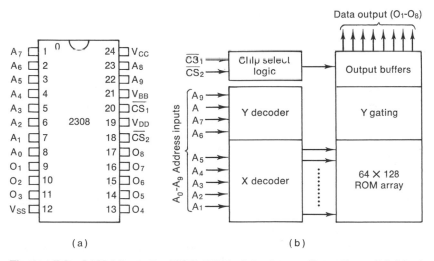

Figure 7.6 8192-bit static MOS ROM. (*a*) pin configuration; (*b*) block diagram. (*From Intel Data Catalog, 1977, pp. 3–14.*)

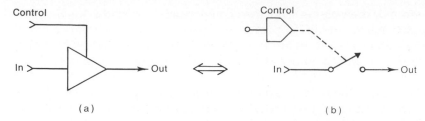

Figure 7.7 Three-state (tristate) logic operation. (*a*) Tristate logic buffer; (*b*) equivalent electrical circuit.

tristate device behaves as though it were an electronic switch (Fig. 7.7). When enabled, it connects the output and input lines together, and when disabled it effectively disconnects the output leads from the rest of the circuit. The use of tristate outputs permits many similar devices to be connected onto the same data bus as long as only one device is enabled at a time.

To interface the ROM to the processor, the eight ROM data output leads are connected directly onto the data bus, and the 10 address leads (A_0 to A_9) to the corresponding points on the processor's address bus. The remaining address leads (A_{10} to A_{15}) are used to select this chip when its address is specified by the processor. For the particular circuit shown in Fig. 7.8*a*, the ROM will be selected only when address bits A_{10} to A_{15} are all 0. Hence this chip is labeled ROM 0. The connection of the memory read operational signal, $\overline{\text{MEMR}}$, ensures that the ROM data will not be placed on the data bus until the processor is ready to receive it. This timing relationship is illustrated in Fig. 7.8*b*.

RAM interfacing is somewhat more complicated than that required for ROMs. RAM circuitry must not only be able to READ data from selected words in memory but when required must also be able to take information off the data bus and store it at the word location indicated by the data on the address bus. A typical second generation 1024-bit static RAM chip is illustrated in Fig. 7.9. It is organized as a 256-word × 4-bit memory unit and has a common data input/output bus ($I/0_1$ to $I/0_4$) which of course is ideally suited for use with bus-oriented systems. When the R/$\overline{\text{W}}$ (read/write) input signal goes LO, this causes the input data present on the I/0 lines to be stored at the addressed location. Bringing the output disable (OD) lead HI tristates the output buffers and keeps the data associated with the addressed RAM word off the data bus unless a read operation is being performed. It is important to note that when data is being written into memory, the RAM output buffers must be disabled or else the incoming data from the processor as well as that at the output of the RAM will both be fighting for control of the data bus. The timing diagram in Fig. 7.10 illustrates how this data is read from and entered into RAM.

Let's consider next how we might construct a 1024-word × 8-bit RAM module using the 2111 RAM chips. By combining two of these ICs in parallel (address and chip select leads commonly connected),

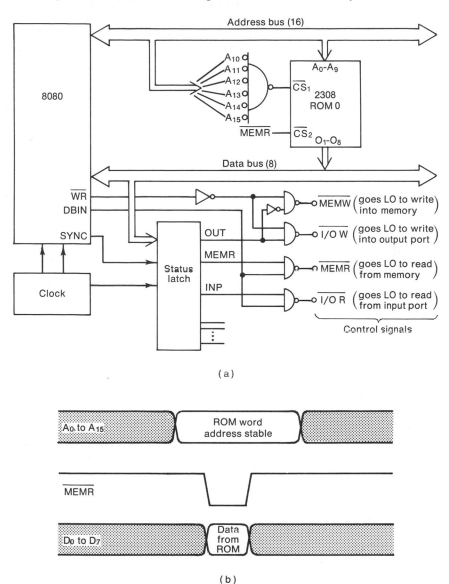

(a)

(b)

Figure 7.8 (a) Interfacing a ROM to the 8080 microprocessor; (b) timing relationships in a ROM.

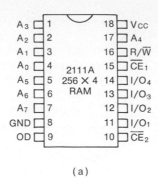

(a)

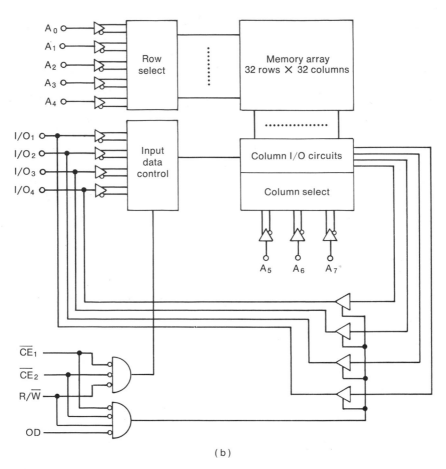

(b)

Figure 7.9 A 256-word × 4-bit static RAM. (a) Pin configuration; (b) block diagram. *(From Intel Data Catalog, 1977, pp. 2–68.)*

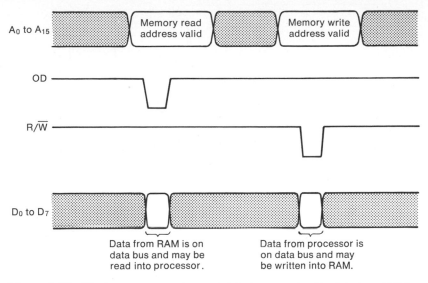

Figure 7.10 Timing sequence to read data from and write data to a RAM.

we can make up a 256-word × 8-bit submodule; four of these submodules are then connected together to complete the 1-kilobyte × 8 RAM design. The overall design of this sytem, also incorporating the 1 kilobyte of ROM from the previous discussion, is given in Fig. 7.11.

As one final example of memory system design, let's consider the construction of an 8-kilobyte memory consisting of three 1-kilobyte RAMs and five 1-kilobyte ROMs. The overall design for this memory is given in Fig. 7.12. To minimize the package count, this circuit makes use of a special one out of eight decoder chip which contains multiple enable inputs. Note that this memory bank is enabled when address leads A_{13} to A_{15} are zero and further that a specific chip in the bank, for example RAM$_3$, is enabled when A_{10} to A_{12} has an address equal to the selected chip number—in this case a 3 or 011. With the exception of the decoder, the remainder of the design follows the guidelines previously discussed.

7.4 DIGITAL DATA RECORDING ON MAGNETIC TAPE

Digital memory can be expensive, and in order to optimize a particular digital design, several different types of memory components are frequently combined in the overall system design.

In the earlier sections of this chapter we introduced semiconductor RAM and ROM and pointed out that semiconductor RAM, though

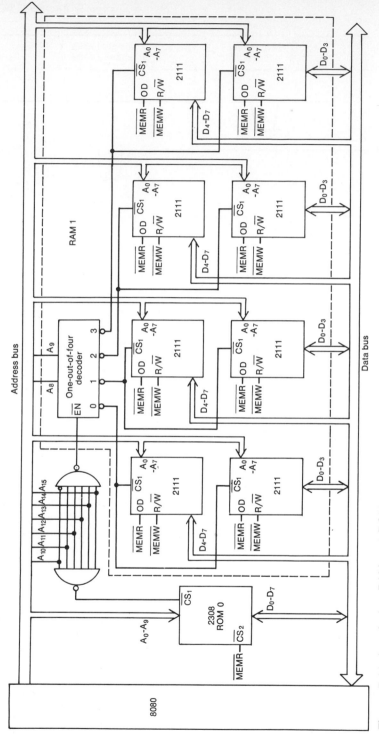

Figure 7.11 Interfacing RAM and ROM memory to the 8080 microprocessor.

168

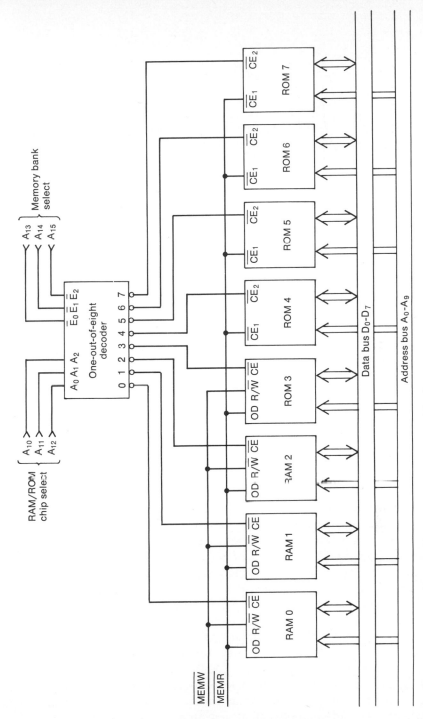

Figure 7.12 An 8-kilobyte RAM and ROM memory block.

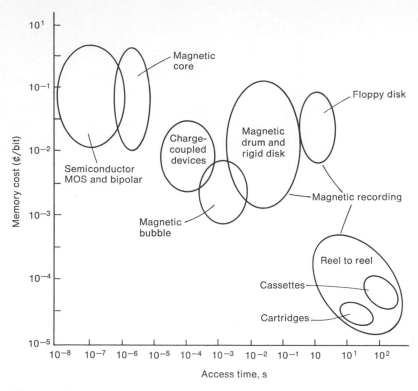

Figure 7.13 Comparison of the cost of different types of memory. *(From Byte Magazine, March 1976, p. 18.)*

volatile, is useful when small amounts of high-speed RWM are required and that ROM is generally employed for permanent storage of programs and data. However, as shown in Fig. 7.13, both of these storage techniques are extremely expensive when compared with data storage on magnetic media. Therefore for many of the newer electronic game designs which feature user programmability or game alteration by changing sections of memory, manufacturers are giving serious consideration to magnetic storage techniques. For the present the Philips-type cassette appears to be most promising for these applications, owing to its low cost, rugged construction, and widespread availability.

At the present time manufacturers find two major applications for magnetic storage techniques: first, to permit the player to create individualized games by writing programs for them and then storing the results on cassettes for later use, and second, as a replacement for more costly ROMs in supplying the user with a multiplicity of sophisticated video games, all stored on a single cassette.

Memories making use of data storage on magnetic tape are referred to as *serial access devices* since bits are generally stored one bit behind the other on the tape. Therefore, in direct contrast to the random access capability of the RAM and ROM semiconductor devices previously discussed, all words on the tape cannot be located (or accessed) in the same amount of time. In fact if you happen to be at the beginning of the tape and want to examine a word at the end of the tape, it may take you minutes to get there. Thus serial memories such as magnetic tapes are characterized by rather large access times. Fortunately for electronic game applications, we don't need true random access capability since we will either be recording or playing back large blocks of data, and for these tasks magnetic tape is nearly ideal, especially when you consider that a standard 60-min cassette costing only $2 or $3 is capable of storing more than 100 kilobytes of digital data.

One problem associated with employing magnetic tape memory in microprocessor-based electronic games is that magnetic tape is inherently bit-by-bit serial in nature, while microprocessors are generally byte-oriented devices. Therefore in order to interface the two together, some type of parallel-to-serial conversion will be required during data recording, and a corresponding serial-to-parallel conversion will be needed during playback. The methods for achieving these types of data transformations are well known and will be presented in Sec. 7.5. The remainder of this section will be devoted to a discussion of the more popular digital data-recording techniques.

Conventional audio cassette recorders are commonplace items today, and it is therefore tempting for the game manufacturer to design systems to function in conjunction with these types of recorders. This reduces the overall cost of the system since the manufacturer need not include the tape transport as part of the video game and the buyer is able to use standard inexpensive cassettes. However, there are several drawbacks to this approach. Audio cassette recorders are designed to record music and voice signals and not digital data. Therefore, in order to use them, some type of tone encoding is frequently employed, and external electronics added to the recorder to encode and decode these signals. In addition, these audio data recording schemes generally result in rather low data transfer rates.

A second alternative open to the manufacturer is to include an inexpensive cassette tape transport as part of the video game. Although costing a bit more than the previous approach, this technique permits direct digital drive of the tape head and considerably simplifies the record and playback electronics. In addition, this approach allows for increased reliability, higher data rates, and some measure of product security since game tapes purchased in these formats cannot be easily duplicated. In the paragraphs that follow we will discuss an example of each of these digital data recording methods.

Data Recording on an Unmodified Audio Cassette Recorder

Many techniques are available for recording digital data on audio cassettes; but, rather than discuss the advantages and disadvantages of each, we will present one example which illustrates the approach typically employed in recording binary information on a conventional cassette tape recorder.

The system shown in Fig. 7.14 operates on the frequency shift

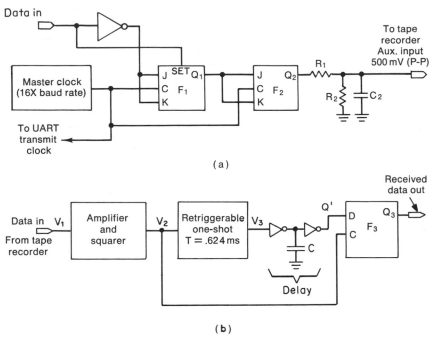

(a)

(b)

Figure 7.14 Digital data audio cassette recorder. (a) Transmitter section; (b) receiver section. *(From Byte Magazine, March 1976, p. 40.)*

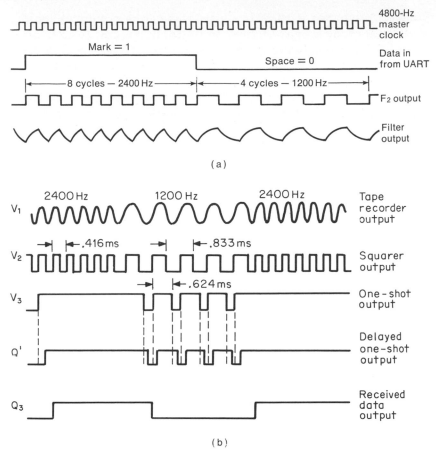

Figure 7.15 Key waveforms for the digital data audio cassette recorder.
(a) Transmitter waveforms; (b) receiver waveforms.

cycles of a 2400-Hz quasi-sine-wave tone and a binary zero by four cycles of a 1200-Hz tone. This particular data recording and playback system requires no software, works with any microprocessor, and will tolerate moderate differences in record and playback speeds without producing data errors. In addition, the system is easily connected to any processor having a universal asynchronous receiver-transmitter (UART) type of serial interface. As will be discussed in Sec. 7.6, this type of interface may be implemented by using either a hardware or a software approach.

As shown in Fig. 7.14a, when the data-in line is HI, the Q_1 output of F_1 is continuously set to one, and F_2 simply acts as a divide-by-2 counter, producing a 2400-Hz square wave at its output. When the data input changes to a LO, the J and K input lines on F_1 go HI, and the F_1-F_2 flip-flop combination behaves like a divide-by-4 counter, producing a 1200-Hz square wave at the Q_2 output terminal. This signal then passes into the R_1-R_2-C_2 filter network, which attenuates the signal to a level suitable for direct connection to the auxiliary (AUX) input on the tape recorder. In addition, this low-pass filter rounds off the corners of the square wave. This is necessary because the poor transient response of most audio recorders would cause overshoot and ringing of the square wave on playback, resulting in data playback errors. With sine waves, or in this case with quasi sine waves, this problem is minimized. The waveforms found at various critical points in the transmitter circuit are indicated in Fig. 7.15a.

On playback, the signal is taken from the earphone output jack on the tape recorder and amplified and squared by the first stage of the receiver circuit (Fig. 7-14b). This signal is then applied to the retriggerable one-shot; the period of the one-shot is adjusted halfway between T and $T/2$, where T is the period of the low-frequency signal recorded (in this case, 0.833 ms). In this way, as long as a 2400-Hz high-frequency signal with its 0.416-ms period is applied, the one-shot will continuously fire, keeping its output HI; while the application of a 1200-Hz low-frequency signal will permit the one-shot to time-out each cycle (Figure 7-15b). The delayed one-shot output Q' is connected to the input on the D-type flip-flop F_3 and causes the output of F_3 to go HI during receipt of a 2400-Hz tone and LO during receipt of a 1200-Hz tone, thus correctly interpreting the received data.

In this receiver system, note that since the transmitter clocking information is not recovered from the received data, the receiver UART will not be able to synchronize its clock to that of the transmitter. As a result, correct data reception will depend on having a tape system whose record and playback speeds differ by no more than ±5%. The overall data rate for this system is 300 baud (bits/s).

Direct Digital Recording on Magnetic Tape

The graph shown in Fig. 7.16 illustrates the relationship between applied magnetizing force and the resulting permanent magnetization of a typical piece of magnetic tape. Clearly this relationship is highly nonlinear. For analog recording, linearity is required to preserve the relationship between the various components of the

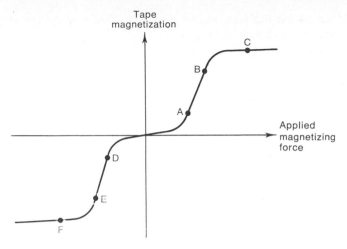

Figure 7.16 Relationship between applied magnetic field (magnetizing force) and resulting tape permanent magnetization. *(From Byte Magazine, Feb. 1977, p. 27.)*

recorded information, and therefore this type of recording is carried out in regions *AB* and *DE* on the tape. To operate in these regions either a dc or high-frequency bias is employed.

For digital recording no such linearity is required, and in fact the tape is driven out to points *C* and *F*, which completely magnetizes it (saturates it) in one direction or the other, depending on whether a binary 1 or 0 is to be stored. This type of recording technique is highly tolerant of large variations in drive signal, since as long as the tape is driven into saturation, the same total magnetization will occur, resulting in identical signals on playback. Furthermore, this recording method, where the tape swings from saturation on one side to saturation on the other, also results in the maximum playback voltage signals, highest signal-to-noise ratio, and minimal electronics since one doesn't have to worry about critical bias levels to keep the tape in the linear region. In short, direct digital data recording is inherently easier, cheaper, and more reliable than audio techniques for the recording of digital data.

As illustrated by the recorder circuit given in Fig. 7.17, the actual direct recording of digital data on magnetic tape is not all that difficult. All that is required is a circuit capable of producing a bidirectional current in the write head large enough to saturate the tape. Typical digital tape heads require peak write currents of from 2 to 5 mA to guarantee tape saturation. The circuit given in the figure converts standard transistor-transistor logic (TTL) digital input signals into the required write currents.

When V_{in} is above 2.4 V (TTL HI input, D_1 conducts, and D_2 zeners so that V_0 is $1.4 - 0.7 - 11 = -10.3$ V. When V_{in} is below 0.8 V (a TTL LO input), D_2 conducts, D_1 zeners, and $V_0 = 1.4 + 0.7 + 8.2 = +10.3$ V. With a value of $R_1 = 2.0 k\Omega$, the write current corresponding to these TTL input signals will be ± 5 mA, more than enough to saturate the tape.

During playback of the recorded signals, the same head may be used to "read" information off the tape. Since the head is basically an inductor, it will have a voltage induced in it only when the magnetic field (or flux) from the tape passing under it is changing, or more specifically, an induced voltage proportional to the rate of change of flux passing under the head. Therefore, if a square wave of current were applied to the write head, producing a corresponding square wave of magnetization on the tape, then on playback the head voltage would appear as an alternating sequence of positive- and negative-going spikes corresponding to the direction of the flux changes (Fig. 7.18a).

The circuit given in Fig. 7.18b illustrates one approach for converting the voltage spikes produced at the tape head back into a signal corresponding to the original data recorded on the tape. IC_1 amplifies the voltage signal and filters it to improve the signal-to-noise ratio. IC_2 and IC_3 are threshold detectors, with IC_2 responding to voltages exceeding a preset positive voltage and IC_3 to a preset negative voltage. R_1 adjusts the threshold amplitude and is set at a level high enough to minimize noise effects and yet low enough to capture all valid flux transition spikes. The output of these detectors is then

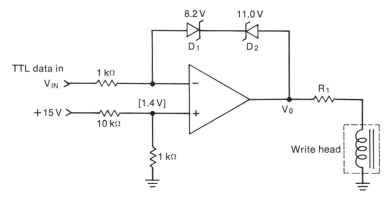

Figure 7.17 Direct recording of digital data on magnetic tape. *(From Byte Magazine, February 1977, p. 27.)*

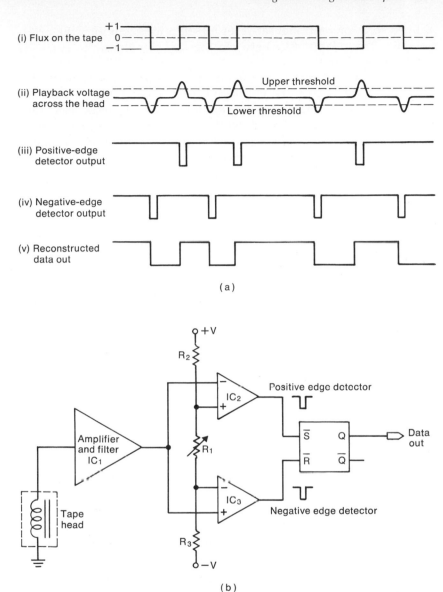

(a)

(b)

Figure 7.18 (a) Key waveforms associated with the direct digital data tape playback circuit given below. *(From Byte Magazine, January 1977, p. 35.)* (b) Playback circuit of direct digital cassette recorder.

applied to a conventional set-reset flip-flop to reconstruct the original data. The relationship between the key signals in the circuit is given in Fig. 7.18a.

One subject completely glossed over in the previous discussion is the actual technique to be employed for encoding the data on the tape, that is, the format of the data on the tape. In the examples given in this section, the so-called NRZ (nonreturn to zero) encoding scheme is employed, and while this method is particularly simple to understand and construct in terms of required electronics, there are many superior recording schemes available. However, a discussion of the relative merits of each of these methods is beyond the scope of this text.

7.5 MICROPROCESSOR INTERFACING TO MAGNETIC TAPE I/O DEVICES

The serial transmission of digital data may be accomplished by using either synchronous or asynchronous methods. Synchronous transmission involves a continuous stream of characters and is used in applications where high data transmission rates and maximum data storage density are of paramount importance. Asynchronous communication techniques, on the other hand, are best suited to applications where the transmission of characters is not necessarily continuous in time, and where low cost of the transmit and receive electronics is a primary concern.

Although the storage of asynchronous data on magnetic tape may not be optimal from the viewpoint of maximizing the data storage density on the tape, one 60-min cassette can still hold upwards of 300 kilobytes of data recorded in this manner, and thus this technique is more than adequate for meeting the storage needs of most electronic games. Therefore, in this section on methods for interfacing a microprocessor to a cassette mass storage system, we will confine our discussion to asynchronous data transmission methods. The block diagram given in Fig. 7.19 indicates the overall scope of the interfacing problem.

To record data on the cassette unit, the tape is started and the word to be recorded is sent to the transmitter; then, on receipt of a control signal from the processor, the transmitter converts the 8-bit data word into a serial stream of data bits. The tape encoder electronics further convert these digital signals into a format appropriate for recording on the tape; for example, one of the methods previously discussed can be used to convert the signals into distinct tones representing the 1s and 0s.

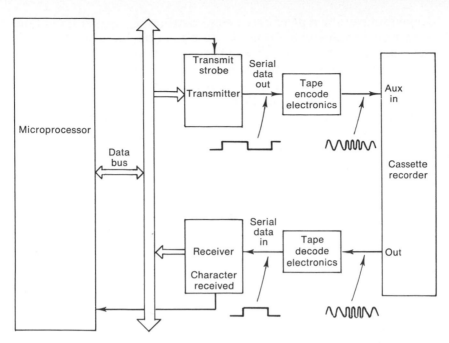

Figure 7.19 A complete mass-storage cassette recorder interface to a microprocessor.

On playback the signals on the tape (the tones in the example given) are decoded, transforming them back into a serial stream of 1s and 0s. This serial data enters the receiver, where it is converted back to its original parallel form. When one complete data word has been collected by the receiver, it sends a signal to the processor, and the word is read into the computer. This process continues until all of the data has been successfully read from the tape.

The general form of the signal used in asynchronous data transmission is shown in Fig. 7.20*a*. Note that the information is transmitted one character (word) at a time and that no clocking information is explicitly transmitted with the signal. Furthermore, the spacing between successive characters is not fixed and can be of any duration, as long as there are *at least* the proper number of stop bits from the end of one character to the start of the next. During the transmitter idle time, that is, during the time when no data is being sent, the output remains HI (logic 1). To begin the transmission of a new character, the output goes LO (logic 0) for a 1-bit time interval; this is known as the start bit and is used to signal the receiver that a new character is beginning. The start bit is followed by the transmission of the data bits, with the least significant bit transmitted first.

Depending on the type of data being transmitted, this portion of the signal may be anywhere from 5 to 8 bits in length; however, for a specific system this is usually fixed at one particular value. Following the data, the user may if desired add a parity bit, choosing to employ either even, odd, or no parity with the transmitted signal. In order to separate one character from the next, the parity bit must be followed by at least 1 stop bit, that is, a return to a logic 1 level before the next character is transmitted. As an example of this form of data transmission, consider the waveform given in Fig. 7.20*b*, in which the 8-bit data word 10110101 is being transmitted. Odd parity has been assumed, and 2 stop bits have been selected.

In order to transmit this type of signal, the data word output from the microprocessor must be loaded into some type of shift register circuit. Additional control circuitry is also needed to cause the transmission of the proper number of data and stop bits, and to insert the proper parity information in the signal. The receiver circuit for this type of signal must also contain some type of shift register. However, since the incoming signal is asynchronous, i.e., can begin at any time, special circuitry needs to be included to detect the occurrence of a start bit. Generally the receiver clock is set at a frequency 16 times higher than the incoming data bit rate. When a start bit is detected, the receiver waits 24 clock times (to get to the center of data bit D0) and then reads in the first data bit; subsequent bits are read

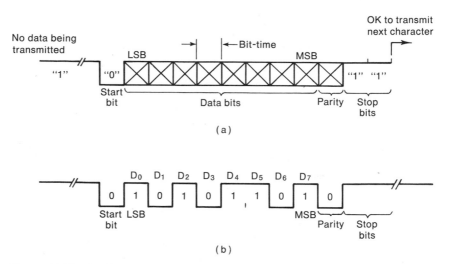

Figure 7.20 (*a*) General format used for asynchronous data transmission; (*b*) asynchronous transmission of the data word 10110101 using odd parity and 2 stop bits.

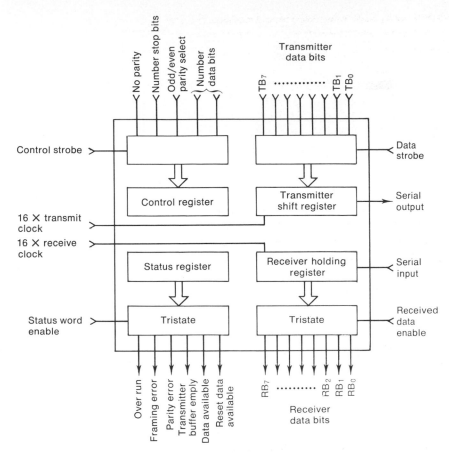

Figure 7.21 Basic internal structure of a UART. *(Adapted from General Instrument AY-5-1013 Data Sheet, March 1974.)*

in every 16 clock cycles. This use of high-frequency clocks allows the transmitter and receiver clocks to differ by as much as ±5% without producing any data transmission errors.

From the previous discussion it should be apparent that a fair amount of digital logic hardware would be required to construct the transmitter shift register, the control and parity generation circuits, and the receiver shift register and control and transmission error-detection circuits. Fortunately all of this hardware has been designed into a single LSI circuit known as a universal asynchronous receiver-transmitter (UART).

The block diagram of a typical UART is given in Fig. 7.21. The device is programmable; that is, by making external connections to it, the user can select the number of data bits per character, the

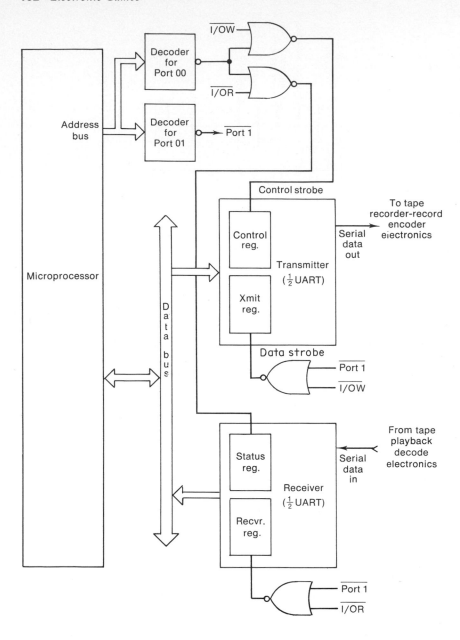

Figure 7.22 (*a*) Interfacing a UART to a microprocessor.

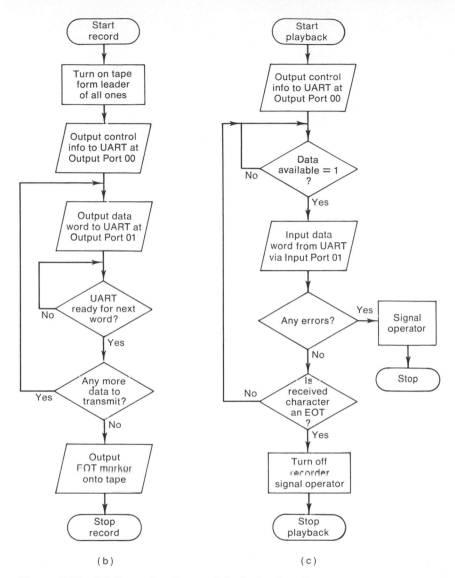

Figure 7.22 (*b*) Record software; (*c*) playback software.

number of stop bits, and the type of parity if any. Either this information can be hard-wired permanently to the UART by connecting the input control lines to the appropriate HI or LO levels or, as shown in Fig. 7.22, the UART control register may be initialized to the proper value at the start of the data transfer operation by treating the register as an output port and writing the proper data into it.

In coupling the UART to byte-oriented microprocessor systems, 8 data bit characters are most commonly employed. When the processor is ready to transmit a character, it places the information on the data bus and signals the UART to transmit it by pulling the "data strobe" line LO. This loads the UART's transmitter shift register and causes the transmit clock to shift the data out onto the serial output line. When the UART is free to accept another character, it signals this fact by bringing the transmitter "buffer empty" line HI. This signal is often fed back to the processor to tell it that the UART is now ready to accept another character for transmission.

At the receiver end of the UART, the incoming signal is loaded into the receiver holding register. When a complete character has been shifted into the UART, the unit signals this fact by bringing the "data available" line HI. In addition, the UART produces a series of error check signals to determine whether or not the character has been received correctly. These signals, along with the data contained in the receiver holding register, are all connected to the outside world via tristate buffers and are therefore easily interfaced to the bus-oriented structure of microprocessors.

The circuit given in Fig. 7.22 illustrates one method for interfacing a UART of the form previously described to an 8080 microprocessor. The flowcharts given in Fig. 7.22*b* and *c* indicate the type of software that would be employed with this hardware in order to construct a complete system for recording and playing back digital data from a magnetic tape recorder. This system would work equally well with either of the recording techniques described in the previous section.

To write information onto tape, the processor first outputs a control word to output port 00. This data is loaded into the UART's control register, and determines the format to be used during the remainder of the data recording. Next the processor outputs the first data word to the UART by writing into output port 01. The control signal produced pulses the UART's "data strobe" line which loads the transmitter shift register with the contents of the data bus and begins transmission of the first character. Unless the microprocessor knows that it won't overload the UART, that is, send characters to it too fast, it should check the UART's transmitter "buffer empty" line to ensure that the UART is ready for another character before outputting to port 01. However, if the UART has a fixed clock rate, then the processor can avoid this testing by using internal time delay routines to guarantee that the processor's data output rate will not exceed the UART's capability. This process continues until all of the data has been transmitted by the microprocessor, and at that point some special character such as an EOT (end of transmission) may be sent and recorded on the tape to serve as a marker for locating the end of the program.

To read data from the UART during tape playback, the processor first reads the contents of the status register from input port 00. When the "data available" line goes HI, this indicates that a complete character is now in the receiver holding register, and the processor responds to this condition by reading in this data from input port 01. This process continues until the EOT character is detected, and at this point the processor terminates the READ operation. Then, depending on its external connections, it may either turn off the tape recorder or simply signal the operator via a light or buzzer that all of the data has been read from the tape.

The technique that has been employed in this section for converting data from parallel to serial form and vice versa by using UARTs may be classified as a hardware approach to this data conversion problem. However, as we shall see in the next chapter, this same task can be accomplished equally well by using software instead of hardware. With this approach special programs are written to take the data words internal to the processor and shift them out one bit at a time or, conversely, to sense data coming in serially on one of the lines of an input port and by means of software check it for errors and simultaneously restructure it into 8-bit data words. In fact, by means of proper software design, most of the tape recorder encoder and decoder electronics discussed in the previous section could also be eliminated. The factors governing these hardware-software trade-offs will be fully discussed in Chap. 8.

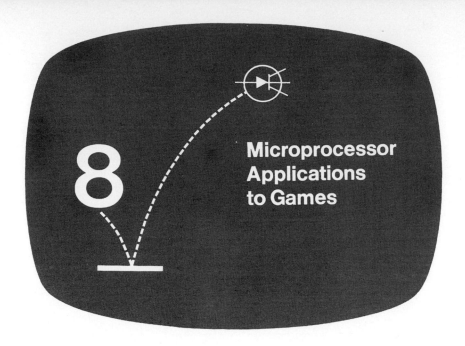

8 Microprocessor Applications to Games

In this chapter we will examine the techniques for employing micro-processors in the design of electronic games. Since, at present, the majority of these games have been developed for use with standard television receivers, considerable attention will be focused on the methods used for display through this medium. In the first section we will discuss how to display digital information raster-type TV scans, and in the sections that follow we will elaborate on the techniques for producing special video and audio effects.

One of the most attractive features of designs based on micropro-cessors is that they often permit considerable savings to the manu-facturer through elimination of excess hardware with replacement of the equivalent functions by software. In Sec. 2 the authors present a complete discussion of this subject and illustrate several typical hardware-software trade-offs encountered in the design of electronic games.

8.1 MICROPROCESSOR REFRESH TECHNIQUES FOR RASTER SCANS

In its simplest form a microprocessor-based video display consists of nothing more than a circuit which permits a section of memory to be displayed on a cathode-ray tube (CRT). The number of memory bytes employed determines the resolution, that is, how much fine detail is present, with the actual data stored determining the specific pattern displayed in the scene.

Some systems, such as RCA's Studio II electronic game, directly display the stored information on a bit-by-bit basis, while others use the word stored at each memory location to address a ROM which contains the set of stored patterns to be generated. Usually the latter method represents a more efficient use of available memory space since one word of memory can be used to create a ROM character field of arbitrary size and complexity.

The block diagram given in Fig. 8.1*a* illustrates how to construct one type of video RAM circuit, employing a ROM character genera-

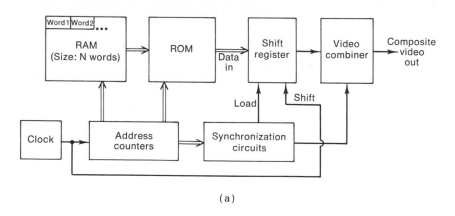

(a)

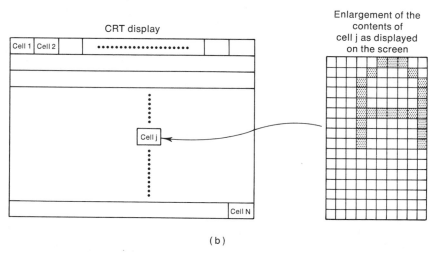

(b)

Figure 8.1 Video RAM display system. (*a*) Block diagram of a typical video RAM circuit; (*b*) mapping of the video RAM output on the CRT.

tor, to create a particular video scene. As shown in the figure, the contents of all *n* words of the RAM are simply *mapped* directly into the *n* video cells on the CRT. The actual pattern displayed in each of the cells on the screen is determined by the data stored in the RAM as well as by the type of ROM employed, and thus the final scene created could contain either alphanumer-ics or graphics data or possibly both.

The specific ROM illustrated in Fig. 8.2 is used for generating alphanumeric char-acters in a standard 7 × 9 dot matrix for-mat. To produce a particular character, the ASCII code for that character is entered on the data input lines (DO to D6). For exam-ple, to generate the letter A, as shown in Fig. 8.1*b*, the input data 1000001 is placed on the data input lines. Note that although the final characters produced fit into a 7 × 9 grid pattern, typically a dot-matrix for-mat of 10 × 15 boxes is allocated for each character, with the empty boxes serving as intercharacter and interline spaces.

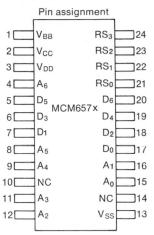

Pin assignment

Figure 8.2a The MCM 6576—a 7 × 9 dot matrix character generator ROM: MCM 6576 ROM pinout.

In order to understand how a typical video RAM system operates it may first be useful to consider the operation of the sys-tem shown in Fig. 8.3, which has been designed to display a single character on a conventional oscilloscope. The ROM illustrated in this figure is the same as that shown in Fig. 8.2 and, while not directly applicable to video games, is very popular for use with systems generating alphanumeric raster scans. Here as in the previous exam-ple the selected character will be displayed in a 10-column by 15-row format in which for the alphanumeric representation presently being considered only 7 × 9 of these dots will be active. The output data from the ROM corresponding to the selected character is available one row at a time. At first the fact that all matrix points are not simultaneously available might appear to create a problem. How-ever, by recalling that a TV raster scans only one line at a time, you should be able to see that this ROM, in fact, is ideally suited to the task at hand.

Returning now to the figure, let's assume that the ROM character data input is a 1000001, or the ASCII entry for the letter A, and that the vertical and horizontal sweep signals generated by the circuit are applied to the respective deflection plates on the oscilloscope. The key waveforms for this circuit are given in Fig. 8.4. For this circuit one complete vertical sweep is produced for every 15 horizontal

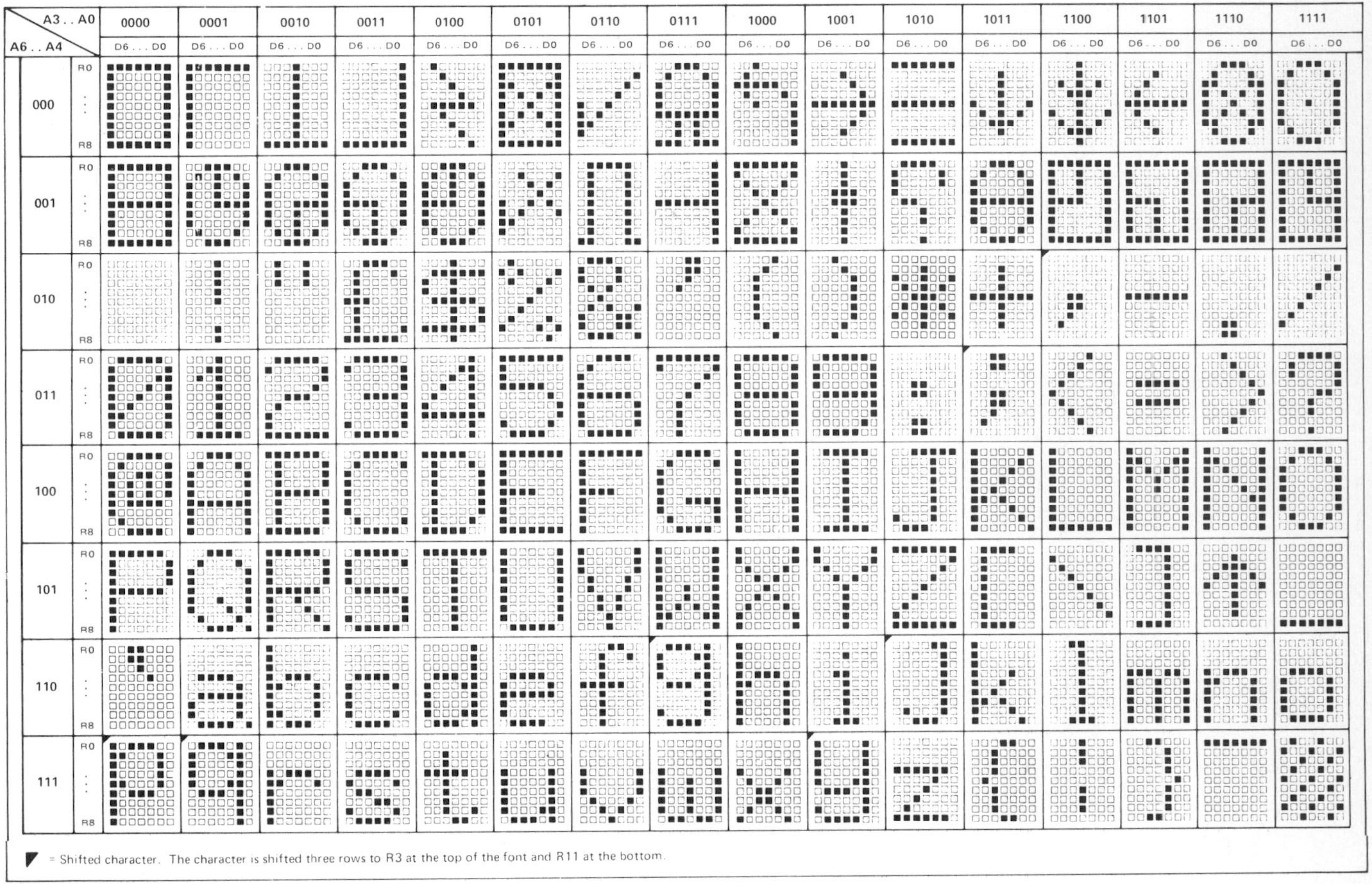

Figure 8.2b MCM 6576 standard ROM patterns. (*Courtesy Motorola Semiconductor.*)

▼ = Shifted character. The character is shifted three rows to R3 at the top of the font and R11 at the bottom.

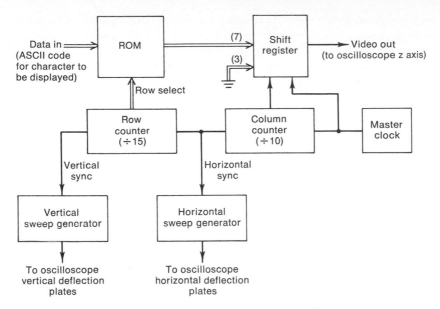

Figure 8.3 Displaying a single character on an oscilloscope.

sweeps of the beam, and this relationship generates a raster containing 15 horizontal scan lines. Each of these scan lines is effectively divided into 10 columns (or dot positions) by the column counter, producing an overall grid pattern of 10 columns by 15 rows, or 150 dots.

At the beginning of each new figure, the row and column counters are initially 0, with the beam starting out at the upper-left-hand side

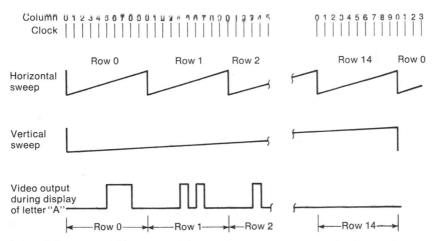

Figure 8.4 Key waveforms of the single-character video display system.

of the screen. Since the row counter contains a binary 0000, the ROM output contains data corresponding to row 0 of the character A, or a 0011100 sequence. These outputs, along with three additional 0s (see Fig. 8.3) are loaded into the shift register and shifted out one bit at a time onto the z-axis input of the oscilloscope to modulate the beam intensity. Here it has been assumed that a 1 turns the beam on and a 0 cuts it off. The three 0 bits entered along with the ROM data bits at the start of each new row blank the beam and serve as the interchar- acter spacing. The reader should also note that rows 10 through 14 are automatically blanked by the character generator to produce the required interline spacing of characters.

The same basic circuitry may also be used to create graphic dis- plays if the character generator ROM and shift register circuit previ- ously discussed are replaced by the ROM-like circuit given in Fig. 8.5. In this display mode each video RAM cell is effectively divided into a 6-box array of 2 columns by 3 rows (Fig. 8.6). By application of the appropriate input code, each of these boxes (dots) may be inde- pendently illuminated or left dark in order to create different graph- ics patterns. The code required to generate a particular pattern is

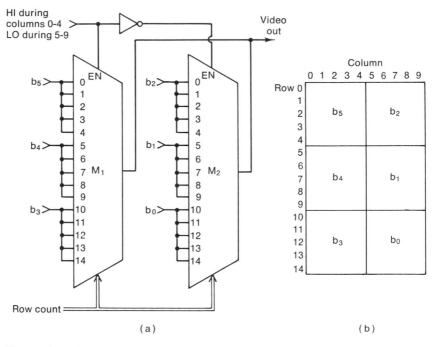

(a)   (b)

Figure 8.5 A graphics "ROM." (a) Electronics of the graphics ROM; (b) cell areas controlled by bit inputs to the graphics ROM. *(Adapted from Polymorphic Systems Video Interface Board.)*

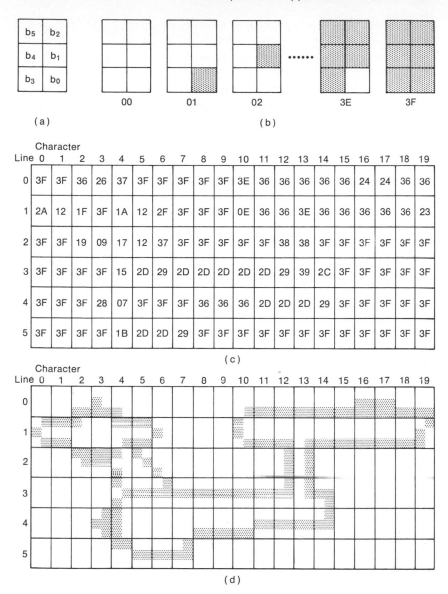

Figure 8.6 Developing graphics images with the graphics ROM. (a) Bit positions used to generate the graphic patterns; (b) hexadecimal code for particular cell patterns; (c) video RAM contents to produce graphics display given in (d) (*Note:* zero in a bit position illuminates the square, one in a bit position darkens the square.); (d) video display produced by the video RAM data given in part (c).

simply the binary equivalent of that pattern using the bit position values given in Fig. 8.6*a*. Several specific cell patterns are illustrated in Fig. 8.6*b,* and in Fig. 8.6*c* an array of these video cells has been combined to form a particular graphics image.

The graphics-generating circuit given in Fig. 8.5 operates in the following manner. For graphics generation all of the 10 by 15 dots in the grid are utilized, and when the scan is on the left-hand side of the character (columns 0 through 4), multiplexer M_1 is enabled. When the scan crosses over to the right-hand side of the character (columns 5 through 9), M_1 is turned off and multiplexer M_2 is enabled. Depending on the particular row count, either bits b5 or b2 (during rows 0 to 4), b4 or b1 (during rows 5 through 9), or b3 or b0 (during rows 10 through 14) are displayed. This type of combined graphics display is especially useful for games in which it is desired to display both graphics and high-quality alphanumeric text material.

If high-resolution alphanumerics are unnecessary for the particular game under consideration, then a simpler, less costly graphics approach of the form illustrated in Fig. 8.7 is indicated. For this case the character generator ROM has been eliminated, and when needed the alphanumerics are created by using a low-resolution graphics approach. Each word in the video RAM is now displayed on a bit-by-bit basis in a sequential fashion on a single scan line, or, as is usually the case, repeated several times on a group of scan lines. For the specific display illustrated in Fig. 8.7*a,* a total video RAM size of five hundred and twelve 8-bit words is used. This display employs a noninterlaced raster scan of 256 lines, with each word line repeated on a group of four scan lines. Thus the display generates 64 word lines having 8 RAM words of 8 bits each, or an overall display of 64 × 64 dots. For many of today's video games this resolution has proved adequate. As shown in Fig. 8.7*b,* the electronics required for this type of direct video display are quite simple, and as a result this has been the approach employed in many of the currently popular low-resolution microprocessor-based video games.

In order to generate a complete video RAM raster scan display of the form previously illustrated in Fig. 8.1, additional circuitry will be needed to permit the generation of multiple characters on a single line and of multiple lines of output in order to form a complete image. The design given in Fig. 8.8 generates an alphanumeric/ graphics display containing 16 character lines with 32 character positions per line. In order to generate both alphanumeric and graphics data, it employs both a standard 7 × 9 character-generator ROM as well as the graphics "ROM" circuit given in Fig. 8.5. Here the RAM is used to store the data to be displayed, with bit b7 in each

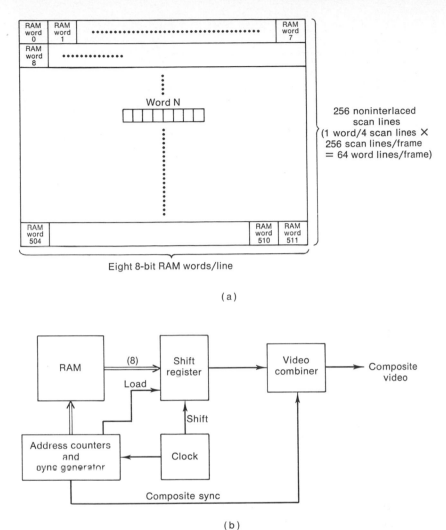

Eight 8-bit RAM words/line

(a)

(b)

Figure 8.7 A direct-display video RAM system. (*a*) 4096 (64 × 64) dot array; (*b*) direct video RAM circuit.

word being used to determine whether the stored word (in bits b0 to b6) is to be converted into an alphanumeric or a graphic character. Additional line and character counters have also been added to the former single character display of Fig. 8.3 in order to generate the complete video image.

As before, at the start of each frame, the electron beam begins at the upper-left-hand side of the screen, and since all of the counters

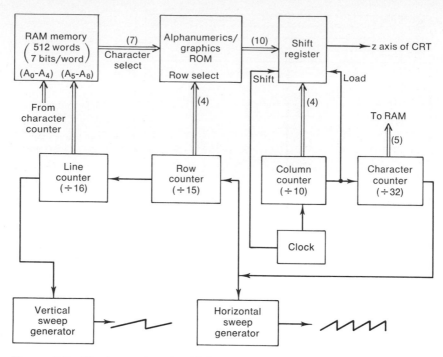

Figure 8.8 Display system for 16 lines of alphanumeric graphics data, 32 characters per line.

are initially zero, the ROM is first addressed with the data from RAM word zero, and a sweep on row 0 is begun. The ROM output data corresponding to row 0 is then loaded into the shift register, and with each subsequent clock pulse the next column output of row 0, character 0, line zero is shifted out onto the z-axis line to modulate the beam intensity. After the first 10 clock pulses, the character counter is incremented, and the next word in RAM is addressed to start the display of the WORD 1 output on row 0. This process continues until the first row of all characters on line zero has been displayed, and at this point the row counter is incremented, and the column and character counters are reset to zero to begin the display of the second row of line 0. At the end of the fifteenth row, one complete line of characters has been displayed, and the line counter increments to begin the display of the second line. When the display of all lines is completed, all counters return to 0, and the process begins again.

In order to change the display, the contents of the video RAM must be altered. Since the RAM "belongs" to the display system, additional circuitry is needed to present the data to be written at the RAM input and then to either jam the address of the word to be modified into the line and character counters prior to application of the WRITE pulse or else, via multiplexers, to switch in a new address register containing the address of the word to be changed. The circuit given in Fig. 8.9 illustrates a microprocessor-based TV video display system employing this latter approach.

In its normal display mode, the video RAM is addressed by using the line and character counters, which also generate the appropriate sync and blanking signals to lock the picture on the screen and to

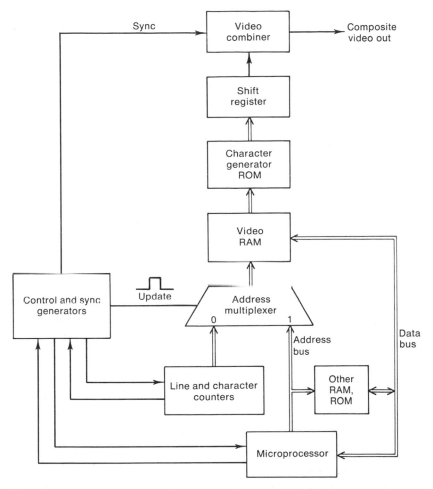

Figure 8.9 A complete microprocessor-controlled video RAM display system.

blank out the beam during retrace. Thus for this mode of operation the system behavior is identical to that of the video RAM previously discussed.

To alter the contents of the memory, the processor issues to the display circuits a command which at the appropriate time in the display cycle causes the multiplexer to switch the video RAM addressing over to the microprocessor. At this point the processor, now temporarily in control of the RAM's address bus, writes the required information into the proper locations within the RAM. In order to prevent the appearance of visual "glitches" on the screen as the RAM contents are updated, this procedure is carried out during the nondisplayed (blanked out) portions of the vertical sweep. This technique is very similar to that employed in Fairchild's Channel F microprocessor-based video game.

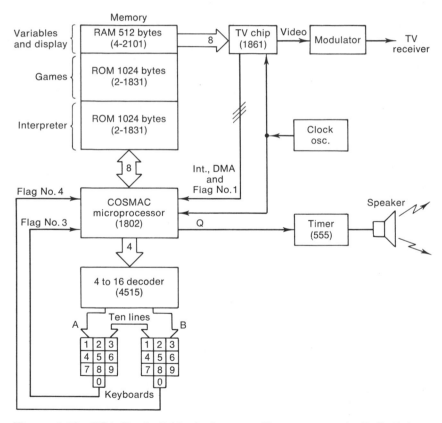

Figure 8.10 RCA Studio II block diagram. *(From a paper by P. K. Baltzer and J. A. Weisbaecker, "Fun and Games with Cosmac," presented at Electro 77, April 1977.)*

In the RCA Studio II electronic video game (Fig. 8.10), most of the hardware associated with the design given in Fig. 8.9 has been eliminated. This paring down of the electronic circuits required may be attributed to the use of a special video display interface IC (the CDP 1861) in conjunction with RCA's own CDP 1802 microprocessor, which has an internal DMA capability. In addition to generating all the required sync and video information, the interface chip initiates a RAM refresh cycle at the beginning of each new frame by sending a DMA request to the processor. When this occurs, the processor enters a special DMA interrupt routine and via its internal DMA hardware transfers the entire video RAM contents one word at a time into the interface chip for display. During the nondisplayed vertical and horizontal time intervals, the processor returns from its DMA mode to carry out the normal data processing and RAM updating associated with the particular game being played.

8.2 HARDWARE-SOFTWARE TRADE-OFFS

Once the decision has been made to incorporate a microprocessor into a particular video game, many side benefits are accrued. Most obvious of these are the versatility of the design, the multiplicity of games available, and the ease with which a particular game design can be modified. Additionally there is the low cost associated with the elimination of the usually considerable number of ICs required to accomplish this same task by means of conventional wired-logic approach. Along these lines, as we shall see in this section, it is also possible to realize many other savings, especially in the systems interfacing circuitry, by replacing this hardware with software routines that carry out the same functions.

In order to illustrate the general form of these hardware-software trade-offs, the authors will discuss four examples of particular relevance to the design of electronic games:

1. An analog joystick interface

2. A keyboard encoder design

3. An LED digit scan design

4. A software UART

Joystick Interface

Many video games employ some type of joystick control to allow the player to position objects (such as tennis paddles, hockey sticks,

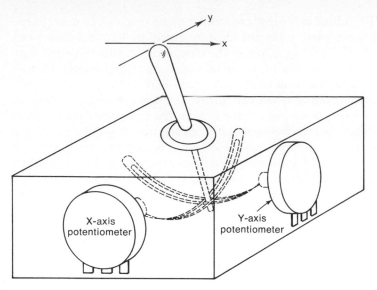

Figure 8.11 A potentiometer joystick control.

tanks and aircraft, and cue sticks) on the screen. Although somewhat less reliable than all-digital controls, the dual-potentiometer joystick illustrated in Fig. 8.11 is inexpensive and does offer the player a "feel" not present in discrete digital controls.

The block diagram given in Fig. 8.12a illustrates how a control of this type might be interfaced to the microprocessor by means of an all-hardware approach. Here, depending on the position of the joystick control, a voltage V_1 is produced. This voltage is then transformed into its digital equivalent by using an external analog-to-digital converter. On completion of each conversion cycle, the A/D

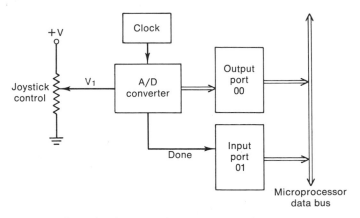

Figure 8.12 An all-hardware joystick interface.

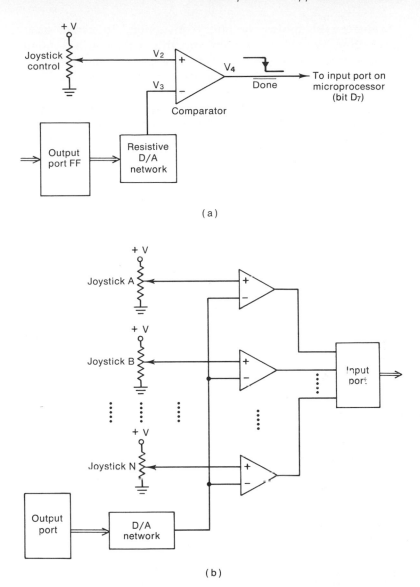

(a)

(b)

Figure 8.13 A reduced-hardware joystick interface. (*a*) A part-hard-
ware–part-software A/D converter; (*b*) interfacing multiple joysticks to
a single A/D converter.

unit signals the processor by means of the DONE flag bit, and, once
recognized, the processor simply reads the converted data in from
one of its input ports. If the A/D unit is much faster than the
processor sampling rate, then the DONE flag bit is unnecessary, and
the unit can convert the signal and wait for the processor to take in

this data before beginning another conversion. In either case, although rather simple to implement, this conversion scheme requires considerable external hardware, is expensive, and is therefore an unlikely candidate for incorporation into mass-produced electronic games.

One way to simplify this hardware somewhat is to perform part of the A/D conversion process within the microcomputer. The circuit illustrated in Fig. 8.13 is that of a typical ramp-type A/D converter in which the ramp generation process is carried out by the computer. To initiate a conversion, the processor places a hexadecimal 00 into output port FF and then begins to increment this number while continually testing the V_4 ($\overline{\text{DONE}}$) line to see if V_3 equals V_2. As the value of V_3 increases, eventually it will equal V_2, and when this occurs the comparator output will go LO. The processor senses this transition as the end of the conversion and at this point has the digital equivalent of the analog input voltage V_2 in its accumulator. A complete sample program for this type of A/D conversion is given in Fig. 8.14.

It is important to note that the basic converter circuit given in Fig. 8.13*a* can easily be interfaced to a multiplicity of joystick controls by simply adding one additional comparator for each joystick control (Fig. 8.13*b*). Furthermore, the resistive D/A network shown in Fig. 8.13*a* is not essential and can be replaced by a much less expensive IC integrator which can be used to produce the ramp voltage. In addition, this latter approach requires only a single control bit from the processor to reset the integrator at the start of each conversion cycle.

A very different approach to the solution of this joystick interfacing problem is illustrated in Fig. 8.15. This technique requires mini-

Hexadecimal code		Mnemonic		
Address	*Instruction*	*Label*	*Instruction*	*Comments*
0000	AF		XRA A	Clear A.
01	3C	LOOP:	INR A	
02	D3FF		OUT #FF	
04	47		MOV B,A	Save A.
05	DBFF		IN FF	Check D7.
07	E680		ANI #80	
09	78		MOV A,B	Put back (flags not
0A	CZ0100		JNZ LOOP	affected).
0D	D3FF		OUT #FF	Display result.
0F	76		HALT	Stop.

Figure 8.14 Software for hardware shown in Fig. 8.13*a*.

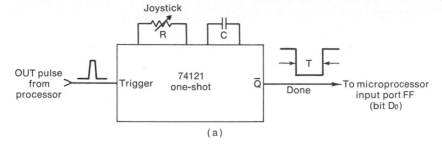

(a)

Hexadecimal code		Mnemonic		
Address	*Instructions*	*Label*	*Instruction*	*Comments*
0000	D3FF	START:	OUT #FF	Write to any output
02	14	LOOP:	INR D	port to initiate pulse.
03	DBFF		IN #FF	Check for timeout
05	E601		ANI #01	completed (bit DO).
07	CA0200		JZ LOOP	
0A	C9		RET	Final answer in D.

(b)

Figure 8.15 (*a*) Minimal hardware joystick interface; (*b*) software for use with circuit in (*a*).

mal hardware and uses the joystick to control the pulse width generated by the 74121 one-shot. The generation of the pulse is initiated by the processor when it executes an OUT operation (that is, writes to *any* output port), after which the processor remains in the counting loop until it receives a DONE signal from the one-shot. In this way the final count in the D register (see Fig. 8.15*b*) is proportional to the joystick resistance R.

Keyboard Interface

Owing to the rather rough treatment received by the interface controls on electronic games, the potentiometer joystick found on today's low-cost games is likely to be replaced by an equivalent control operating by means of a keyboard or by some type of switching arrangement having a joysticklike appearance. Examples of each of these latter approaches are found in RCA's Studio II and Fairchild's Channel F games respectively.

The principal advantages of keyboards and switches over resistive-type joysticks are enhanced reliability, versatility, and ease of interfacing to microprocessor-controlled games. Here again, as with the joystick interface previously discussed, many opportunities are

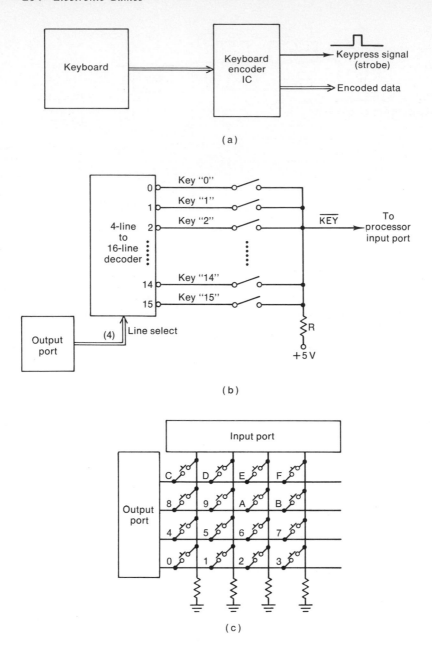

Figure 8.16 Interfacing a keyboard to a microprocessor. (*a*) All hardware; (*b*) partial hardware; (*c*) minimal hardware.

afforded for eliminating excess hardware at the expense of an increased software overhead.

The block diagram given in Fig. 8.16*a* illustrates one of the more conventional approaches for encoding keystroke information into its equivalent binary code. These special keyboard encoder ICs, in addition to encoding the data, also can debounce the key information and eliminate erroneous outputs due to multiple key rollover (depression). Unfortunately, they are rather expensive. The circuit illustrated in Fig. 8.16*b* goes a long way toward eliminating most of the hardware by involving the processor in the keyboard encoding task.

The operation of this circuit may be explained as follows. When no key is depressed, as the processor continually tests each of the key lines (see Fig. 8.16*b*), a HI output will be continuously obtained in the $\overline{\text{KEY}}$ line. Should any key be struck, then a LO will be found on the $\overline{\text{KEY}}$ line when that line is tested by the processor via the demultiplexer. At this point the processor waits for a small amount of time for the key bounce to die out, checks all other keys (for rollover effects), and then if no other keys have been simultaneously hit, generates and stores the binary code equivalent of the key pressed.

An even greater hardware simplification of this circuit may be obtained by replacing the individual switch contacts used in the previous example with a keyboard matrix of the form given in Fig. 8.16*c*. With this type of keyboard, the entire encoding operation can be performed in software, and hardware requirements are cut to the bone.

As before, in its resting mode the processor continually checks the keys to see if one has been struck. However, in this case, the scanning operation is accomplished by having the processor pulse one row at a time and then check the column lines for nonzero outputs. Should a HI be detected on any of the column lines, then, as before, the processor enters a WAIT loop for debouncing and then rechecks all of the other key positions to prevent multiple key rollover effects. If none exist, the keystroke information is then considered valid and the data is input to the processor.

Digit Scan

In nonvideo electronic games, the game's progress is frequently indicated on 7-segment LED displays. This interfacing problem affords another opportunity for the elimination of considerable hardware at the expense of additional software.

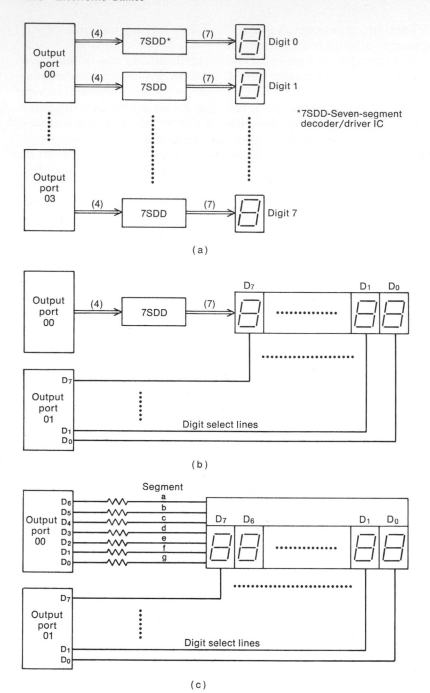

(a)

*7SDD–Seven-segment decoder/driver IC

(b)

(c)

The circuit given in Fig. 8.17*a* illustrates one conventional approach that might be utilized to interface a microprocessor to an 8-digit LED display. As shown, this sytem requires four 8-bit output ports and eight 7-segment decoder driver ICs (7SDD in the figure). We can eliminate much of the hardware by using a scanned approach to this problem. With this technique, each LED is illuminated in turn, and the scan operation repeated at a high enough rate that all of the digits appear to be lit simultaneously. The circuit illustrated in Fig. 8.17*b* shows how the displays would be interfaced to the processor for the 8-digit case.

A further simplification in the hardware required may be obtained by storing the digit decode information in ROM. With this approach, only two output ports and no additional hardware, other than current limiting resistors, would be needed to interface the 8-digit display to the processor.

The complete software for generating this type of display is illustrated in Fig. 8.18. For simplicity, only the 2-digit case is shown, but with minor revisions the program can be expanded to handle any number of digits. The hardware connections associated with this program are given in Fig. 8.17*c*.

Following the comments given with the program, we see that the program uses the data corresponding to the decimal number to be displayed to form the address for the 7-segment table look up. The corresponding 7-segment code for the character is then sent to bits DO through D6 of output port 00, while the number in bits DO and D1 of output port 01 determines which of the two digits is to be illuminated.

Returning now to the 8-digit case in which all the lines of output port 01 are connected to the corresponding digit select lines on the display, consider for example the sequence of steps required to light a "3" in digit 6 of the display. Initially while the data in port 00 is being changed, all digit displays are momentarily blanked by sending an FF to port 01 to prevent digit smearing. Next the "3" is used to form the proper ROM address (0033 in this case), and its contents are sent to output port 00. This, a 01001111, or 4F in hexadecimal code, will cause segments a, b, c, d, and g to light up in the selected digit, producing a "3".

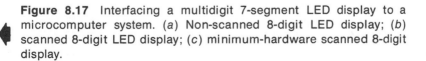

Figure 8.17 Interfacing a multidigit 7-segment LED display to a microcomputer system. (*a*) Non-scanned 8-digit LED display; (*b*) scanned 8-digit LED display; (*c*) minimum-hardware scanned 8-digit display.

Hexadecimal code		Mnemonic		
Address	Instruction	Label	Instruction	Comments
				Assume 2-digit number to be displayed is in A.
0000	2600	START:	MVI H,#00	
02	47		MOV B,A	Save A.
03	E60F		ANI #0F	Strip away MSH.
05	C630		ADI #30	Form look-up ad-
07	6F		MOV L,A	dress for D0.
08	3EFF		MVI A,#FF }	Blank all digits.
0A	D301		OUT #01 }	
0C	7E		MOV A,M	Look up 7-seg-
0D	D300		OUT #00	ment code.
0F	3EFE		MVI A,#FE }	Turn on D0.
11	D301		OUT #01 }	
13	78		MOV A,B	Recall original num-
14	E6		ANI #F0	ber. Strip away LSH.
16	07		RLC ⎤	
17	07		RLC ⎥	Move MSH to LSH
18	07		RLC ⎥	position.
19	07		RLC ⎦	
1A	C630		ADI #30	
1C	6F		MOV L,A	
1D	3EFF		MVI A,#FF	Blank all digits.
1F	D301		OUT #01	
21	7E		MOV A,M	Look up 7-segment
22	D300		OUT #00	code for D1.
24	3EFD		MVI A,#FD }	Turn on D1.
26	D301		OUT #01 }	
28	78		MOV A,B	
29	C30000	4F	JMP START	
0030	3F065B	07		Decoder Table
34	666D7D	7C		
38	7F6777	71		
3C	395E79			

Figure 8.18 Software for use with digit scan hardware of Fig. 8.17*c*.

To select digit 6, a 10111111, or BF, is sent to output port 01, extinguishing all digits other than 6 in this common cathode display. In a similar fashion, the other digits in the display are illuminated by simply rotating the single 0 in output port 01 through all bit positions while simultaneously presenting the information to be displayed at port 00. Since this scanning operation takes place at a high rate, all digits will appear to be simultaneously lit.

A Software UART

In the previous chapter the universal asynchronous receiver-transmitter (UART) was introduced and was shown to be a powerful device for minimizing the hardware needed to permit the serial transmission and reception of data. The program given in Fig. 8.19 illustrates how this UART may be replaced by using software. The program given duplicates only the UART's transmit function, but a similar one could also be written to replace the receiver portion of the UART.

As shown, when a character is to be transmitted, the computer first sends out the zero start bit, delays 9.09 ms, loads the word to be transmitted into the accumulator, and then sends the first bit to a single-bit output port for transmission. After each 9.09-ms delay, successive bits are rotated into the least significant bit (LSB) position of the accumulator and sent to the output port until the entire word has been transmitted. This data is followed by two 9.09-ms stop bits,

Hexadecimal code		Mnemonic			
Address	*Instruction*	*Label*	*Instruction*		*Comments*
0040	0608		MVI	B,#08	Initialize bit count.
42	AF		XRA	A	Clear accumulator.
43	D3FF		OUT	#FF	Transmit start bit.
45	CD6000		CALL	DELAY	
48	79		MOV	A,C	
49	D3FF	NEX BIT:	OUT	#FF	Transmit data.
4B	1F		RAR		
4C	05		DCR	B	
4D	C24900		JNZ	NEX BIT	
50	3EFF		MVI	A,#FF	
52	D3FF		OUT	#FF	
54	CD6000		CALL	DELAY	
57	CD6000		CALL	DELAY	
5A	C9		RET		
0060	11E502	DELAY:	LXI	D,#02E5	Load D with 02,E with E5 or 245_{10}.
63	1B	LOOP:	DCX	D	
64	7B		MOV	A,E	
65	B2		ORA	D	Check if both 0.
66	C26300		JNZ	LOOP	
69	C9		RET		

(a)

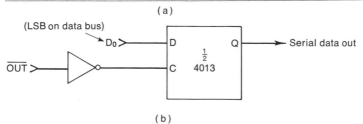

(b)

Figure 8.19 (*a*) A software UART: program and flowchart; (*b*) hardware required for the software UART.

Hexadecimal code		Mnemonic		
Address	Instruction	Label	Instruction	Comments
1010	210088	BEGIN:	LXI H,#8800	
13	E5	NEW MAN:	PUSH H	
14	CDF200		CALL CLR SCRN	See Appendix, p. 330.
17	117010		LXI D,#1070	Initialize MAN 1.
1A	E1		POP H	
1B	CD4710		CALL MAN	
1E	CD9010		CALL DELAY	
21	23	LIN CHK	INX H	
22	7D		MOV A,L	
23	FE40		CPI #40	
25	C21010		JNZ BEGIN	
28	E5		PUSH H	
29	CDF200		CALL CLR SCRN	
2C	118010		LXI D,#1080	Initialize MAN 2.
2F	E1		POP H	
30	CD4710		CALL MAN	
33	CD9010		CALL DELAY	
36	23		INX H	
37	7D		MOV A,L	
38	FE40		CPI #40	
3A	C21310		JNZ NEWMAN	
3D	C31010		JMP BEGIN	
0047	0603	MAN:	MVI B,#03	Row count
49	0E03	NEX LIN:	MVI C,#03	Line character count
4B	1A	NEX CHAR:	LDAX D	
4C	77		MOV M,A	
4D	13		INX D	
4E	23		INX H	
4F	0D		DCR C	
50	C24810		JNZ NEX CHAR	
53	05		DCR B	
54	C26410		JNZ FIX L	
57	7D		MOV A,L	
58	D680		SUI #80	
5A	6F		MOV L,A	
5B	C9		RET	
0064	7D	FIX L:	MOV A,L	Move to start of next line.
65	C63D		ADI #3D	
67	6F		MOV L,A	
68	C34910		JMP NEX LIN	
0090	01FFFF	DELAY:	LXI B,#FFFF	
93	0B	LOOP:	DCX B	
94	79		MOV A,C	
95	B0		ORA B	
96	C29310		JNZ LOOP	
99	C9		RET	

Figure 8.20a A walking man display.

completing the transmission of the character. Since each character contains 11 bits of 9.09-ms duration, the maximum data transmission rate for this case is 10 characters per second.

8.3 MICROPROCESSOR CONTROL OF VIDEO EFFECTS

Probably one of the most important aspects of all video games is the manner in which video information is presented on the screen, for this represents the principal user-game interface medium. Therefore the quality, variability, and types of images displayed will, to a large extent, determine the overall success of a particular game. Here again, the microprocessor's innate ability to store, manipulate, and control the presentation of data make it a prime candidate for incorporation into the newer, more sophisticated electronic games.

In this section we will discuss the microprocessor's role in generating various types of video effects. Specifically we will demonstrate how the processor may be utilized to simulate motion of an object on the screen, to produce blinking of a particular object in order to draw attention to it, to rotate an object, to simulate the collision of an object with an obstacle or projectile, and lastly to add color to the display. Throughout this section, as discussed in Sec. 1, it will be assumed that the display interface is a 16-line video RAM capable of producing 64 characters per line. Each character cell will be considered to be made up of a 6-dot array of the form illustrated in Fig. 8.6.

In order to generate motion on the screen, a technique quite similar to that employed in motion pictures is utilized. Basically what the system does is sequentially present a series of still pictures which when rapidly flashed in succession create the illusion of motion on the screen.

The program given in Fig. 8.20*a* illustrates how the processor may be employed to create the appearance of motion on the CRT—in this case generating the image of a man walking across the screen. To

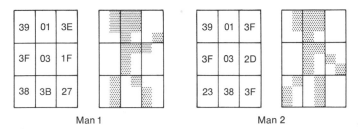

Man 1   Man 2

Figure 8.20b Actual construction of the figures.

Hexadecimal code		Mnemonic			
Address	*Instruction*	*Label*		*Instruction*	*Comments*
1000	AF		XRA	A	
01	329010		STA	#1090	
04	216089	START:	LXI	#8960	
07	E5		PUSH	H	
08	CDF200		CALL	CLR SCRN	See Appendix, p. 330.
0B	117010		LXI	D,#1070	
0E	E1		POP	H	
0F	CD2010		CALL	TANK	
12	CD9000		CALL	DELAY	See Fig. 8.20a.
15	3A9010		LDA	#1090	
18	2F		CMA		
19	329010		STA	#1090	
1C	C30410		JMP	START	
1020	0604	TANK:	MVI	B,#04	Row count
22	0E06	NEX LIN:	MVI	C,#06	Line character counter
24	3A9010	NEX CHAR:	LDA	#1090	
27	B7		ORA	A	Set flags.
28	1A		LDAX	D	
29	CA2F10		JZ	NOCOMP	Check flag.
2C	2F		CMA		⎫ Inverts video.
2D	E63F		ANI	#3F	⎬
2F	77	NOCOMP:	MOV	M,A	⎭
30	13		INX	D	
31	23		INX	H	
32	0D		DCR	C	
33	C22410		JNZ	NEX CHAR	
36	05		DCR	B	
37	C23B10		JNZ	FIX LIN	
3A	C9		RET		
3B	7D	FIX LIN:	MOV	A,L	
3C	C63A		ADI	#3A	
3E	6F		MOV	L,A	
3F	C32210		JMP	NEX LIN	

Figure 8.22 Producing an object on the screen in inverse video.

the vertical axis and then about the horizontal axis. Thus to produce any one of the object orientations shown, at most only two programs (one for the vertical and one for the horizontal reflection) need be called.

One such program which can be employed to produce a horizontal transformation of the images is given in Fig. 8.24. Basically the program operates by interchanging the data contained in the rows of the object display. Since each of the object images consists of four rows, two passes through the subroutine are required to completely transform the image. On the first pass the data contained in the top and bottom rows are interchanged. The address information for each of these rows is contained in the HL and DE register pairs respectively. On the second pass (indicated by the fact that the carry is 0), the data found in the two inner rows is exchanged. The entire program to produce this mirror reflection of the object about the horizontal axis requires only 33 bytes of memory. At first it might seem that it would take less memory space to store all of the object orientations directly in ROM than to make use of these transformation programs. Were there only one type of object to be displayed, this might in fact be true; however, when one considers that the game set might employ 10 or 20 different objects, the utility of these transformation techniques becomes apparent.

Many electronic games involve the collision of projectiles with objects and also objects with objects, and it is therefore necessary to have a technique available for detecting collisions. In terms of software requirements, it is relatively easy to determine when a collision has occurred. Whenever a portion of the projectile image and the object image occupy the same location in the video RAM, a collision has taken place. The program given in Fig. 8.25 provides a simple demonstration of how a collision may be detected by software. Here, when the program is run, a target is displayed at the center of the screen at address 8820, and a projectile is launched at the target from

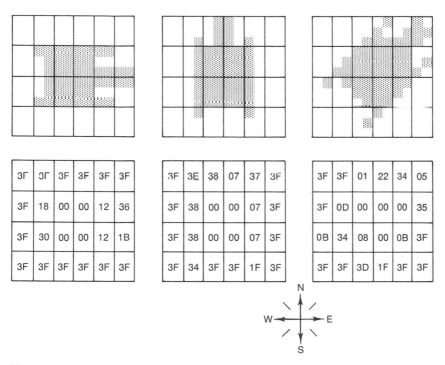

Figure 8.23 Rotated tank ROM patterns.

Hexadecimal code		Mnemonic		
Address	Instruction	Label	Instruction	Comments
1080	37	SUB HOR:	STC	Set carry to 1.
81	216089		LXI H, #8960	Upper row address
84	11208A		LXI D,#8A20	Lower row address
87	0E06	NEX ROW:	MVI C,#06	
89	7E	XCHG:	MOV A,M	
8A	EB		XCHG	
8B	46		MOV B,M	
8C	77		MOV M,A	
8D	EB		XCHG	
8E	70		MOV M,B	
8F	23		INX H	
90	13		INX D	
91	0D		DCR C	} Check for row switch
92	C28910		JNZ XCHG	} completed.
95	3F		CMC	
96	D8		RC	Returns on 2d pass.
97	7D		MOV A,L	
98	C63A		ADI #3A	
9A	7B		MOV A,E	
9B	D646		SUI #46	
9D	5F		MOV E,A	
9E	C38610		JMP NEX ROW	

Figure 8.24 A horizontal reflection subroutine for pattern inversion.

the left. In this case both the projectile and target are represented by the same symbol—a rectangular box (video RAM code 00); of course, in an actual game they could be represented by any type of video display. The projectile moves toward the target at a rate determined by the DELAY subroutine. In this particular program the projectile advances toward the target at a rate of about 6 mm/s (¼ in/s).

In each REFRESH cycle, as with the previous programs discussed, the screen is cleared, and the new target and projectile locations displayed. At this point a check is made to see if a collision has occurred. To do this, the contents of the HL and DE register pairs are compared. Since these registers contain the object and target screen position locations respectively, if a match exists then the projectile has hit the target. To indicate this fact, at this point the projectile disappears from the screen and the object begins to blink at about a 1-Hz rate, signifying that it has been hit. In a more sophisticated program this portion of the routine could be replaced by one calling forth a sound-generation program for an explosion as well as a sequential video update routine showing the object flying apart as a result of the hit.

Thus far all of the video effects discussed have centered around the generation of black-and-white images; however, as we all know, the effect of adding color to a video game, or for that matter to any video display, dramatically increases spectator (or player) interest. In the remainder of this section, we will discuss one particularly simple approach for adding color to a video RAM system.

As discussed in Chap 2, in order to form a complete color TV signal, color information (*chromiance*) is added to the standard black and white (*luminance*) information in the form of a phase-modulated signal centered about a 3.58-MHz carrier. The phase of this signal is compared with that of a reference sine wave transmitted on the back porch of the horizontal synchronization pulses. This 8-cycle 3.58-MHz burst is removed from the sync pulse by the receiver and used to phase-lock the local 3.58-MHz oscillator in the receiver. The relationship between the phase difference of the incoming chromiance signal and the corresponding color produced on the screen is given in Table 8.1. The last column in the table indicates the approximate time delay which is needed between the burst reference sine wave and the chromiance signal in order to produce these different colors. Thus, for example, in order to create a red color on a particular area of the screen, the chromiance color signal generated during that portion

Hexadecimal code		Mnemonic			
Address	Instruction	Label	Instruction		Comments
1000	112088		LXI	D,#8820	Initialize target location.
03	210088		LXI	H,#8800	Initialize projectile location.
06	E5	START:	PUSH	H	
07	CDF200		CALL	CLR SCRN	See Appendix, p. 330.
0A	E1		POP	H	
0B	3E00	NEX MOV:	MVI	A,#00	
0D	77		MOV	M,A	Place target and
0E	EB		XCHG		projectile on screen.
0F	77		MOV	M,A	
10	EB		XCHG		
11	7D		MOV	A,L	
12	BB		CMP	E	
13	C22910		JNZ	OK	Check for collision.
16	7C		MOV	A,H	
17	BA		CMP	D	
18	C22910		JNZ	OK	
1B	3E3F		MVI	A,#3F	If here, collision has
1D	77	BLINK:	MOV	M,A	occurred.
1E	F5		PUSH	PSW	
1F	CD3010		CALL	DELAY	
22	F1		POP	PSW	
23	2F		CMA		
24	E63F		ANI	#3F	
26	C31D10		JMP	BLINK	
29	23	OK:	INX	H	
2A	CD3010		CALL	DELAY	
102D	C30610		JMP	START	

Figure 8.25 Target collision program.

TABLE 8.1   RELATIONSHIP BETWEEN CHROMIANCE PHASE
DELAY AND THE RESULTING SCREEN COLOR PRODUCED

Color	Approximate phase delay from reference, deg	Approximate time delay, ns
Burst	0	0
Yellow	15	12
Red	75	58
Magenta	135	105
Blue	195	151
Cyan	255	198
Green	315	244

SOURCE: Don Lancaster, *TV Typewriter Cookbook,* H. W. Sams, 1976, p. 205.

of the video display is simply a replica of the 3.58-MHz color reference delayed by 58 ns in time.

The circuit given in Fig. 8.26 illustrates that the chromiance signals associated with various colors may be simply obtained by
passing the 3.58-MHz color reference through a series of CMOS 4050
buffer gates since these each typically have internal propagation
delays on the order of 40 ns. If necessary to fine-tune the colors,
additional delays can be obtained by adding small resistors in series

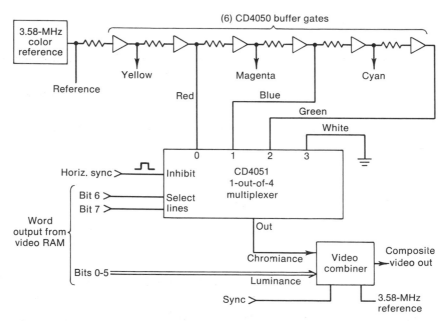

Figure 8.26   Adding color to a video display.(*Adapted from Don Lancaster,
TV Typewriter Cookbook, H. W. Sams, 1976, p.206.*)

with each input gate. Although the circuit indicates that a total of seven different colors are available, for most video games only the four principal colors, red, blue, green, and white, are employed. In this way the selection of a particular color on the screen may be achieved by adding only two color control bits to each video RAM cell, increasing its word size to 8 bits. The lower portion of Fig. 8.26 indicates how these bits are used to control the selection of a particular color for the cell. Note that a zero chromiance signal produces a white image as long as a nonzero luminance signal is present.

8.4 SOUND EFFECTS

The addition of sound effects to an electronic game dramatically increases the realism of the game and greatly enhances player interest and enjoyment. In microprocessor-based games three different techniques are employed for generating these sound effects: waveform creation through the use of a specific algorithm, waveform creation through the use of a look-up table, and lastly sound generation by using the processor to control an external sound-effects creation circuit. An example of each of these approaches is given below.

In Chap. 4 the authors discussed the fundamentals of sound generation and indicated that white-noise sources were particularly useful for creating many familiar sounds. Generally this type of signal is produced by reverse-biasing a diode or transistor junction near its breakdown region; however, this type of signal source is at best somewhat unreliable. One digital alternative to this approach is indicated in Fig. 8.27a, in which a large shift register is connected to a particular feedback network in order to produce a pseudorandom sequence of pulses at the output. The circuit shown is that of a 16-bit shift register configuration producing a sequence which repeats itself every 65,000 shift pulses. A small portion of this sequence is given in Fig. 8.27b. This same circuit can, however, be duplicated in software. The program given in Fig. 8.28 illustrates one method of achieving this duplication.

In this program an equivalent 16-bit shift register is formed from the HL register pair, and the exclusive-OR feedback algorithm is implemented by temporarily transferring the H and L registers to the accumulator in order to carry out the required exclusive-OR operations on the various bits in the HL pair. A careful examination of the software reveals that it operates by "exclusive-ORing" bits 15, 14, 12, and 3 in the equivalent 16-bit register, with the final answer obtained being entered in the b_0 side of the register as each shifting

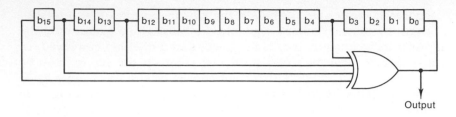

Output

(a)

Shift pulse number	Shift register bit values															
	b_{15}	b_{14}	b_{13}	b_{12}	b_{11}	b_{10}	b_9	b_8	b_7	b_6	b_5	b_4	b_3	b_2	b_1	b_0
	0	0	0	0	0	0	0	0	0	0	0	0	0	0	0	1
1	0	0	0	0	0	0	0	0	0	0	0	0	0	0	1	0
2	0	0	0	0	0	0	0	0	0	0	0	0	0	1	0	0
3	0	0	0	0	0	0	0	0	0	0	0	0	1	0	0	0
4	0	0	0	0	0	0	0	0	0	0	0	1	0	0	0	1
5	0	0	0	0	0	0	0	0	0	0	1	0	0	0	1	0
6	0	0	0	0	0	0	0	0	0	1	0	0	0	1	0	0
7	0	0	0	0	0	0	0	0	1	0	0	0	1	0	0	0
8	0	0	0	0	0	0	0	1	0	0	0	1	0	0	0	1
9	0	0	0	0	0	0	1	0	0	0	1	0	0	0	1	0
⋮																
65,791																

(b)

Figure 8.27 Generating digital white noise. (a) Shift register configuration to produce digital white noise; (b) partial output listing for the $N = 16$ pseudorandom sequence generator in (a).

(DAD D) operation is carried out. One interesting feature of this particular program is that it doesn't use any ports to output the generated information. Instead, it makes use of the interrupt enable (INTE) status signal from the processor as an output control line. This eliminates the extra latch required to store the data if a port approach is adopted. When the HL pair's most significant bit is 1, interrupts are enabled; they are reset when it is 0. This signal is then coupled to an amplifier which is used to create the actual audio output.

For generating more complex waveforms, a different approach is required. For instance, if a sine-wave audio signal is needed, the algorithm to create it is extensive, so much so, in fact, that this type of signal can be more efficiently produced by using a look-up-table approach. The program given in Fig. 8.29 illustrates how this may be accomplished. The program is basically a block transfer program which sends data sequentially from memory (in this case the data in ROM corresponding to the sine-wave amplitude) to the selected output port. If a D/A converter is connected to the output port, the original sine waveform will be re-created at this output.

This particular waveform generator uses 48 data points; however, depending on resolution requirements of the system, this number can of course be modified to any value. The program as shown requires 54 clock cycles per pass through the program, or a total of 2592 clock cycles to complete on sine-wave output display. For an 8080 system using a 2-MHz clock this results in the generation of a 770-Hz sine wave. Of course, to produce sine waves having lower frequencies, simple delays may be added to the main program loop. However, to increase the repetition frequency beyond 700 Hz, either a faster processor or fewer data points would be required.

Hexadecimal code		Mnemonic		
Address	Instruction	Label	Instruction	Comments
1040	110000		LXI D,#0000	
43	210100		LXI H,#0001	
46	7C	LOOP:	MOV A,H	
47	E6		ANI #01	
49	FB		EI	
4A	C24E10		JNZ SKIP	
4D	F3		DI	
4E	0F	SKIP:	RRC	
4F	AC		XRA H	
50	0F		RRC	
51	0F		RRC	
52	AC		XRA H	
53	0F		RRC	
54	AC		XRA L	
55	0F		RRC	
56	0F		RRC	
57	0F		RRC	
58	E601		ANI #01	
5A	29		DAD H	
5B	5F		MOV E,H	
5C	19		DAD D	
5D	C34610		JMP LOOP	

Figure 8.28 Simulating a pseudorandom (white-noise) sequence generator in software. *(Adapted from a program by H. Chamberlain, "Computer Music," Popular Electronics, September 1976, p. 116.)*

Hexadecimal code		Mnemonic		
Address	Instruction	Label	Instruction	Comments
0000	210001	START:	LXI H,#0100	Initialize to first address
03	7E	NEX WORD:	MOV A,M	in table.
04	D3FF		OUT #FF	
06	23		INX H	
07	7D		MOV A,L	} Check for last address
08	FE3F		CPI #3F	} in table.
0A	C20300		JNZ NEXWORD	
0D	C30000		JMP START	
0100	808C99	A5		Sine-wave table
04	B1BCC7	D1		
08	DAE3EA	F1		
0B	F6FAFD	FF		
10	FFFFFD	FA		
14	F6F1EA	E3		
18	DAD1C7	BC		
1B	B1A599	8C		
20	807467	5B		
24	4F4439	2F		
28	261D16	0F		
2B	0A0603	01		
30	010103	06		
34	0A0F16	1D		
38	262F39	44		
3B	4F5B67	74		

Figure 8.29 Waveform generation via table look-up methods.

In some instances tying up the processor in the minute details of the waveform generation process may place such a burden on the device that it does not have sufficient time to carry out its chores in the other parts of the game. In addition, certain sounds can be generated more economically in hardware than in software. In fact, several special-purpose complex sound generation ICs of the form illustrated in Fig. 8.30 are already available. Here in a single IC we find a white-noise generator, a voltage-controlled oscillator (VCO), and an envelope generator for controlling the attack and decay of the signal generated as well as its overall amplitude. Most important of all, these parameters of the signal generated can all be varied from a set of external digital controls. Thus, by combining this type of IC with the microcomputer, the overall system can be made capable of inexpensively generating a wide variety of sophisticated sounds under complete processor control, and, since the control signals do not have to be varied that frequently, the processor remains free to accomplish its other tasks.

One example of this approach is given in Fig. 8.31, in which the microprocessor is being used to gate one of several signals into an

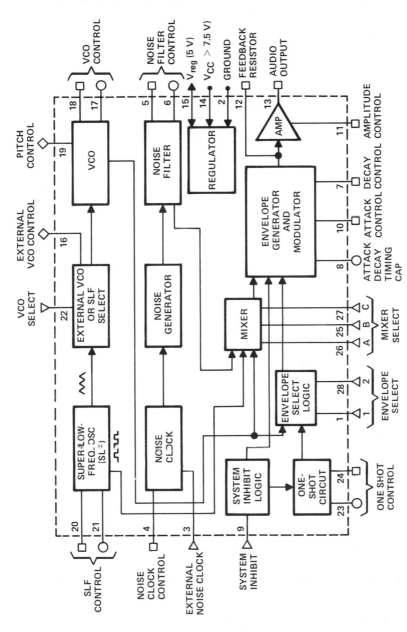

Figure 8.30 Texas Instruments SN76477 complex sound generator IC: block diagram. *(Texas Instruments.)*

223

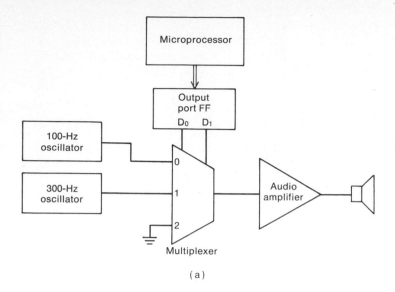

(a)

Hexadecimal code		Mnemonic		
Address	Instruction	Label	Instruction	Comments
1000	AF	HIT:	XRA A	
01	11___		LXI D,#___	Load 10 ms delay time.
04	D3FF		OUT #FF	
06	CD1710		CALL DELAY	
09	C9		RET	
100B	3E01	MISS:	MVI A,#01	
0D	11___		LXI D,#___	Load 300 ms delay time.
10	D3FF		OUT #FF	
12	CD1710		CALL DELAY	
15	C9		RET	
1017	10	DELAY:	DCR E	
18	C21710		JNZ DELAY	
1B	15		DCR D	
1C	C21710		JNZ DELAY	
1F	C9		RET	

(b)

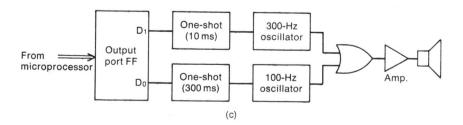

(c)

audio amplifier. By sending a 00 to output port FF, the multiplexer gates the 100-Hz oscillator into the audio amplifier. The presence of a 01 connects the 300-Hz signal, while a 02 results in an extinguishing of all sound. While the audio tones in the figure are generated by separate oscillator circuits, there is no reason why these signals couldn't be derived from part of the horizontal and vertical timing signals.

The program given in Fig. 8.31*b* is used to control the audio amplifier sounds produced in Fig. 8.31*a*. When the HIT subroutine is called, the 300-Hz signal is gated into the audio amplifier for 8 to 10 ms and produces a sound similar to that found in Pong-style paddle games when the ball strikes either the paddle or one of the walls. When the player misses the ball and the ball goes off the screen, the MISS portion of the program is called. In this routine the processor gates the 100-Hz oscillator into the amplifier for a much longer time period on the order of 300 ms. This long low-frequency tone burst generates a hornlike sound which, being completely different from the HIT sound, is used to signal the player that something has gone wrong. If the processor's time is too valuable to be spent waiting for the software loop to "time-out," a hardware one-shot may be added to the external electronics to control the duration of the tones generated (Fig. 8.31*c*). When configured in this manner, the processor only needs to emit a single control pulse in order to initiate the entire sound-generation sequence.

Figure 8.31 Microprocessor control of external sound-generation hardware. (*a*) Processor control of an external sound-generation circuit; (*b*) subroutines for controlling circuit given in (*a*); (*c*)additional circuitry added to sound generator to reduce processor idle time.

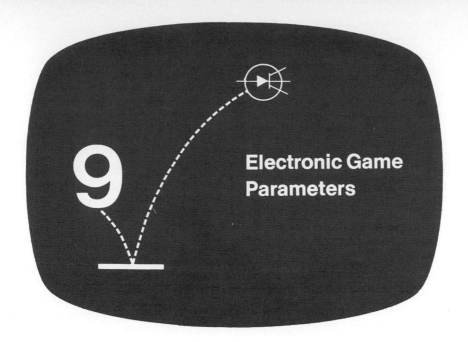

9 Electronic Game Parameters

As pointed out in Chap. 1, games, whether electronic or live, have certain specific parameters which make them attractive to us. The element of uncertainty, the chance to win, knowledge of the rules, keeping the score—all of these factors are essential to maintain player interest. The electronics professional involved in designing, installing, or maintaining electronic games should have some understanding of these game parameters, and this chapter is therefore devoted to the nature of these characteristic game elements.

Electronic games can be broadly divided into games of physical skill, games of mental skill, games of chance, and educational games. Using specific examples of popular electronic games in each category, the reader can compare them to their live versions and become familiar with the essential parameters of each type of game. Each category has many common features; these are discussed in some detail, after which a summary of the key electronic features in each category is given.

9.1 GAMES OF PHYSICAL SKILL

In this category we consider all those electronic games which are based primarily on coordination between eyes and hands, on quick reflexes, on nimble fingers—in short, on physical skill. Most of these games are based on three-dimensional "live" games in which the players move around a lot and are occasionally injured during the course of the game. The electronic versions of these games are played in two dimensions, and the players move only their hands—in comfort and safety.

Electronic games of physical skill can be conveniently divided into ball games, war games, and racing games. Electronic versions of such popular ball games as tennis, hockey, soccer, squash, basketball, bowling, volleyball, baseball, football, and handball are available in both microprocessor-based and dedicated-logic TV and arcade games. There are also some electronic ball games, such as Grid Ball and Pong, for which there is no exact live analog. War games include a variety of tank battle, aerial dogfight, missile attack, submarine hunt, and other games which simulate some aspect of the live action. Target shooting is certainly a game of physical skill, and although it differs somewhat from the other war games, it will be considered in this category. Most racing games involve cars, motorcycles, or some other vehicles, but there are some racing games that simulate horseracing. Depending on the particular version of the game, horseracing could also be considered a game of chance, as in its live version.

Tennis

Figure 9.1 shows the screen display for one of the most widely used tennis games. In this game the "rackets" can move anywhere on a given player's side of the net, and a number of options for the ball's

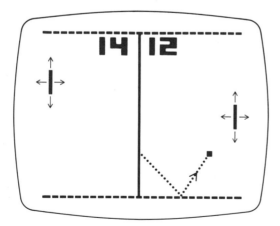

Figure 9.1 Screen display for Tennis (General Instruments).

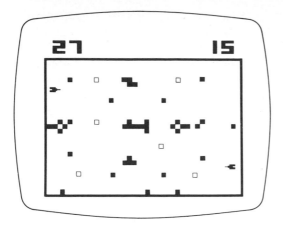

Figure 9.2 Screen display for Battle (General Instruments).

trajectory are available. The length of the racket is electronically divided into two or four parts, and the angle at which the ball leaves the racket depends on the portion it has contacted. This allows either two or four different angles. Each miss results in a point scored by the opponent, and 15 is the winning score.

In contrast to live tennis, the ball always goes over the net in electronic versions. If the ball reaches the top or bottom boundaries, it is reflected at the same angle, and the game continues. Where sound is provided, there is usually a brief click when the ball touches the racket or the boundaries and a different sound to indicate changes in the score. Different versions of this game contain black, white, grey, or selected colors for the field, the boundaries, the net, and the opposing player's racket. Some versions do not have horizontal motion of the racket, some permit the use of different racket lengths, and some have a special push button on the racket control that permits the player to select a curved trajectory as the ball is contacted. This latter feature is often called the *English* or *slam* button.

War

The game Battle is typical of many different war games such as Tank Warfare, Combat Squares, Desert Fox, etc. As illustrated in Fig. 9.2, the screen displays the two opposing tanks and a series of obstacles and mines. Each player controls the motion of a tank and aims its cannon by rotating the tank in the desired direction. The obstacles serve as shields from enemy tank shells, but they can also be hazards. If a tank collides with an obstacle, it is disabled for a short time and must reverse to get clear again. If a tank collides with a mine, an explosion is simulated, the tank is disabled for a fixed time, and a hit is scored for the opponent. While the number of shells that can be fired is not limited, the rate of firing is. The range of a shell is about two-thirds of the width of the screen. When a tank is hit by an opponent's shell, an explosion is simulated, and the score is changed.

In one version of this game it is possible to direct the shell in a curved path by rotating the tank as the shell is fired. The winning score in that version of the game is 31, but scoring varies with different games. Some games use more than two tanks and more than two players. Some games do not use mines, and in some a tank, once hit by a shell, is out of the game. Some games show shell-burst patterns, some show tank explosions only, and some show different colors of explosion patterns depending on the color of the tank. Sound effects range from highly realistic battlefield noises, with different sounds for different tank speeds, collisions, explosions, and shell firing, to much less complex sounds in the simpler games.

Roadrace

This TV racing game is typical of those called Indy 500, Freeway, Dragstrip, etc., and appears on the screen as illustrated in Fig. 9.3. The illusion of motion is created by other cars moving downward while the two player-controlled cars are stationary near the bottom of the screen. The player controls the horizontal motion of the car to

Figure 9.3 Screen display for Roadrace (General Instruments).

avoid colliding with other cars and with the side rails. When a player speeds up, the slower cars in his or her portion of the roadway seem to approach as the player-controlled car goes faster. A collision changes the score and, in most games, results in slowing down the player's car. In some versions of this game, a collision stops the game, and the score is displayed. In other versions, the score is continuously displayed, or else the elapsed time and the number of collisions are displayed.

In one variation of this game, a complex racecourse is displayed on the screen, and each player steers a car through it. Scoring is based on the number of laps completed and on the number of collisions. Scoring varies greatly with each version of this game, as do the symbols for the vehicles and the controls used for steering them. Sound effects range from simulated engine noises, varying with vehicle speed, and realistic crashes to simple buzzes and clicks.

Common Features

In all games of physical skill the players control the motion of objects assigned to them in order to either contact or avoid contact with other objects on the screen. In the ball games the contact is between the ball and the player's racket, bat, stick, etc. Each player tries to affect the trajectory of the ball so as to make it difficult for an opponent to do the same.

In war games the players also control an object, whether tank, missile, or airplane, and the idea is again to either contact or avoid contact with other objects on the screen. Instead of a ball, shells or missiles are launched, and instead of being returned, the tank, missile, or airplane is damaged or destroyed

All of the racing games emphasize the possibility of contact between the player's car, motorcycle, etc., and another vehicle or the guard rail. Contact results in a change in score in all these games. In all of them there are clearly defined boundaries and clearly defined rules. In each case a violation of the rules results in a change of score. In each case the player with the best score wins.

Almost all of the games of skill are intended for two or four players, but most of them also have a practice, automatic, or robot mode in which one player effectively plays against the machine.

Key Electronic Functions

All the games of physical skill involve motion of various objects on the display, and scores change as these moving objects appear to contact or miss each other. Electronic circuits or programs are therefore required to generate this motion in response to player controls and to detect contact. Chapter 3 describes some basic circuits that perform these functions, and typical programs to generate trajectories and detect contact between objects are discussed in Chap. 8. Circuits are also required to translate the action of the player controls into suitable control signals for the game selected. Sound effects can be an important feature in games of physical skill because they add to the realism of the particular game. As a result, some games, particularly the coin-operated types, contain elaborate audio sections, including magnetic tape decks. Scorekeeping and display also vary for different games, but changes in this area usually only require presetting the scorekeeping counters differently for each type of game selected. Finally, those games that feature a practice, automatic, or robot mode must, of course, have a program or special logic circuits for that purpose.

9.2 GAMES OF MENTAL SKILL

It can be argued that all games require some mental skill, but there is clearly one category of games in which mental skill alone determines the winner. Educational games, discussed in Sec. 9.4, are based primarily on factual knowledge and are intended to promote learning rather than logical reasoning. Games of mental skill, such as chess, checkers, scrabble, and backgammon, are well known, and their electronic versions usually use the same game parameters, with the electronics acting as one of the players. In Chap. 11 we describe Chess Challenger and Code Name: Sector, both electronic board games. Two popular TV games which depend only on mental skill are discussed below as examples of the game parameters and key electronic functions of this category of games.

Nim

This ancient game, which presumably originated in the Orient, is deceptively simple. It can be played with sticks, straws, beads, or any kind of object. In the two-person live variety, there are several piles of objects, and each player, in turn, takes any number of objects out of one of the piles. The player who removes the last object wins. In the electronic version of this game, as illustrated in Fig. 9.4, each pile is indicated by a rectangular box, and the number in that box represents the number of sticks, straws, or objects in that pile. The player selects the box from which to remove something by moving the black dot (red in color TV sets) under the selected box. In the Fairchild F-8 TV game, the joystick is used to maneuver the dot and

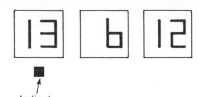

Figure 9.4 Screen display for NIM (Fairchild).

Indicator

also to indicate to the microprocessor what number to subtract from the number shown in the selected box. Since the player plays against the computer, a time limit is set for the player's response. The computer indicates its moves immediately.

At first, Nim appears a very simple game, but it really requires some very careful logical thinking to beat the computer. As a matter of fact, the Fairchild booklet describing this game introduces the reader to binary logic in order to illustrate one method of beating the computer.

Guess the Number

This game can be played by one or two players and requires careful attention to computer-generated clues. RCA's Studio II offers this game through the TV Arcade II cartridge, and the TV screen display appears as shown in Fig. 9.5. In the single-player mode, the computer picks a random 3-digit number, and the player enters a guess on the keyboard. This guess and the clue number appear on the screen for a few seconds, then the number of guesses remaining changes, and the player is ready to guess again. The game ends either when the player has guessed the secret number or when all 20 guesses are used up. At that point the secret number is displayed.

This game must be classified as a game of mental skill because of the way in which the computer presents its clues. After each guess the computer displays a number which represents the sum total of the following:

000	None of the digits is correct
001	One digit correct, but in wrong position
002	One digit correct and in proper position, *or* two digits correct but both in wrong position
003	Any feasible combination of 001 and 002
004	Any feasible combination of 001, 002, and 003
005	Any feasible combination of 001, 002, 003, and 004
006	Correct guess.

One way to approach this game is by means of a truth table, such as logic-circuit designers use, with each combination of possible clues listed. Clearly, mental skill is required for this game.

Secret number
(shown at end)

Number
guessed

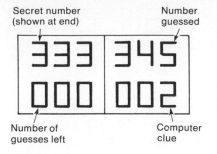

Number of
guesses left

Computer
clue

Figure 9.5 Screen display
for Guess the Number (RCA).

   In the two-player version each player enters a secret number by means of the keyboard while the other player cannot see the screen. The computer stores both secret numbers and then generates the clues as in the single-player version. Both players' guesses and the computer's clues for each are displayed, with a small rectangle above the number assigned to the player whose turn is next.

Common Features

All games of mental skill are microprocessor-based. Even an arcade-type game like the Tic Tac Quiz, described in Chap. 11, which poses questions recorded on magnetic tape to entitle players to enter the X or O, depends on the microprocessor. Another common feature is the digital input and output. For the Chess Challenger, a board game described in Chap. 11, the input is through a keyboard, and the output is an LED display. TV games, as the above examples indicate, are usually based on numeral displays. Uncertainty, a key element in making any game interesting, is provided mostly by the interaction between the electronic game and the player. The relative importance of rules and scoring varies in different games of mental skill. The rules of chess, for example, are a major part of the chess program, but the scoring is limited to checkmate or draw. The scoring in the game of Nim is similarly trivial, but in a game like Guess the Number the scoring is important since it will determine the player's strategy.

Key Electronic Features

As we noted above, all games of mental skill are microprocessor-based and use digital input and output. As a matter of fact, the games in this category are really computer-type games, most of which have been played on time-shared and small dedicated computers for years.

   Next to the hardware, the actual programs which can "play" games of mental skill are the focus of the game designer's efforts.

Programs for playing almost every known game of mental skill have been developed in all popular computer languages, but the adaptation of these programs to the limitations imposed by the microprocessor in an electronic game is still under way. There are always new shortcuts, new program-step-saving ways, and new modifications of the game rules which can provide hardware economies.

Sound effects do not add realism to games of mental skill and are usually omitted.

9.3 GAMES OF CHANCE

As we pointed out in Chap. 1, in playing games of chance, the players generally focus on intuition or luck rather than skill. The belief in luck is really a superstition, and we all know that games of chance depend on probability, which is another way of determining the odds. In playing dice, for example, the probability of throwing two dice so that both show the identical number is much smaller than the probability of getting a total of 7, which can be made up of 1 and 6, 2 and 5, or 3 and 4. As any real dice player knows, this probability is reflected in the odds.

From the engineering point of view, all games of chance are based on the relative randomness of a group of numbers. An illustration of this is found in the Monte Carlo wrist watch sold by Unitrex of New York. This watch contains, in addition to the time control, a game and a display switch which permit the display of random numbers to simulate either a slot machine, the rolling of dice, or the roulette wheel. Inveterate gamblers can play these games while traveling, while waiting for the dentist, or whenever they wish. As in all games of chance, the betting and the payoff, actions that are quite separate from the electronic game, provide the real fun. Two examples of TV games of chance, Draw Poker and War, are presented here, and a detailed discussion of Blackjack is the subject of Chap. 10.

Draw Poker

This TV game can be played either by two players against each other or by one player against the microprocessor. As illustrated in Fig. 9.6, the TV screen displays each player's hand of five cards face up. The bankroll (BR) assigned to each player decreases and increases as bets are made and games won or lost. There is an automatic $5 ante whenever a new game is started. Each player can raise by depressing the button designated "Yes" or call or drop out by depressing the button marked "No." When one of the players calls, an indicator appears on the screen and moves between the two players' cards,

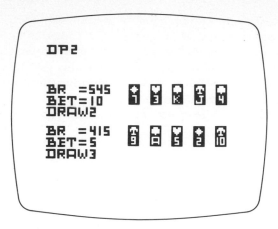

Figure 9.6 Screen display for Draw Poker. (General Instruments.)

allowing the players in turn to secretly depress their "Yes" buttons to indicate the cards they wish to replace. When the indicator has moved past all 10 cards, the selected cards are replaced, and the microprocessor evaluates each hand. The winning hand is then awarded the loser's bet, both bankrolls are updated, and the winner's BR flashes. In the single-player version the object is to achieve the best poker hand. The amount wagered is multiplied by the odds and then added to the player's bankroll in accordance with a table of factors ranging from even for a single pair of jacks or better, to 100 to 1 for a royal flush.

War

Based on a simple children's card game, this microprocessor-controlled TV game starts out with two sets of five cards displayed on the TV screen face down, as shown in Fig. 9.7. An indicator moves sequentially between the two rows of cards, allowing each player to select one card by pressing the button indicating "Yes." When each player has selected one card, both cards are shown, the higher-value card wins two points for its player, and two new cards appear, face down. If both cards match, a state of "war" exists. Each player makes a new selection, and the winner gets 12 points. A total of four decks (208 cards) are used, and the game ends when all cards have been displayed. The winning score will then flash on the screen. There is also a single-player version in which both the player's and the game's card are selected following the player's decision. The scoring is the same as in the two-player version.

Common Features

All of the TV games which offer games of chance use microprocessors and plug-in cartridges. As in the case of games of mental skill, computer programs have long existed for many of the games of chance, with special emphasis on the randomness of numbers which is at the heart of any such game. All the controls of games of chance are digital, but the displays in many popular games are pictures of playing cards. This latter feature adds realism, but doesn't change the actual numerical nature of the game.

The player's focus is usually on the odds and the resulting chances of winning money. While players of other games compete against each other or against the machine in terms of physical or mental skill, in games of chance the key motivation is really greed, the desire to win money. We may fool ourselves into believing that there is some skill in playing poker or dice, but in reality they require only blind luck and a knowledge of the odds.

Key Electronic Features

As in games of mental skill, the microprocessor, the RAM, the ROM, and the I/O section are the key circuits. Randomness is usually achieved by programming, although, as explained in earlier chapters, the difference between the clock speed and the human response of pressing a button can also be used to provide this effect. Some programs take the different probabilities for different events into account, but, as concerns the players, this is not an essential feature.

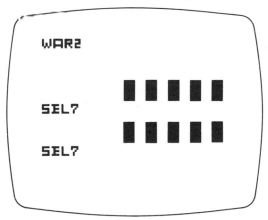

Figure 9.7 Screen display for War (General Instruments.)

Where scoring is part of the game, as in Draw Poker, these probabilities appear as the odds in the payoff shown on the screen. In TV games showing playing cards, the circuits that generate that display are usually part of the character generator, just as they are for other games displaying complex objects. Realistic color displays require red, white, and black, possibly on a green background, and the only motion is that of the indicator or cursor. Sound effects are of little importance in games of chance and are limited to special sounds which indicate a win or a loss.

9.4 EDUCATIONAL GAMES

This is the last category of games that has become popular, but many marketing experts predict that the educational aspects of TV games will prove to be a major sales factor. They point to the popularity of the special pocket calculators designed to teach children arithmetic and the increasing acceptance of TV as a source of education. While the majority of educational electronic games involve the home TV screen, a number of manufacturers offer board-type games featuring a pocket calculator. Typical of these are Calculator Squares and Check Out, two games made by Texas Instruments and based on their model 1400 five-function pocket calculator. Both games include educational material combined with arithmetic problems for the calculator and are intended for children over 12.

The two examples of educational TV games presented below are typical of the microprocessor-controlled, cartridge-based games. One major difference between them is that RCA's TV School House series depends on a set of booklets for its variety of educational material while the Fairchild F-8 system uses the booklets primarily for game instructions with the problems displayed and solved on the screen. Both systems are open to innovation and future expansion for almost any kind of educational material.

Multiplication

In this Fairchild TV game the Videocart-7C cartridge is used to present simple multiplication and division problems for one player. The booklet furnished with this cartridge also describes a number of competitive games for several players, based on solving the multiplication or division problems. As illustrated in Fig. 9.8, the two types of problems appear on the screen as they would on paper, with the score of correct and incorrect answers in the lower corners. The answer is entered on the screen by twisting the joystick-type hand controller left or right, with each momentary twist changing a digit

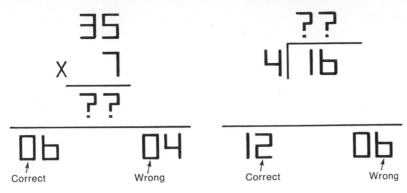

Figure 9.8 Screen display for Multiplication (Fairchild).

by one. When the desired answer is displayed, it is entered by pushing the control knob down. If the answer is correct, the word "RIGHT" will appear. If the answer is wrong, the message "TRY AGAIN" gives the player a second chance. If the second attempt fails, the game will show the player step by step how the correct answer is obtained. New problems are started by pulling the control knob up, but only after the player has either solved the problem correctly or after the game has displayed the solution.

School House

In this game, a single cartridge contains the data for 36 separate quizzes, 9 each in elementary and advanced social studies and 9 each in elementary and advanced mathematics in RCA's TV School House game. Each quiz consists of eight questions, and the key to the entire series is the set of booklets supplied with the cartridge.

The following example (Fig. 9.9) illustrates "European Geography," part of advanced social studies, and explains the technique used in this educational game. For quiz 1 the booklet shows a map of Europe, with eight countries identified by letter. Below the map there is a list of ten countries with a numeral, 0 through 9, next to each. A letter, A through H, appears on the screen next to an empty box, and the player selects the right answer by pressing the appropriate number on the keyboard. In setting up the game, the player has a choice of two levels of difficulty, allowing either 10 or 20 s for an answer. When two people play, the objective for each player is to answer a question before the other can. If a player answers incorrectly, the word "NO" appears, and the player is locked out. Correct answers earn from 1 to 10 points, depending on how quickly the answer is entered. If there is no correct answer after the allotted time,

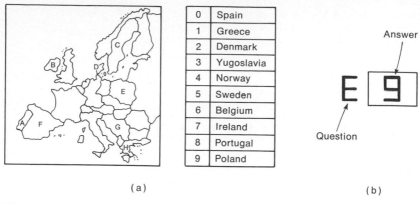

0	Spain
1	Greece
2	Denmark
3	Yugoslavia
4	Norway
5	Sweden
6	Belgium
7	Ireland
8	Portugal
9	Poland

(a)

(b)

Figure 9.9   European Geography (RCA).

the next question is shown. Each time the game is played, the questions appear in a different, random sequence.

The same game, with the same letters A through H on the TV screen, is played to teach civics, history and, of course, mathematics. In this last subject the problems are shown in the booklet with their identifying letters, and the solutions are keyed to corresponding numbers. There are always 8 questions and 10 answers, and they cover addition, subtraction, series, multiplication, division, measurements, Roman numerals, and fractions.

Common Features

Like games of mental skill and games of chance, educational games are essentially based on numbers. Again, microprocessors and plug-in cartridges are common features for all TV games, and some kind of arithmetic ability is also required of the board-type games. All controls are digital, and the display is also digital, whether numbers or letters are used. The educational TV games can easily be adapted to parallel conventional classroom teaching, and they could even replace or supplement homework assignments. There is a narrow line between TV homework and a TV game, but once students become conditioned to sit in front of the TV set, they might learn to do homework without complaining.

Key Electronic Features

The key circuits in educational games are again the RAM, the ROM, the I/O portion, and the processor itself. Although the sequence in which problems are presented appears random, randomness features are not as important as in games of chance. The coincidence of an internal clock pulse and some player's input is generally sufficient to assure randomness in this type of game. Simple alphanumerics are the key display elements, and, in most games now on the market, color adds little to the display value. The plug-in ROM, contained in the cartridge, is a key element because its program structure determines the number and complexity of educational games available. In the example of the RCA TV School House educational series, we have seen how a single ROM can be used to provide a program for 36 different quizzes, each having eight questions. The program only has to match up a set of eight numbers and display only a few alphanumerics. Scorekeeping is done in conjunction with timing. The meaning of each letter and answering number is determined by booklets which can be printed to cover any topic at any level of difficulty.

Sound effects are of little importance in educational games, and most TV games are silent when used for educational purposes.

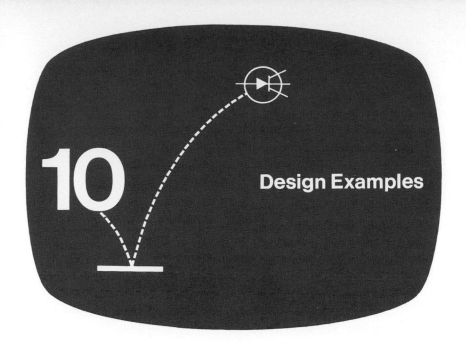

Design Examples

The electronic games industry experienced a phenomenal growth during the 1970s as the IC and later the microprocessor made the development of these games economically feasible. Earlier games, most notably the Pong variety, relied heavily on standard TTL digital ICs and later on special LSI chips for their operation, while the second generation of electronic games, the so-called intelligent games, have made extensive use of microprocessors. In this chapter the authors will present an example of each of these two styles of game design, as well as a third example illustrating how to convert an all-hardware design of Sec. 10.1 to microprocessor control.

10.1 PIT AND THE PENDULUM—AN ALL-HARDWARE ELECTRONIC GAME

Pit and the Pendulum is a game of skill in which a player challenges the machine. In operation, a pendulum, or to be more precise a bar with an opening in it, moves back and forth across the screen approximately once every second. As the pendulum moves, the opening in it is also seen to move, but in a pseudorandom fashion.

As the bar comes toward the player (see Fig. 10.1), the player must move through the opening in it or else be struck by the pendulum,

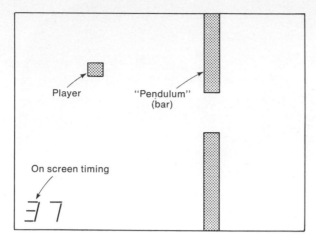

Figure 10.1 Video display for the Pit and the Pendulum game.

ending the game. Separate on-screen scoring keeps track of how long the player has been able to avoid being hit by the pendulum. The game may be played at three skill levels: novice, intermediate, and expert. Depending on the game level selected, the pendulum speed, size of the opening, and rate at which the opening moves are correspondingly changed.

A block diagram of the overall game design is shown in Fig. 10.2. To create the player position, two one-shots, OS_1 and OS_2, whose widths are determined by the position of the player's joystick control, produce pulses at the horizontal and vertical sweep rates, respectively. These pulses determine the location of the player on the screen. To permit the player to be positioned anywhere on the screen, their widths must be joystick-variable from about 0 to 63 μs for the horizontal position and from 0 to 16.7 ms for the vertical. OS_3 and OS_4 control the width and height of the player respectively. The actual video signal for the player is produced by "ANDing" the vertical and horizontal pulses together so that the player video image occurs only at the point on the screen where the vertical *and* horizontal pulses (from OS_3 and OS_4) simultaneously occur (See Fig. 10.3).

The pendulum is produced in a similar fashion, except that a pulse-width modulator is used to vary the bar position on the screen. The control signal for this modulator is a 1-Hz triangle-wave generator. This varies the width of the pulse generated by OS_5 and thus slowly sweeps the bar back and forth across the screen about once every second. A similar modulator is used to position the hole in the bar, but the control signal for this modulator varies pseudorandomly

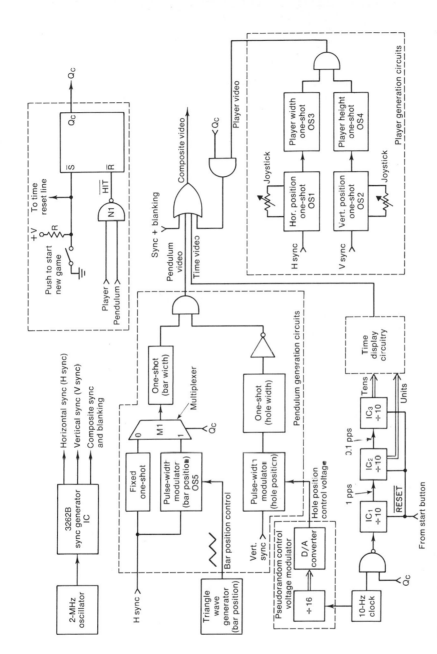

Figure 10.2 Overall game design for Pit and the Pendulum.

245

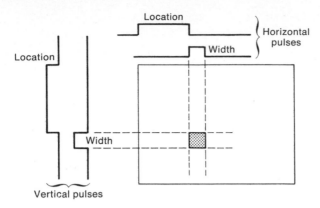

Figure 10.3 Generation of the player video image.

at a rate determined by the clock input to the divide-by-16 counter shown in the figure. As a result of the connection of the capacitor C across the D/A converter op amp, the output control voltage does not change immediately but instead slews from one point to the next at a rate appropriate to the game. This gives the player an opportunity to get through the hole even though it's moving to a new location.

To understand how the D/A converter operates, consider the circuit in Fig. 10.4*a*, illustrating an ordinary D/A converter which when connected to a simple binary counter produces an analog output voltage proportional to the binary number stored in the counter. In this way as the counter is continuously incremented by the clock, the resulting output is a ramp. By interchanging the bit values and specifically in this case by reversing all the bit position locations, a pseudorandom output can be obtained. The outputs for this circuit connection are given in Fig. 10.4*b*, and the resulting waveform is shown in Fig. 10.4*c*.

Let's trace through the operation of an actual game. At the start of the game, the control flip-flop Q_c is set to one, the bar begins to move, the player appears on the screen, and the timer begins to count, displaying the elapsed time in seconds in the lower left-hand corner of the screen. As the game progresses, the player continuously attempts to avoid a collision with the pendulum. Should a collision occur, that is, should the player and pendulum video images exist at the same point on the screen at the same time, the output of N_1 goes LO and resets the game control flip-flop.

Once $Q_c = 0$, further counting is inhibited, and the player's final time remains on the screen. In addition, the player video signal is gated off, and furthermore the multiplexer M_1 switches in a final fixed one-shot to control the bar position. Thus, in response to a collision, the timer freezes, the "player" disappears from the screen, and the bar remains locked at the center of the screen. To begin a new game, the player simply hits the start button, which again sets $Q_c = 1$, and which also resets the time counter register, IC_1, IC_2, and IC_3. A complete wiring diagram for the game is given in Fig. 10.5. Most of the circuitry is straightforward, except perhaps for the pulse-

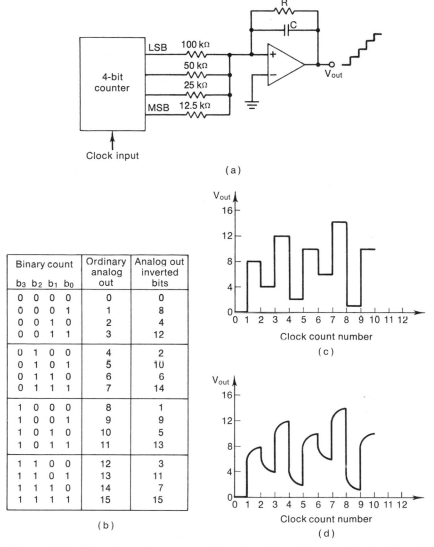

Binary count				Ordinary analog out	Analog out inverted bits
b_3	b_2	b_1	b_0		
0	0	0	0	0	0
0	0	0	1	1	8
0	0	1	0	2	4
0	0	1	1	3	12
0	1	0	0	4	2
0	1	0	1	5	10
0	1	1	0	6	6
0	1	1	1	7	14
1	0	0	0	8	1
1	0	0	1	9	9
1	0	1	0	10	5
1	0	1	1	11	13
1	1	0	0	12	3
1	1	0	1	13	11
1	1	1	0	14	7
1	1	1	1	15	15

(b)

Figure 10.4 Pseudorandom generation circuit for hole position in Pit and the Pendulum. (*a*) Basic D/A converter; (*b*) relation between binary count and op amp analog output; (*c*) output without slew computer; (*d*) output with slew capacitor.

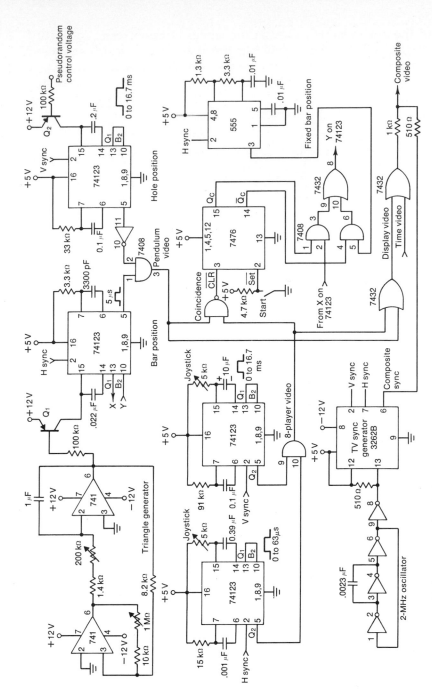

Figure 10.5a Main electronics for the Pit and the Pendulum.

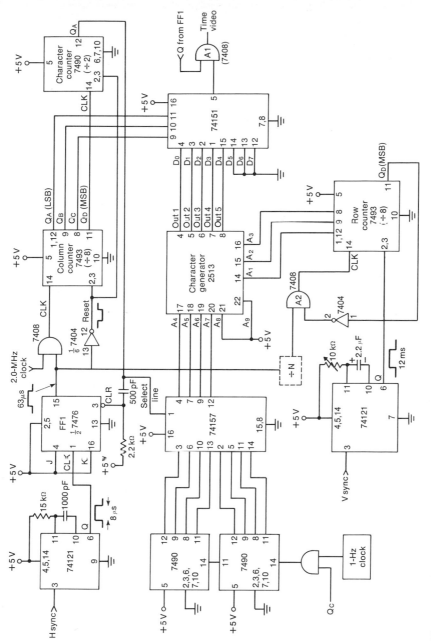

Figure 10.5b Timer electronics for Pit and the Pendulum.

width modulators and time-display circuitry whose operation will be explained further.

The pulse-width modulators are basically standard TTL one-shots, except that the timing resistor R usually found in the circuit has been replaced by a voltage-controlled current source (transistors Q_1 and Q_2). For this case the charging current I is approximately given by the expression

$$I = h_{FE} \frac{11.3 - V_{control}}{R_B}$$

where h_{FE} is the transistor current gain and R_B the base resistance. The fact that the one-shot times out when the voltage across C reaches 2.5 V suggests the following relationship between the control voltage and the resulting one-shot period:

$$T = \frac{2.5 R_B C}{h_{FE} (11.3 - V_{control})}$$

By changing $V_{control}$ the resulting one-shot pulse width can easily be varied over a 100 to 1 range, providing more than adequate resolution for this game.

To understand how the elapsed game time is displayed on the screen, consider that the circuit block diagram given in Fig. 10.6 is essentially the same as the video RAM circuits discussed in Chap. 8. Here, however, the RAM only contains two "words," corresponding to the data stored in the decade counters IC_2 and IC_3. The one-shots OS_1 and OS_2 control this position of the display on the screen.

At the beginning of a new video scan, the vertical synchronization pulse triggers OS_2, and its output pulse resets and holds the row counter at row 0 and thus effectively blanks the TIME VIDEO, since all character-generator column outputs corresponding to row 0 are 0. When OS_2 times out, which in this case takes about 12 ms, display of the characters is ready to begin. Of course, this places the characters near the bottom of the screen (three-fourths of the way down). On the next horizontal sync pulse, marking the beginning of a new sweep line, OS_1 is triggered, and after it has timed out (about 5 μs in this case), flip-flop Q_1 is set and the 2-MHz dot-clock gated into the column counter. OS_1 and OS_2 control the horizontal and vertical character display position on the screen, respectively, with the clock frequency determining the "dot width" of the characters.

Initially FF_2 is reset to 0, and M_2 sends the tens data into the character generator data input lines. As the column counter is incremented by the clock via the multiplexer M_1, it selects the appropriate column information from the character generator and gates it onto

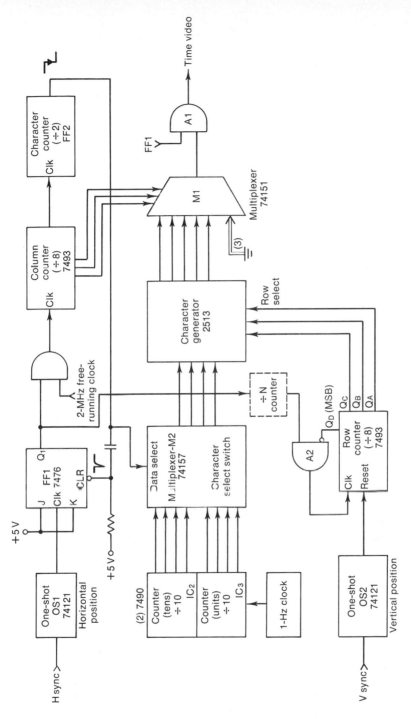

Figure 10.6 Block diagram for on-screen time display for Pit and the Pendulum.

the TIME VIDEO line. The last three counts send out 0s into the video which serve as intercharacter spacing. When the column counter returns to column 0 (a 000 count), it toggles FF_2, the character counter, and this causes M_2 to select the units counter information as the data input to the character generator. This information is then displayed column by column in the same fashion as the previous character. Once the units information has been displayed, the output of FF_2 returns to 0 and this edge transition is used to reset FF_1, which inhibits further clocking. At this point AND gate A1 is disabled, and the beam is held off until the next horizontal scan line. On the next horizontal sync pulse, the row counter is incremented and the display of row 1 begins. This process continues until all eight rows have been displayed, that is, until the time has been output onto the screen. At this point Q_D (the most significant bit in the row counter) is set, A2 is disabled, clocking of the row counter is inhibited, and the row counter is locked at row 0 until the next vertical field begins. As before, the TIME VIDEO signal is 0.

If a divide-by-N counter is inserted between the output of FF_1 and the row counter clock (Fig. 10.6), then the row count will only be incremented every N scan lines. This means that the video output will be the same on N consecutive horizontal scan lines and the resulting display will be N times taller. Thus the counter serves as a vertical size adjustment.

10.2 SOFTWARE IMPLEMENTATION OF PIT AND THE PENDULUM

In the previous section we described the design of a typical first-generation electronic game and demonstrated how it could be constructed from standard off-the-shelf ICs. However, as explained in Chap. 8, if this game is converted to microprocessor-based control, most of the external hardware can be eliminated. In fact when this is done, other than the microcomputer and video RAM circuitry, only a single joystick control and 2 one-shots will be needed to construct the entire game.

The basic program sequence for this software version of Pit and the Pendulum is illustrated in Fig. 10.7, and the complete program listing is given in Fig. 10.8. Owing to its length, a detailed explanation of each portion of the program will be needed if it is to be understood. In this program a set of six "memory registers" is employed in addition to the normal internal registers in the processor. These registers, denoted as R0 through R5, are actually memory locations in which data is stored, examined, and modified by using

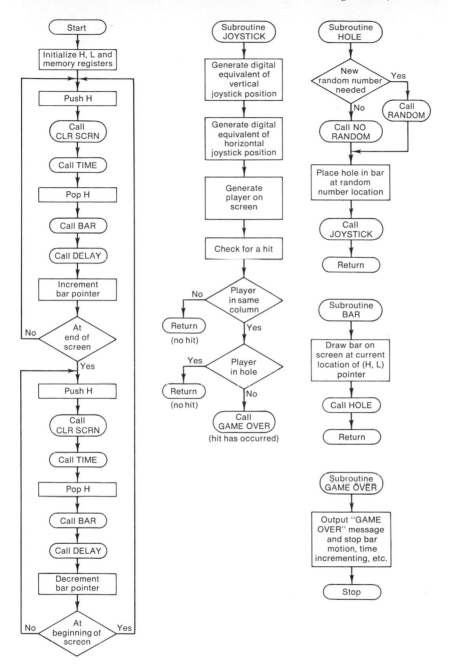

Figure 10.7 Flowchart for software version of Pit and the Pendulum.

Hexadecimal code		Mnemonic		
Address	Instruction	Label	Instruction	Comment
1000	AF		XRA A	Initialize registers.
01	32F510		STA #10F5	R5 = 00 Modulo-64 counter
04	32F210		STA #10F2	R2 = 00 Screen time
07	3C		INR A	
08	32F010		STA #10F0	R0 = 01 Random number seed
0B	3C		INR A	
0C	3C		INR A	
0D	32F110		STA #10F1	R1 = 03 Hole repeat
10	210088		LXI H,#8800	
13	E5	MOV RITE:	PUSH H	
14	CDF200		CALL CLR SCRN	See Appendix, p. 330.
17	CD4310		CALL TIME	
1A	E1		POP H	
1B	CD8010		CALL BAR	
1E	CD7010		CALL DELAY	
21	23		INX H	
22	7D		MOV A,L	} Check for end of line.
23	FE39		CPI #39	
25	C21310		JNZ MOV RITE	
28	E5	MOV LEFT:	PUSH H	
29	CDF200		CALL CLR SCRN	
2C	CD4310		CALL TIME	
2F	E1		POP H	
30	CD8010		CALL BAR	
33	CD7010		CALL DELAY	
36	2B		DCX H	
1037	7D		MOV A,L	
38	E63F		ANI #3F	} Check for beginning of new line.
3A	FE00		CPI #00	
3C	C22110		JNZ MOV LEFT	
3F	C31310		JMP MOV RITE	
1043	3AF510	TIME:	LDA #10F5	R5 is modulo 64 or
46	3C		INR A	pass counter.
47	E63F		ANI #3F	
49	32F510		STA #10F5	
4C	3AF210		LDA #10F2	Bring in R2 (time count).
4F	C25810		JNZ No CHG	Only increment time
52	C601		ADI #01	once each pass.
54	27		DAA	Increment and set flags for DAA.
55	32F210		STA #10F2	
58	E5	NO CHG:	PUSH H	
59	21048B		LXI H,#8B04	Screen time location.
5C	57		MOV D,A	Unpack and display
5D	E60F		ANI #0F	decimal characters.
5F	F6B0		ORI #B0	
61	77		MOV M,A	
62	2B		DCX H	
63	7A		MOV A,D	
64	0F		RRC	
65	0F		RRC	
66	0F		RRC	
1067	0F		RRC	
68	E60F		ANI #0F	
6A	F6B0		ORI #B0	
6C	77		MOV M,A	
6D	E1		POP H	
6E	C9		RET	

Figure 10.8 Program for software version of Pit and the Pendulum.

Hexadecimal code		Mnemonic			
Address	Instruction	Label		Instruction	Comment
1070	111010	DELAY:	LXI	D,#1010	
73	1D	LOOP:	DCR	E	
74	C27310		JNZ	LOOP	
77	15		DCR	D	
78	C27310		JNZ	LOOP	
7B	C9		RET		
1080	014000	BAR:	LXI	B,#0040	Next-line increment size
83	3E00	NEX BLK:	MVI	A,#00	A = 0, basic bar building
85	77		MOV	M,A	block
86	09		DAD	B	
87	7C		MOV	A,H	⎫ Check for end of bar.
88	FE8C		CPI	#8C	⎬
8A	C28310		JNZ	NEX BLK	⎭
8D	2688		MVI	H,#88	Initialize to beginning of a
8F	E5		PUSH	H	new line.
90	CD9610		CALL	HOLE	
93	E1		POP	H	
94	C9		RET		
1096	3AF110	HOLE:	LDA	#10F1	Generate new random
99	3C		INR	A	hole number only if
9A	32F110		STA	#10F1	R1 = 0. Occurs once every
9D	E603		ANI	#03	fourth pass.
9F	CCB510		CZ	RANDOM	
A2	C3AB10		JMP	JOY CALL	
A5	3AF010		LDA	#10F0	Use old random number to
A8	CDC410		CALL	NO RAND	generate hole in same
AB	CD0011	JOY CALL:	CALL	JOYSTICK	location. Do not generate
AE	3E3F		MVI	A,#3F	new random number.
B0	77		MOV	M,Λ	
B1	09		DAD	B	
B2	77		MOV	M,A	
B3	C9		RET		
10B5	3AF010	RANDOM:	LDA	#10F0	Eight-bit shift register
B8	57		MOV	D,A	pseudorandom sequence
B9	07		RLC		generator.
BA	AA		XRA	D	
BB	07		RLC		
BC	AA		XRA	D	
BD	2F		CMA		
BE	17		RAL		
BF	7A		MOV	A,D	
C0	17		RAL		
C1	32F010		STA	#10F0	
10C4	E60F		ANI	#0F	
C6	C8	RTRN:	RZ		
C7	09		DAD	B	
C8	3D		DCR	A	
C9	C3C610		JMP	RTRN	
1100	06FF	JOYSTICK:	MVI	B,#FF	
02	D300		OUT	#00	Trigger one-shots.
04	04	VERT LOOP:	INR	B	
05	DB00		IN	#00	⎫ Test vertical one-shot
07	E601		ANI	#01	⎬ to see if timed out.
09	CA0411		JZ	VERT LOOP	⎭
0C	78		MOV	A,B	Vertical done, Store
0D	32F410		STA	#10F4	result in R4.

Hexadecimal code		Mnemonic			
Address	Instruction	Label	Instruction		Comment
10	06FF		MVI	B,#FF	
12	D300		OUT	#00	
14	04	HOR LOOP:	INR	B	
15	DB00		IN	#00	Test horizontal one-shot
17	E602		ANI	#02	to see if timed out.
19	CA1411		JZ	HOR LOOP	
1C	78		MOV	A,B	
1D	32F310		STA	#10F3	
20	5F	PLAYER:	MOV	E,A	Fill D0 to D5 with column number.
21	3AF410		LDA	#10F4	Generate player on
24	0F		RRC		screen from joystick data
25	0F		RRC		stored in R3 and R4.
1126	57		MOV	D,A	
27	E6C0		ANI	#C0	Add in two LSBs
29	B3		ORA	E	of row number into two
2A	5F		MOV	E,A	MSBs of E.
2B	7A		MOV	A,D	
2C	E603		ANI	#03	
2E	F688		ORI	#88	
30	57		MOV	D,A	Finished with player address.
31	AF		XRA	A	
32	12		STAX	D	Put player on screen.
1135	7D	HIT:	MOV	A,L	Check for collision.
36	E63F		ANI	#3F	Mask off bar column.
38	57		MOV	D,A	
39	3AF310		LDA	#10F3	Player column number (R3)
3C	BA		CMP	D	Are player and bar column same?
3D	C0		RNZ		Return if not same.
3E	29		DAD	H	
3F	29		DAD	H	Shift row number into H-4 LSBs.
40	7C		MOV	A,H	
41	E6OF		ANI	#0F	Mask off hole row number.
43	57		MOV	D,A	Save hole row number.
44	3AF410		LDA	#10F4	Player row number (R4)
47	BA		CMP	D	
48	C8		RZ		Return if player is
49	3C		INR	A	in hole.
4A	BA		CMP	D	
114B	C84*		RZ		
4C	CD5011		CALL	GAME OVER	If here, player has hit bar.
1150	11108A	GAME OVER:	LXI	D,#8A10	Starting address for message display
53	217011		LXI	H,#1170	Starting address for message location
56	0609		MVI	B,#09	Message size
58	7E	MESSAGE:	MOV	A,M	
59	EB		XCHG		
5A	77		MOV	M,A	
5B	EB		XCHG		
5C	23		INX	H	
5D	13		INX	D	
5E	05		DCR	B	
5F	C25811		JNZ	MESSAGE	
62	C36211	SELF:	JMP	SELF	
1170	C7C1CD	C5			"GAME OVER" message
74	A0CFD6	C5			
78	D2				

Figure 10.8 (Continued)

the direct-addressing LDA and STA instructions. Although these instructions are awkward in that they require 3 memory bytes and take 13 clock cycles to execute, this approach frees the processor's internal registers for use in the main program and allows for data storage operations that would be extremely difficult if only the standard registers and the stack were employed.

The program begins by setting the HL register to point to the memory location corresponding to the upper-left-hand corner of the video RAM. In addition the memory registers R0, R1, R2, and R5 are initialized to their appropriate values. For later reference the function of each of these registers is identified in Table 10.1.

To begin the display of a new frame of video, the screen is first cleared via the CLR SCRN subroutine, which fills the entire video RAM with blanks (3F in hexadecimal code). Next the TIME routine is called and displays the total number of successful noncollision passes through the bar made by the player. This information is displayed in the lower-left-hand corner of the screen in video RAM locations 8B03 and 8B04. Since the KOUNT routine is called each time the position of the vertical bar is incremented or decremented (64 times per pass), a modulo-64 counter (R5) is used so that the count displayed on the screen is updated only once per pass.

The vertical bar is constructed by completely illuminating a vertical segment of the video RAM. The bar's location on the screen is determined by the initial value in the HL register pair at the time the BAR routine is called. Since adjacent vertical RAM cells differ by 64_{10} memory locations, or 40_H, successive addresses for the bar's construction are obtained by double adding the BC register contents,

TABLE 10.1 MEMORY REGISTERS USED WITH PIT AND THE PENDULUM GAME

Register name	Function	Range of data stored	Stored at memory location
R0	Random number for hole generation	01–FF	01F0
R1	Hole repeat factor	03 (single value)	01F1
R2	Screen time	00–99 (base 10)	01F2
R3	Digital equivalent of horizontal joystick position	00–3F (hex)	01F3
R4	Digital equivalent of vertical joystick position	00–0F (hex)	01F4
R5	Modulo-64 counter	00–3F (hex)	01F5

initialized to 0040 at the beginning of this routine, to the HL address pointer register pair. Once the bar's construction has been completed and the end detected by the presence of an 8C in the H register, the HL pair is reinitialized to the beginning of the next column before the processor continues with the next portion of the program, which places the hole in the bar. For reference purposes a listing of the important memory locations within the video RAM is given in Fig. 10.9.

The generation of the hole in the bar makes use of a pseudorandom number generation routine similar to that described in Chap. 6. Here an 8-bit shift-register scheme is employed along with the generation algorithm $\overline{DO = D7 \oplus D6 \oplus D5}$. This routine, known as RANDOM, is located in memory at address 10B5 and is called by the HOLE routine when needed, with the resulting random number generated being placed in R0. In order to avoid a continuous updating of the hole position each time the bar moves one column to the left or right, the contents of R0 are updated only once for every four times that the HOLE routine is called. This is accomplished by incrementing R1 on each pass through the HOLE routine while changing the random number in R0 only when the 2 least significant bits in R1 are zero. Since this occurs once every four passes through the routine, the hole remains in the same location on the bar for four successive bar column locations, giving the player an opportunity to move through the hole even after it has moved to a new position. In addition, in order to give the player a better chance to make it through the opening in the bar, the hole size is made two spaces high for this specific program (see program addresses 10AE through 10B3). In principle, of course, this size could easily be changed to vary the difficulty of the game. The reader should note that the joystick interfacing routine is also a part of this portion of the program so that the player's position on the screen is updated each time a new bar is drawn.

The technique employed to interface the joystick to the processor is the same as that previously described in Sec. 8.2, in which one-shots are employed whose generated pulse-widths are proportional to the resistance of the joystick. As illustrated in Fig. 10.10, the player's location on the screen is effectively obtained by determining the x and y coordinates of the joystick control.

Each time the processor executes an OUT instruction, pulses are generated by both the horizontal and vertical one-shots. When the processor is in the vertical portion of the JOYSTICK routine, it continually tests the output of the vertical one-shot (bit D1 on input port 00) and generates a count proportional to the position of the

	Character 0	Character 1		Character 62_{10}	Character 63_{10}
Line 0	8800	8801	───────────────────	883E	883F
Line 1	8840	8841	───────────────────	887E	887F
Line 2	8880				
•	88C0				
•	8900				
•	8940				
	8980				
	89C0				
	8A40				
	8A00				
	8A80				
	8AC0				
	8B00				
•	8B40				
•	8B80				
•					
Line 15	8BC0	8BC1		8BFE	8BFF
Off screen ⟹	8C00	8C01		8C3E	8C3F

Figure 10.9 Important video RAM locations for Pit and the Pendulum.

vertical potentiometer on the joystick control. A count of 00 placed in R4 corresponds to the player location at the top of the screen (row 0), and a 0F to the player position at the bottom of the screen (row 15). Since this routine requires 32 clock cycles per pass, or 16 μs per pass, to execute, at the top of the screen a one-shot output of about 10 μs is needed while at the bottom of the screen a 250-μs pulse will result in a maximum count in R4 of 0F.

A similar program is utilized to generate the digital equivalent of the horizontal position of the joystick control, except that for this case the number eventually stored in register R3 indicates in which of the 64 possible columns to place the player. Since this routine will require four times as long to accumulate the maximum count, for this case a 10-μs pulse width from the one-shot will correspond to the left-hand side of the screen (a count of 00 in R3) while a 1-ms pulse will be needed for the right-hand position to produce a count of 3F in R3.

The problem of generating the player's location on the screen from the joystick-generated x and y coordinates (row and column values) is a little complex and is best explained with the aid of Fig. 10.11 and a closer examination of the PLAYER GENERATION routine which begins at address 1120. Basically what is done is to reconfigure the original data stored in registers R3 and R4 into the final form illus-

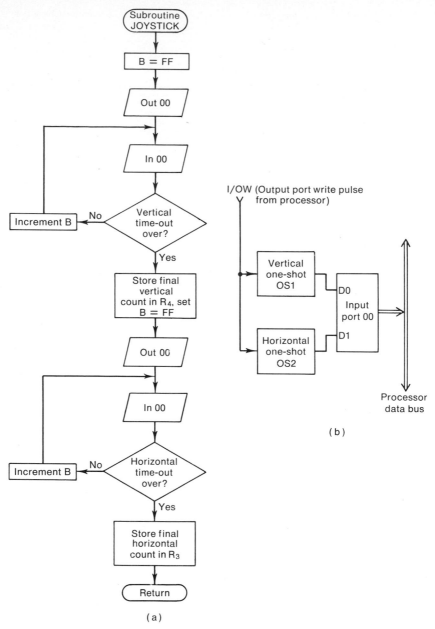

Figure 10.10 (a) Flowchart for the joystick subroutine; (b) electronics interface for the joystick control.

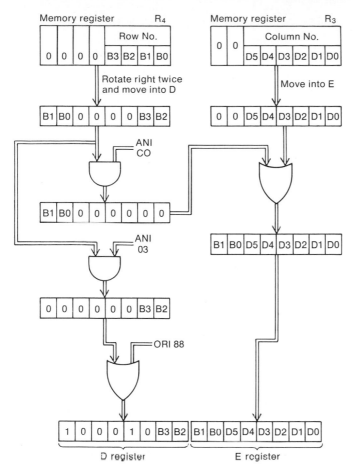

Figure 10.11 Generating the player screen address from the individual horizontal and vertical joystick controls.

trated in the bottom of the figure. As shown in the figure, this requires considerable bit shifting, masking, and "ORing" operations, but the process is not really too difficult to understand. As an example let's suppose that the player's position is row 1 (0001), column 62 (111110). This would place the player in the upper right-hand corner of the screen, one row from the top and one column from the extreme right. The corresponding video RAM address for the player's location may be formed by placing the row and column information in the DE register pair as illustrated in the bottom of Fig. 10.11. This results in a 1000 1000 0111 1110 in the DE pair, or an 887E address for the player. Comparing this result with the corresponding address for this position given in Fig. 10.9 illustrates the correctness of this algorithm.

Once the player address has been created, it is next displayed on the screen and checked to see if a collision has taken place with the bar. To do this, the player and bar location are first compared to see if they are in the same column. Since at this point in the program the bar hole position is in HL and the player location in DE, the column check may be made by comparing the first 6 bits of the L and E registers. If they do not match, the player column is different from that of the bar and no collision could have taken place. If they do match, a collision has occurred unless the player's location is the same as that of the hole in the bar. To check for this, the hole row information in bits D1 and D0 of H and in bits D7 and D6 of L is shifted into the 4 least significant bits of H by double adding HL to itself twice. These bits are then masked off and compared with the contents of R4, which contains the hole row number. If a match is found with either this row number or that below it (since this is also part of the hole), again no collision has occurred. If no match is found, a hit has taken place and the GAME OVER routine is called to terminate the game.

Should the latter event occur, the message starting at memory location 1170 is simply transferred to the video RAM, signaling "GAME OVER," the lap counter is frozen, the player disappears, the bar position is frozen, and the game terminates. To initiate a new game, the player must merely reset the computer to begin program execution at location 1000.

10.3 BLACKJACK—A FULL-FLEDGED MICROPROCESSOR CONTROLLED VIDEO GAME

Blackjack, or twenty-one as it is also called, has a history dating back to the Dark Ages; yet in spite of its apparently dated origins it remains the most popular card game at the Nevada gaming tables. Although deceptively simple in its objective, the game offers the player an excellent opportunity to combine both luck and skill in "beating the house" and is in fact one of the few games of chance for which a real system exists to enable the player to actually come out a winner. To be sure, the casinos are ever watching for those individuals who appear to know this system.

In blackjack all players compete against the dealer, the object being to obtain the highest possible score without going over 21.

Should a player's final score exceed 21, he or she is "bust" and loses the bet regardless of the dealer's final score. In tallying the score, aces may be counted as either 1 or 11 points at the discretion of the holder of the card. Picture or face cards (i.e., kings, queens, and jacks) count as 10 points each, while the remaining cards have point values corresponding to their numerical values. Thus, for example, a player holding an ace, a queen, and a five could claim a score of either 16 or 26, and since the latter tabulation would cause a bust, should choose the 16 for a final score.

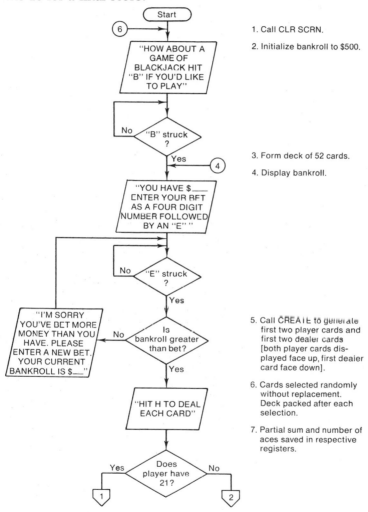

1. Call CLR SCRN.

2. Initialize bankroll to $500.

3. Form deck of 52 cards.

4. Display bankroll.

5. Call CREATE to generate first two player cards and first two dealer cards [both player cards displayed face up, first dealer card face down].

6. Cards selected randomly without replacement. Deck packed after each selection.

7. Partial sum and number of aces saved in respective registers.

Figure 10.12 Flowchart for the blackjack program.

To begin a game of blackjack, two cards are dealt to each player—
one face up and the other face down. The combination of an ace with
either a 10 or a face card produces a score of 21 and is known as a
natural or a "blackjack." A dealer with a natural wins all bets from
those players without naturals and ties with those players also having naturals. If, on the other hand, the player has a blackjack while
the dealer does not, then the player collects $3 for every $2 in the
original bet.

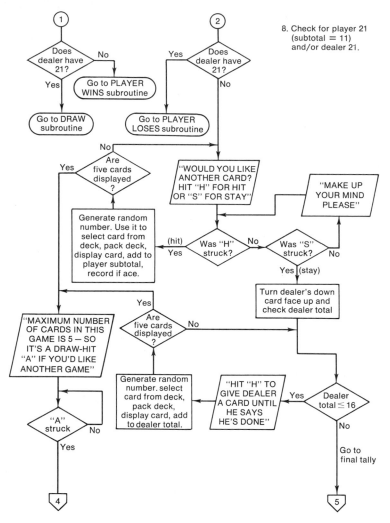

Figure 10.12 (Continued)

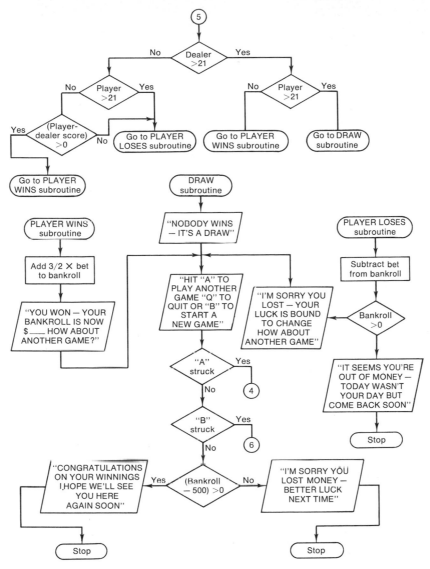

Figure 10.12 (Continued)

If no one receives a blackjack on the first two cards dealt, then each player in turn may request additional cards face up by asking the dealer to "hit me" in order to get a score nearer to 21. A player who feels unable to draw additional cards without going over 21 will tell the dealer to "stay," and will receive no further cards. In a similar

TABLE 10.2 SUMMARY OF SUBROUTINES USED IN BLACKJACK
PROGRAM

Subroutine name	Information required by routine	Information delivered by routine	Routine starting address	Appendix page no.
GEN CARD	Card display point in HL register pair. Suit and point in B register.	Displays selected card on screen (uses OUTLINE, SUIT SELECT, AND POINT SELECT subroutines).	1020	325
SUIT SELECT	Card display point in HL register pair. Suit and point in B register.	Generates address of suit pattern location to be displayed. Address placed in DE register pair.	1060	325
POINT SELECT	Card display point in HL register pair. Suit and point in B register.	Generates address of card face value pattern to be displayed. Address placed in DE register pair.	1080	326
OUTLINE	Card display point in HL register pair.	Constructs outline of a playing card on the screen.	0100	326
PATTERN DISPLAY	Pattern screen destination in HL register pair. Pattern source in DE register pair.	Displays 12-character pattern inside previously drawn card outline.	0131	327
FORM DECK	None	Forms deck of 52 cards stored at memory locations 1100–1133. LSH contains point value; MSH, suit value.	1040	327
PACK DECK	Card location in HL register pair.	Remove card from deck and place in register B. Pack remaining cards together. Decrement C (deck size) register.	1F20	327
MESSAGE	HL register pair contains message start point in memory.	Displays message on screen, starting at location 8800 (can modify to start at other locations).	1F40	328

Subroutine name	Information required by routine	Information delivered by routine	Routine starting address	Appendix page no.
INPUT	None.	Inputs character from keyboard into A register. Use in conjunction with RANDOM subroutine to generate each card	1F00	328
KBD IN	None.	Inputs character from keyboard (used in conjunction with INPUT routine).	1F10	328
RANDOM INIT	None.	Generates random numbers in B register from 1 to C (current deck size) until key is struck on keyboard.	1F50	328
BET	Player enters 4-digit bet on keyboard, followed by an E to enter bet.	Bet appears on screen as it is typed in and on receipt of E is entered in BET storage register.	1F63	328
PACK	ASCII character to be packed in A register.	Takes successive ASCII numeric characters from A register and packs them into B register from left.	0090	329
UNPACK	Two BCD digits to be displayed in A register. Display address in HL register pair.	Unpacks word in A register and displays it on screen in two successive screen locations.	00C0	329
CHECK BET	None.	Checks if bet is bigger than bankroll. If bet is too large, tells player to enter another bet.	1FA0	329
CREATE	None.	Pulls card from deck and places card point value in A register. Packs deck.	1FD0	330
CLR SCRN	None.	Enter all blanks on video display.	00F2	330

fashion, the other players may request additional cards. When all players have decided to stay, the dealer completes his or her own hand.

If the dealer's two original cards are less than 17, another card must be drawn, and if the dealer's total is still below 17, cards must continue to be drawn until either a bust or a score greater than 16 is obtained. Should the dealer's two original cards exceed 16, no more cards may be drawn; that is, the dealer must "stand on 17." If no one hits 21 by the time all players including the dealer have completed their hands, the one who comes closest to this number without going bust (exceeding 21) is the winner.

The electronic-game version of blackjack to be discussed in the remainder of this chapter follows all of the rules previously presented and basically operates in accordance with the game flowchart given in Fig. 10.12. Unfortunately the software requirements for this game are rather extensive (nearly 2 kilobytes), and therefore to understand its operation, it would appear best to first discuss the organization of the more important program subroutines and later integrate these into the description of the overall game design. A listing of these subroutines is given in Table 10.2 along with a brief description of their functions. The entire program listing for each of these routines is contained in the Appendix. In addition, a memory map is presented in Fig. 10.13 which illustrates the location of the various subroutines in memory and indicates their relative sizes.

To begin the discussion of the game subroutines, let's again review the basic display system—the video RAM. As discussed in Sec. 8.1, the RAM displays a total of 16 video lines containing 64 characters per line for a total of 1024 symbols. These symbols may be either alphanumeric or graphic in nature and follow the format discussed in Chap. 8. The alphanumeric messages used in conjunction with this game are presented on the first two video RAM lines, with LINE 0 spanning locations 8800 to 883F and LINE 1 locations 8840 to 887F. Each playing card displayed on the screen occupies a screen area 6 lines high by 10 characters wide. The game allows a single player to compete against the dealer and can display up to 5 player cards and 5 dealer cards.

The player's cards are presented on lines 2 through 7. The upper-left-hand-corner starting addresses for each of the player's cards are 8881, 888D, 8899, 88A5, and 88B1 for cards 1 through 5, respectively. The corresponding dealer cards are presented on lines 8 through 13 at addresses 8A41, 8A4D, 8A59, 8A65, and 8A71 for cards 1 through 5, respectively.

The process of generating a particular playing card consists of three separate steps. First, the outline of the selected card is drawn at

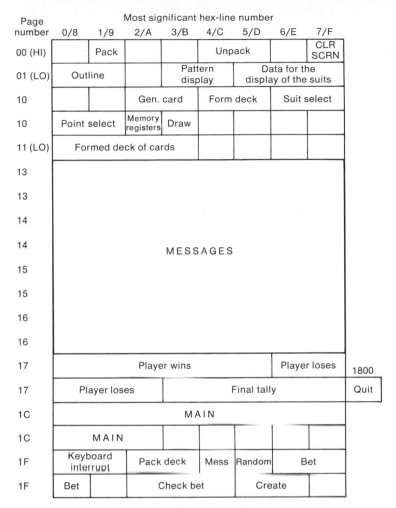

Figure 10.13 Memory map for the blackjack program.

one of the ten starting addresses given in Fig. 10.14. Next, depending on the particular card selected from the deck, the suit of the card is placed in the upper portion of the card outline and finally the face value is entered on the lower portion of the card. The complete set of 18 symbols (1 card outline, 4 suits, and 13 point values) used in conjunction with the particular game is stored in ROM at locations 0151 through 0290, and a sample of these patterns is given in Fig. 10.14.

To play an actual game of blackjack, program execution is begun in the main program at memory location 1C00. The purpose of this section of the program is to deal out the first two cards to both the

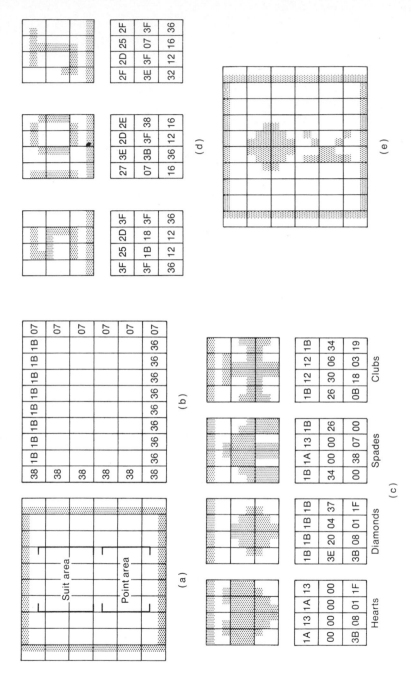

Figure 10.14 Card drawings used with the video RAM. (*a*) Card outline; (*b*) data stored in video RAM to produce display shown in (*a*); (*c*) card suit displays and their corresponding video RAM data. (*d*) point displays for several selected face values; (*e*) complete graphics display of a king of diamonds.

player and the dealer. This routine begins by clearing the screen, i.e., by entering blanks in all video RAM locations. This is accomplished by the CLR SCRN subroutine (see Appendix). For simplicity, as with the previous game discussed, a specific set of memory locations will be used as "memory registers" for holding certain data to be used during the game. This approach turns out to be more convenient than using the stack for storing this information. The register listing employed with this game is given in Table 10.3. At the start of a new game the player bankroll (R3 and R4) is initialized to $500 and the player and dealer ace counters (RE and RF) are both cleared to zero.

Once the screen has been cleared, the first game message is displayed: "HOW ABOUT A GAME OF BLACKJACK—HIT B IF YOU'D LIKE TO PLAY." To accomplish this, the contents of a section of memory (that section containing the message) are simply transferred onto the message portion of the screen. Rather than fix the message size to a specific length, this transfer operation continues until a special symbol, in this case the @, is detected, terminating the message. The specific subroutine for generating all of the messages associated with this game is given in the Appendix, and the actual ASCII entry for this specific message is given for illustrative purposes in Fig. 10.15. One point is clear: storing messages for use with video games can use up a large number of memory locations. In fact, the messages associated with this game occupy nearly 1 kilobyte of data storage.

Some screen messages contain variable as well as fixed information. For example, in the message "YOU WON $500—YOUR BANKROLL IS NOW $850. HIT A IF YOU'D LIKE TO PLAY ANOTHER

TABLE 10.3 MEMORY REGISTERS USED IN THE BLACKJACK GAME

	Player			*Dealer*	
Address	*Name*	*Function*	*Address*	*Name*	*Function*
10A0	R0	Card subtotal	10A7	R7	Card subtotal
1021	R1	LO } Bet value	10A8	R8	Hidden card
10A2	R2	HI } Bet value	10AC	RC	LO } Current card screen
10A3	R3	LO } Bankroll	10AD	RD	HI } address
10A4	R4	HI } Bankroll	10AD	RF	Dealer ace count
10A5	R5	LO } Current card screen address			
10A6	R6	HI } Current card screen address			
10AE	RE	Player ace count			

"HOW ABOUT A GAME OF BLACKJACK HIT B IF YOU'D LIKE TO PLAY"

(a)

C8	CF	D7	AO	C1	C2	CF	D5	D4	AO	C7
C1	CD	C5	AO	CF	C6	AO	C2	CC	C1	C3
CB	CA	C1	C3	CB	BR	AO	AO	C8	C9	D4
D4	AO	A2	C2	A2	AO	C9	C6	AO	D9	CF
D7	A4	C4	AO	CC	C9	CB	C5	AO	D4	CF
AO	DO	CC	C1	D9	CO					

(b)

Figure 10.15 (a) Introductory message used with blackjack game; (b) ASCII equivalent of the message (note that the last byte, the CO, is the ASCII code entry for the symbol @).

GAME AND Q IF YOU WANT TO QUIT," all of the message information with the exception of the bet winnings and bankroll is fixed. Thus to create this message, what is done is to first display the fixed portion of the message, inserting blanks in those sections where variable data information must be entered. Next a special UNPACK routine is called (see Appendix) and is used to display the contents of a specific memory location on the screen. For an example of this technique, the reader's attention is directed to the portion of the main program contained in memory locations 1C1C to 1C30 (Fig. 10.16) where the player's bankroll information (contained in memory registers R3 and R4) is displayed on the screen.

Returning now to the main program, after the screen has been cleared and the game request message displayed, should the player strike key B, indicating an interest in playing a game of blackjack, the program will create a new deck of 52 playing cards in memory locations 1100 to 1133. This is accomplished by the FORM DECK subroutine which is located at address 1040 in the actual program and is listed in the Appendix. The format used for the cards is similar to that previously discussed in Sec. 6.4 in which the most significant hexadecimal character in the card-byte determines the card's suit, with a 1 corresponding to a heart, 2 to a spade, 3 to a club, and 4 to a diamond, while the lower 4 bits are used to indicate the point value of the card.

This routine is followed immediately by a message requesting the player to enter a bet as a 4 digit number followed by an E for enter. Once the bet has been entered, the program checks the size of the bet to see if it exceeds that of the player's bankroll. Should this be the case, a message will appear on the screen announcing this fact and requesting entry of a proper bet.

If the bet is not excessive, its value will be stored in the player bet registers R1 and R2, and a message will come up on the screen: "HIT H TO DEAL A CARD." At this point the program enters the random number generation (RANDOM) routine in order to determine the first card to select from the deck (see Appendix, page 328). Unless interrupted by the player striking a key on the keyboard, the program remains in a loop in this routine and continues to generate random numbers between 1 and N, where N represents the number of cards remaining in the deck. Thus initially this routine generates numbers between 1 and 52, and as the game progresses and the deck size decreases, so does the range of these numbers.

When the player requests a card by typing an H on the keyboard, the program leaves the RANDOM routine, with the final number stored in the B register corresponding to the card selected from the deck. Immediately following this card request by the player (see address 1C40 in the main program of Fig. 10.16), the screen is cleared and the CREATE subroutine called. This routine pulls the selected card from the deck, packs the deck, and places the card's point value in the A register. The point value is stored in the card subtotal register (R0), and furthermore, should the card be an ace, this fact is recorded in the player's aces register (RE) for later use. Immediately following these checks, the card is displayed on the screen in the first card position (screen location 8881). In a similar fashion, when the player requests another card by typing H on the keyboard, the second card is also displayed on the screen, with the subtotal of the player's cards updated and stored in R0.

The next two Hs typed by the player will cause the dealer's first two cards to be displayed on the screen. However, the first of these cards will be shown face down; that is, only the outline for this card will be drawn. As with the player, the dealer's point subtotal and ace count will be stored in the appropriate data memory registers (R7 and RF).

At this point a check is made (see program steps 1C8F through 1CAA) to determine whether or not the dealer, the player, or both have blackjack. This is done by comparing each of their subtotals with an 11 (since at this point in the game any aces will have been considered as ones) and branching to the appropriate game-ending routine (PLAYER-WINS, PLAYER-LOSES, or DRAW) if anyone has obtained a blackjack. If no one has 21, then at this point the main program is exited and a branch to the REMAINING CARDS routine is made (Fig. 10.17).

Upon the start of this routine, a message immediately comes up on the screen indicating that the player should "HIT H FOR A HIT AND S TO STAY." In this portion of the program, each time a key is struck it is tested to see if it is an H or an S. Each time the player requests a hit, the card selected by the RANDOM subroutine is placed at the appropriate screen location. In addition, the player subtotal and ace

Hexadecimal code			Mnemonic		
Address	Instruction	Label		Instruction	Comment
1C00	CDF200	BEGIN:	CALL	CLR SCRN	Begin entire new game.
03	210005		LXI	H,#0500	Initialize bankroll to $500.
06	22A310		SHLD	#10A3	
09	210013		LXI	H,#1300	Message: "HOW ABOUT A GAME
0C	CD401F		CALL	MESS	OF BLACKJACK''
0F	CD501F		CALL	RANDOM INIT	
12	AF	ANOTHER:	XRA	A	⎫ Start another round.
13	21AE10		LXI	H,#10AE	⎪
16	77		MOV	M,A	⎬ Clear ace count of
17	23		INX	H	⎪ player and dealer.
18	77		MOV	M,A	⎭
19	CD4010		CALL	FORM DECK	
1C	215013		LXI	H,#1350	Message: "YOU HAVE $ . . . "
1F	CD401F		CALL	MESS	
22	2AA310		LHLD	#10A3	Load bankroll to HL pair.
25	5D		MOV	E,L	⎫
26	7C		MOV	A,H	⎪
27	215A13		LXI	H,#135A	⎬ Displays bankroll message
2A	CDC500		CALL	UNPACK	⎪ on screen in space left
2D	7B		MOV	A,E	⎪ by previous message.
2E	CDC500		CALL	UNPACK	⎭
31	CD631F		CALL	BET	Enter bet in dollars.
34	CDA01F		CALL	CHK BET	Check if bet < bankroll.
37	CDF200		CALL	CLR SCRN	If here, bet is OK and are
3A	21001D		LXI	H,#1D00	ready to deal cards.
3D	CD401F		CALL	MESS	Message: "HIT H TO DEAL CARD"
1C40	CD501F		CALL	RANDOM INIT	Generate random number for
43	CDF200		CALL	CLR SCRN	1st player card.
46	CDD31F		CALL	SUB CREATE	Create new card, pack deck,
49	FE01		CPI	#01	⎫ place point value in A.
4B	CA511C		JNZ	NO ACE	⎬ Check for ace.
4E	32AE10		STA	#10AE	Record ace value.
51	3AA010	NO ACE:	STA	#10A0	Store partial sum.
54	218188		LXI	H,#8881	Initialize 1st player card location.
57	CD2010		CALL	GEN CARD	Display card on screen.
5A	CDD01F		CALL	CREATE	Pull 2d card from deck.
5D	FE01		CPI	#01	Check for ace.
5F	CA651C		JNZ	NO ACE	
62	32A010		STA	#10AE	Save in ace register if drawn.
65	21A010	NO ACEY:	LXI	H,#10A0	Update player point total.
68	86		ADD	M	
69	27		DAA		
6A	FE11		CPI	#11	Does player have 21?
6C	F5		PUSH	PSW	Save result for later.
6D	77		MOV	M,A	Store point total.
6E	218D88		LXI	H,#888D	Initialize 2d card location.
71	CD2010		CALL	GEN CARD	Display 2d player card.
74	CDD01F	DEALER CARDS:	CALL	CREATE	Pull 1st dealer card.
77	21A710		LXI	H,#10A7	
7A	77		MOV	M,A	Store dealer partial sum.
7B	23		INX	H	
7C	70		MOV	M,B	Store 1st card for later.

Figure 10.16 Main program of Blackjack—deals first two cards to player and dealer.

Hexadecimal code			Mnemonic		
Address	Instruction	Label		Instruction	Comment
1C7D	21418A		LXI	H,#8A41	Dealer card screen location.
81	C5		PUSH	B	
82	E5		PUSH	H	
85	CD0001		CALL	OUTLINE	Hide card value but show outline.
86	E1		POP	H	
87	C1		POP	B	
8A	CDD01F		CALL	CREATE	Pull dealers 2d card
8D	21A710		LXI	H,#10A7	Initialize dealer subtotal location.
8E	86		ADD	M	Form subtotal.
8F	27		DAA		
91	FE11		CPI	#11	Check for dealer 21.
92	77		MOV	M,A	Save partial sum.
93	F5		PUSH	PSW	Save 21 answer on stack.
96	214D8A		LXI	H,#8A4D	Set up 2d card address.
99	CD2010		CALL	GEN CARD	
9A	F1		POP	PSW	Check for dealer 21.
9D	CAA41C		JZ	DEAL 21	
9E	F1		POP	PSW	If here, dealer does not have
A1	CA0017		JZ	PLAY WIN	21. Check for player 21.
A4	C3201E		JMP	NEX PLAYCARD	
A5	F1	DEAL 21:	POP	PSW	If here, dealer has 21. Check
A8	C26517		JNZ	PLAY LOSE	for player 21.
	C3F717		JMP	DRAW	If here, both have 21.

Figure 10.16 (Continued)

count are updated, and a check is made to see if the maximum number of cards allowed on the screen (five) has been exceeded. Should this be the case, a message will appear on the screen indicating that "MAXIMUM NUMBER OF CARDS IN THIS GAME IS FIVE—SO IT'S A DRAW—HIT A IF YOU'D LIKE ANOTHER GAME OR Q TO QUIT."

Besides the card count check, the player subtotal is tested to see if it is BUST, that is, if it exceeds 21. If this is the case, the program branches to the PLAYER-LOSES routine, and the game is over. If his subtotal is still under 22, however, the program simply loops back to location NEX-CARD and asks whether or not the player wishes another card. When the player requests to stay, the program exits the player mode and enters the DEALER-CARDS portion of the program.

At the start of this routine, the dealer's face-down card is turned over and displayed, and a check is made on the point total to see if it is less than 17. Should this be the case, the following message is displayed: "HIT H TO GIVE DEALER A CARD UNTIL HE SAYS HE'S DONE." Each time an H key is depressed, another dealer card will be displayed and the dealer's subtotal and ace count updated. If the total number of dealer cards exceeds five, the game terminates

Hexadecimal code			Mnemonic		
Address	Instruction	Label		Instruction	Comment
1E20	218D88	NEX PLAY CD:	LXI	H,#888D	
23	22A510		SHLD	#10A5	Store address for 3d player.
26	21401D	NEX CARD:	LXI	H,#1D40	Message: HIT H FOR HIT, S card.
29	CD401F	BACK:	CALL	MESS	for STAY
2C	CD521F	ONE MORE:	CALL	RANDOM	Picks card for next cycle.
2F	FED3		CPI	#D3	} Check for "STAY".
31	CA801E		JZ	DEALER CARD	
34	FE		CPI	#CB	} Check for "HIT".
36	CA401E		JZ	HIT ONE	
39	212010		LXI	H,#1020	
3C	C3291E		JMP	BACK	
1E40	2AA510	HIT ONE:	LHLD	#10A5	
43	70		MOV	A,L	} Update address on
44	C60C		ADI	#0C	screen for next card.
46	6F		MOV	L,A	
47	FEBD		CPI	#BD	Check for too many cards.
49	C2521E		JNZ	OK	
4C	219011		LXI	H,#1190	Message: " . . . HIT A IF
4F	CD401F		CALL	MESS	YOU'D LIKE ANOTHER GAME . . ."
52	22A510	OK:	SHLD	#10A5	Save address.
55	E5		PUSH	H	Save address of card on stack.
56	CDD31F		CALL	SUB CREATE	Generate another card.
59	CDDO1E		CALL	ACE CHK	Bring in previous subtotal.
5C	86		ADD	M	} Form new subtotal
5D	27		DAA		and save.
5E	77		MOV	M,A	
1E5F	E1		POP	H	Get back screen address.
60	F5		PUSH	PSW	
61	CD2010		CALL	GEN CARD	Display next player card.
64	F1		POP	PSW	} Check for player over 21.
65	FE22		CPI	#22	
67	DA2C1E		JC	ONE MORE	Ask if player wants another card.
6A	C36517		JMP	PLAYER LOSES	Player is over 21.
1E80	3AAB10	DEALER CARD:	LDA	#10A8	Bring back 1st card.
83	47		MOV	B,A	
84	21418A		LXI	H,#8A41	Screen location of 1st card.
87	CD2010		CALL	GEN CARD	Turn over 1st dealer card.
8A	3AA710		LDA	#10A7	} Check if dealer total ≤ 16.
8D	FE17		CPI	#17	
8F	D2BO17		JNC	FINAL TALLY	Message "HIT H TO GIVE DEALER
92	216014		LXI	H,#1460	CARDS UNTIL HE SAYS HE'S
95	CD401F		CALL	MESS	DONE".
98	214D8A		LXI	H,#8A4D	Set up address for 3d dealer card.
9B	22AC10		SHLD	#10AC	
9E	7D	NEW CARD:	MOV	A,L	Move card address pointer
9F	C60C		ADI	#0C	one card to right.
A1	6F		MOV	L,A	Check for too many cards.
A2	FE7D		CPI	#7D	
A4	C2AD1E		JNZ	OK1	
A7	219011		LXI	H,#1190	Too many cards message.
AA	CD401F		CALL	MESS	
1EAD	22AC10	OK1:	SHLD	#10AC	
B0	E5		PUSH	H	

Figure 10.17 REMAINING CARDS routine for the Blackjack program.

Hexadecimal code			Mnemonic		
Address	*Instruction*	*Label*		*Instruction*	*Comment*
B1	CDD01F		CALL	CREATE	Generate next card.
B4	CDD01E		CALL	ACE CHK	Bring in dealer subtotal.
B7	86		ADD	M	⎫
B8	27		DAA		⎬ Update dealer subtotal.
B9	77		MOV	M,A	⎭
BA	E1		POP	H	
BB	F5		PUSH	PSW	
BC	CD2010		CALL	GEN CARD	Place card on screen.
BF	F1		POP	PSW	Check if dealer ≥ 17
C0	FE17		CPI	#17	(no carry).
C2	D2B017		JNC	FINAL TALLY	
C5	2AAC10		LHLD	#10AC	Bring in for new card address.
C8	C39E1E		JMP	NEW CARD	
1ED0	FE01	ACE CHK:	CPI	#01	Check for ace.
D2	C2D81E		JNZ	NO ACE	
D5	3AAF10		STA	#10AF	Record ace in player ace.
D8	21A710	NO ACE:	LXI	H,#10A7	Bring in dealer register subtotal.
DB	C9		RET		

Figure 10.17   (Continued)

and ends in a draw. Once the dealer's point score is greater than 16, the program branches to FINAL-TALLY routine, where a final decision is made on the outcome of the game. A complete listing of this portion of the blackjack program is contained in Fig. 10.18. It consists of three major subprograms: PLAYER-WINS, starting in memory location 1700; PLAYER-LOSES, starting at 1765; and the FINAL-TALLY routine itself, beginning at memory location 17B0.

At the start of the latter subprogram, both the player and dealer point counts are maximized by checking their respective ace counters and, where appropriate, adding 10 to the point tallies in order to maximize each of the scores without going over 21. Next the player and dealer point totals are compared, with branching to the appropriate subprogram determined as shown in Table 10.4. Note that at this point in the game the player's score cannot be over 21 since had this occurred earlier, a branch would immediately have been made to the PLAYER-LOSES routine. Should a draw occur, the message "NOBODY WINS—IT'S A DRAW" is displayed and a branch back to the CHECK-KEYBOARD routine (address 1754) is made to see if the player wants to initiate another round of play, start a new game entirely, or perhaps even discontinue further playing of the game by quitting.

If the player decides to quit, the program starting at address 1800 compares the current bankroll with the initial $500 stake and,

Hexadecimal code		Mnemonic			
Address	Instruction	Label		Instruction	Comments
					Message: "YOU WON, YOUR
1700	216115	PLAYER WINS:	LXI	H,#1561	BANKROLL IS NOW $ . . .".
03	CD401F		CALL	MESS	
06	119999		LXI	D,#9999	Initialize dividend register.
09	2AA110		LHLD	#10A1	Bring in bet and multiply
0C	7D	LOOP:	MOV	A,L	by 3/2.
0D	CC98		ADI	#98	
0F	27		DAA		
10	6F		MOV	L,A	
11	7C		MOV	A,H	Subtract two via 10s
12	CE99		ACI	#99	complement from
14	27		DAA		HL pair.
15	67		MOV	H,A	
16	F5		PUSH	PSW	When done, HL = 0 (Save flags).
17	3E01		MVI	A,#01	
19	83		ADD	E	
1A	27		DAA		Increment DE by 1
1B	5F		MOV	E,A	decimally.
1C	3E00		MVI	A,#00	When done looping,
1E	8A		ADC	D	1/2 bet is in DE.
1F	27		DAA		
20	57		MOV	D,A	
21	F1		POP	PSW	Check if done looping.
22	DA0C17		JC	LOOP	
25	2AA110		LHLD	#10A1	Put bet in HL.
28	7D		MOV	A,L	
29	83		ADD	E	
2A	27		DAA		
172B	5F		MOV	E,A	Form 3/2 bet and
2C	7C		MOV	A,H	put answer in DE.
2D	8A		ADC	D	
2E	27		DAA		
2F	57		MOV	D,A	
30	2AA310		LHLD	#10A3	Bring in bankroll.
33	7D		MOV	A,L	
34	83		ADD	E	
35	27		DAA		
36	6F		MOV	L,A	Add winnings to
37	7C		MOV	A,H	bankroll.
38	8A		ADC	D	
39	27		DAA		
3A	67		MOV	H,A	
3B	22A310		SHLD	#10A3	Save new bankroll.
3E	45		MOV	B,L	Save L in B,H still in A.
3F	212588		LXI	H,#8825	Bankroll screen position.
42	CDC500		CALL	UNPACK	Display bankroll within
45	78		MOV	A,B	winnings message.
46	CDC500		CALL	UNPACK	
49	210988		LXI	H,#8809	BET screen position
4C	7A		MOV	A,D	
4D	CDC500		CALL	UNPACK	Display bet within
50	7B		MOV	A,E	winnings message.
51	CDC500		CALL	UNPACK	
54	CD101F	CHECK KBD	CALL	KBD IN	

Figure 10.18 The PLAYER-WINS, PLAYER-LOSES, and FINAL-TALLY sub-program for Blackjack.

Hexadecimal code		Mnemonic			
Address	Instruction	Label	Instruction		Comments
1757	FED1		CPI	#D1	Check for "Q".
59	CABA10		JZ	QUIT	
5C	FEC2		CPI	#C2	Check for "B".
5E	CA001C		JZ	BEGIN	
61	C3121C		JMP	ANOTHER	Go here if key A or any other struck.
		PLAYER			
1765	2AA310	LOSES:	LHLD	#10A3	Bring in bankroll.
68	EB		XCHG		Put bankroll in DE.
69	2AA110		LHLD	#10A1	Bring in bet.
6C	37		STC		
6D	3E99		MVI	A,#99	
6F	CE00		ACI	#00	
71	95		SUB	L	
72	83		ADD	E	
73	27		DAA		Subtract bet from
74	6F		MOV	L,A	bankroll.
75	3E99		MVI	A,#99	
77	CE00		ACI	#00	Final result in HL.
79	94		SUB	H	
7A	82		ADD	D	
7B	27		DAA		
7C	67		MOV	H,A	
7D	22A310		SHLD	#10A3	Store updated bankroll.
80	5B	ZERO CHECK:	ORA	L	
81	C28E17		JNZ	YOU LOST	
					Message: "IT SEEMS YOU ARE
84	211516		LXI	H,#1615	OUT OF MONEY"
1787	C39117		JMP	MESS1	
					Message: "I'M SORRY YOU LOST,
					YOUR LUCK IS BOUND TO
178E	21B315	YOU LOST:	LXI	H,15B3	CHANGE. . . ."
91	CD401F	MESS 1	CALL	MESS	
				CHECK	
94	C35417		JMP	KBD	
17B0	3AA010	FINAL TALLY:	LDA	#10A0	Bring in player point total
B3	FE12		CPI	#12	if > 11, then count aces as
B5	47		MOV	B,A	1's so don't add 10
				DEALER	
B6	D2C517		JNC	POINTS	
B9	3AAE10		LDA	#10AE	Load ace count and add 10 if any.
BC	B7		ORA	A	Set flags.
				DEALER	
BD	CAC517		JZ	POINTS	
C0	3E10		MVI	A,#10	Add 10 to score.
C2	80		ADD	B	
C3	27		DAA		
C4	47		MOV	B,A	Final player point score in B.
		DEALER			
C5	3AA710	POINTS:	LDA	#10A7	Bring in dealer points total.
C8	FE12		CPI	#12	Is score > 11?
CA	4F		MOV	C,A	
CB	D2D817		JNC	NO FIX	

Figure 10.18 (Continued)

Hexadecimal code			Mnemonic		
Address	Instruction	Label		Instruction	Comments
CE	3AAF10		LDA	#10AF	Any aces?
D1	B7		ORA	A	
D2	CAD817		JZ	NO FIX	
D5	3E10		MVI	A,#10	
D7	81		ADD	C	
17D8	FE22	NO FIX:	CPI	#21	Is dealer >21?
DA	D2E717		JNC	DEALER OVER	
DD	4F		MOV	C,A	If here, dealer not over. Save
DE	78		MOV	A,B	dealer points in C. Check
DF	FE22		CPI	#22	player for >21.
E1	D26517		JNC	PLAYER LOSES	
E4	C3F017		JMP	COMPARE	If here, neither is over.
E7	78	DEALER OVER:	MOV	A,B	Check if player over.
E8	FE22		CPI	#22	
EA	D2F717		JNC	DRAW	
ED	C30017		JMP	PLAYER WINS	
F0	BA	COMPARE:	CMP	C	Player is in A; dealer in C.
F1	DA6517		JC	PLAYER LOSES	
F4	C20017		JNZ	PLAYER WINS	
F7	21A914	DRAW:	LXI	H,#14A9	Message: "NOBODY WINS—IT'S A DRAW."
FA	CD401F		CALL	MESS CHECK	
FD	C35417		JMP	KBD	
1800	2AA310	QUIT:	LHLD	#10A3	Bring in bankroll.
03	3E05		MVI	A,#05	Compare current bankroll
05	BC		CMP	H	with starting bankroll ($500).
06	212F16		LXI	H,#162F	Message: "I'M SORRY YOU
09	D20F18		JNC	OUT	LOST MONEY . . ."
0C	212C15		LXI	H,#152C	Message: "CONGRATULATIONS ON YOUR WINNINGS . . ."
0F	CD401F	OUT:	CALL	MESS CHECK	
12	C35417		JMP	KBD	Look for a new game.

Figure 10.18 (Continued)

depending on whether the player has won or lost money in the game, displays either the "CONGRATULATIONS ON YOUR WIN-NINGS—I HOPE WE'LL SEE YOU HERE AGAIN SOON" or "I'M SORRY YOU LOST MONEY—BETTER LUCK NEXT TIME" message.

If the player has beaten the dealer, a branch to the PLAYER-WINS routine occurs and the player's bet is multiplied by 1.5. These winnings are then added to the player's bankroll, with both the winnings and new bankroll displayed in the message "YOU WON

TABLE 10.4 BRANCHING DECISIONS FOR
FINAL-TALLY PORTION OF THE BLACKJACK
GAME

Condition	Branch to
Player ≤ 21 and Dealer > 21	PLAYER-WINS
Both < 21 But	
Player > Dealer	PLAYER-WINS
Player = Dealer	DRAW
Player < Dealer	PLAYER-LOSES

$\underline{\quad}$ —YOUR BANKROLL IS NOW $\underline{\quad}$ HOW ABOUT ANOTHER GAME? Since this portion of the program is somewhat complex, a brief description of its operation will be given.

In order to multiply the bet by 1.5, the bet is first divided by 2 and then this result simply added to the original bet. Were this bet information available in pure binary form, the division by 2 could simply be accomplished by shifting the information 1 bit to the right. However, since this data must be displayed in conventional decimal dollar notation, the bet information is stored in memory registers R1 and R2 in BCD format. As a result, this division process is accomplished by seeing how many 2s there are in the bet, that is, by successively subtracting 2 from the bet value while keeping track of the number of subtractions required to reduce the original bet to zero. Of course this subtraction must be done in 10s-complement (see program steps 1706 through 1724). When completed, half of the original bet is stored in the DE register pair, and this is simply added to the original bet to form the player's winnings for the round.

On the other hand, should the player lose, then the amount of the bet is subtracted from the player's bankroll and the message "I'M SORRY YOU LOST—YOUR LUCK IS BOUND TO CHANGE—HOW ABOUT ANOTHER GAME?" is displayed, followed by the message "HIT A TO PLAY ANOTHER GAME, Q TO QUIT, OR B TO START A NEW GAME." If the player's bankroll was reduced to zero by the previous loss, then the game is terminated and the following condolence message issued: "IT SEEMS YOU'RE OUT OF MONEY—TODAY WASN'T YOUR DAY, BUT COME BACK SOON."

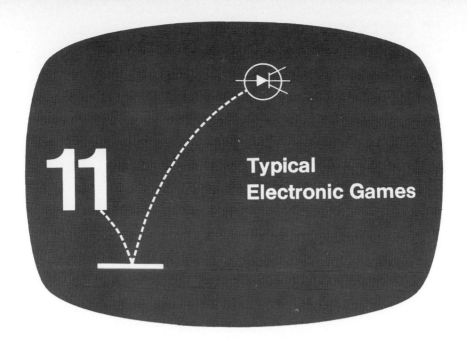

Typical Electronic Games

In the preceding 10 chapters we have discussed the technical principles and functions of electronic games as well as game parameters and special features. This chapter is devoted to a description of actual electronic games now on the market. All three categories, board games, TV games, and arcade, or coin-operated, electronic games are represented, but space limitations dictate a selection of those electronic games that are most typical. In the presentation that follows, a general description of the basic game and its variations is followed by a brief technical discussion. Special features are included, as are the name and address of the manufacturer for those who wish to write for more details.

CODE NAME: SECTOR (Parker Brothers)

This board game is produced by the manufacturers of the original Monopoly real estate trading game. As illustrated in Fig. 11.1, the game consists of a board resembling a grid map of a portion of the ocean, a control panel, and a display panel. Up to four players can participate, and the object is to hunt down the hidden submarine. Each player plots a destroyer's course in a different color on the grid map. Crayons, a parallel ruler, and a cloth to wipe out the crayon

Figure 11.1   CODE NAME: SECTOR (© 1977 Parker Brothers).

markings are included with the game. Locations of surface ships and of the hidden submarine are stored by the microcomputer.

A 6-digit LED display indicates which ship is being controlled, what its speed is, and what its range to the hidden submarine is. In addition, four pinpoint LEDs show the direction of the controlled ship with reference to eight compass points (N, S, W, E and NE, NW, SE, SW). The game contains many realistic features, such as the submarine's ability to change location each time a pursuit ship moves. When a submarine is sunk, another appears, and the length of the game can range from half an hour to many hours. Although advertised for children of 12 years and older, this game will undoubtedly be played by adults because of the great potential of mental challenge.

Technical Description   Code Name: Sector contains a single integrated circuit. This is a custom-made IC which Texas Instruments has designed specifically for Parker Brothers. Based on the TI family of TMS-1000 microprocessors, this IC includes a RAM which can store 64 four-bit words and a ROM which stores 1000 eight-bit words. Also included in the IC are all of the LED drivers. Eleven pushbuttoms comprise the keyboard, and, in addition, two more controls can be reached by pressing a small, recessed button with a ball-point pen. One control adds complexity to the regular program of evasive tactics of the hidden submarine. The other displays the submarine's location and heading.

Special Features   By depressing the "teach" mode button, the players can start the special teaching program. In this mode a complete submarine hunt is enacted, with each action carefully explained in the game's instruction book and each LED display precisely programmed to match the instruction book. All possible courses, features, and errors occur in this teaching program.

Code Name: Sector can be played by one individual as commander of as many as four ships against the computer, or it can be played by as many as four individual players competing against each other as to who can sink the hidden sub first.

Manufacturer   Parker Brothers, Division of General Mills Fun Group, Inc., 190 Bridge Street, Salem, MA 01970.

CHESS CHALLENGER (Fidelity Electronics)

This electronic game actually represents one of the classic board games because it permits the individual to play chess, on a regular chessboard, against a computer. As illustrated in Fig. 11.2, data is entered on a 12-button keyboard and displayed on four LED numerals. Two additional LED lights indicate "check" or "I lose."

Each of the squares on the chessboard is identified by a numeral and letter so that only eight keys are required to specify any square. The remaining four keys are used to enter moves into the computer, to clear out unwanted moves before pressing "enter," to make double moves, such as castling, and, finally, to reset the game.

When a game starts, the positions of the white and black pieces are stored automatically in the computer's memory. Each time a move is made, the computer stores the newly entered position of the particular piece. When the next move is made, you only have to enter the position from which you are moving a piece and that to which you are moving it. The rules of chess are stored in the computer's memory, and the computer will indicate when illegal moves have been made. For every move the player enters, the computer will indicate its best countermove.

Technical Description   All of the electronics of the Chess Challenger are contained on a single printed-circuit board. For the advanced version, these electronics consist of 14 ICs and 28 transistors, which are used as LED drivers, one per segment. The heart of the Chess Challenger is a type 8080 microprocessor, made by Nippon Electric Co., with 2 kilobytes of ROM for the basic version and 4 kilobytes of ROM for the advanced version. Chess rules programs are stored in

Figure 11.2   Chess Challenger (Fidelity Electronics Ltd.).

the ROM, and, because the advanced version has three levels of difficulty, the larger memory is required. Both versions contain 512 bytes of RAM, which stores the positions and the individual moves of the chess pieces. All ICs are standard, off-the-shelf parts, but the manufacturer expects to perform all repairs at the factory.

Special Features   In the updated version of Chess Challenger it is possible to select three levels of sophistication. When the game is normally turned on, the designation "CL1" (chess level 1) will appear in a display window, indicating the first level of complexity. By pressing the clear button once, this can be increased to "CL2"; by depressing it a second time, "CL3," maximum difficulty is obtained.

Ordinarily the computer plays the dark and the player the light pieces. It is possible, however, for the player to select the dark pieces and have the computer play the offense. This special feature is particularly helpful in learning chess and provides variety for the experienced player.

Manufacturer   Fidelity Electronics Ltd., 5245 Diversy Avenue, Chicago, IL 60639.

MISSILE ATTACK, AUTORACE, AND FOOTBALL (Mattel Electronics)

While these three games come under the category of board games, they are much more like hand-held calculators. None of them requires a TV set, and all of them have basically the same type of display and control circuits. As illustrated in Fig. 11.3, Missile Attack lets the player manipulate a missile from the bottom of the display in order to intercept an enemy coming down from the top. There are three possible paths for either the enemy missile or the antimissile missile. The position of the antimissile missile is controlled by the player, while the enemy missile's position is controlled by the internal logic. A "fire" button starts the antimissile missile in response to whatever missile the computer sends down. The display consists of a 3 × 9 matrix of small, rectangular, LED dots. Movement is simulated by lighting up one LED after the next. The dot indicating the antimissile missile is brighter than that for the enemy missiles. A 2-digit numerical LED display shows the score. When one of the enemy missiles reaches its target, the first few bars of taps are played.

The same type of 3 × 9 LED matrix display is used for Autorace and Football. In the Autorace game, the player controls the steering of a car, indicated by a bright LED, to avoid oncoming cars. Speed is controlled by a four-position gearshift switch. The buzzing sound

Figure 11.3 Missile Attack (Mattel Electronics).

heard whenever the car is running increases in pitch with the speed. As in most racing games, there is some penalty due to loss of time after each collision, and the car may even be returned to the starting point. Each time the car reaches the top of the display, one lap is completed. A 2-digit LED display shows the elapsed time in seconds.

In the football game, the LED matrix display is arranged horizontally and placed in a representation of a football stadium. The player controls the movement of the running back, while the game logic controls the defensive players of the opposite team. The scores of both teams and the elapsed time are indicated by numerical LED displays and can be accessed by depressing either the "status" or the "score" push button. The motion of the running back is controlled by three push buttons, one for forward or backward and the other two for up or down. A separate "kick" button permits the use of the goal kick. As in real football, the referee's whistle is heard whenever you lose the ball.

Technical Description   Each of the three games uses the same basic display module. Apparently fabricated by a process similar to that used for the 7-segment LED numeral, the 3 × 9 matrix of LED rectangles and its interconnections are mounted on a single substrate and covered by a plastic sheet. Aside from a small filter capacitor and 1/4-watt resistor, the only other component is a custom-made IC. This LSI device contains all of the control logic, the drivers for the numerical LED indicators, and the LED dots, as well as an audio circuit which drives a small diaphragm-type speaker. A 9-V transistor-type battery is sufficient to power each of these three games.

Manufacturer   Mattel Electronics, 5150 Rosecrans Avenue, Hawthorne, CA 90250.

INDY 500 (Universal Research Laboratories)

This is a TV game, in color, for road racing, tennis, and hockey. The standard TV, hockey, and tennis games are played in the conventional way, with potentiometer controls to permit up to four players to move the hockey stick or tennis racket in a vertical direction. As shown in Fig. 11.4, the same four controls can be used by one or two players in the "road racing" mode. In this mode, the player-controlled cars are moved horizontally to avoid the other traffic, which appears to move from the top of the screen to the bottom, and the

Figure 11.4 INDY 500 (Universal Research Laboratories).

score depends on the number of collisions with other cars. Speed increases during the race, but returns to zero after a collision.

Technical Description The INDY 500 game uses four ICs, one of which is a special LSI-CMOS made specifically for this manufacturer. It is not a standard microprocessor, but contains some memory. Three of the ICs are standard op amps. There is a 3.58-MHz crystal for the color features, and a number of transistors are used for various special circuits. A small audio section generates paddle-hit, rebound, and score sounds for tennis or hockey and motor and crash sounds for racing. A small speaker is located in the player-controlled console. The RF oscillator and output circuit use two transistors which are contained in a shielded case. The antenna switch does not control the game's power. Either 9-V battery operation or a separate ac adaptor is available to power this unit.

Special Features One of the special features is the ability to select "robot," which is in effect a practice mode, allowing the electronic game to play hockey or tennis against one or two players. In the latter mode the robot, in effect, plays doubles. The degree of skill of the robot is adjustable by a potentiometer. Another special feature is the capability to put English on the ball in tennis by using segmented rackets.

Manufacturer Universal Research Laboratories, Elk Grove Village, IL 60007. Att.: Mr. W. E. Olliges

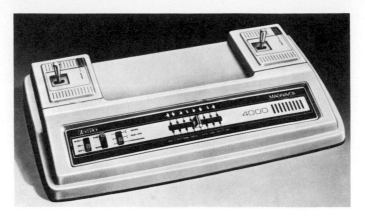

Figure 11.5   Odyssey 4000 (Magnavox).

ODYSSEY 2000, 4000, and 5000 (Magnavox)

These games are the latest in the Odyssey series and feature the basic tennis-hockey-smash games as well as a variety of other games and special features. The basic games are provided in the 2000 model, while the 4000 model offers eight games in full color with two separate, hand-held joystick controls. In addition to tennis, hockey, and smash, this model also contains gridball, basketball, baseball practice, soccer, and smash practice. In gridball the player has to move the ball through a series of barricades. In the practice mode, one player can play against the game itself. There are separate sounds for each of the games, random movement of players, "serve" buttons, a three-level handicap selection, fast and slow speed adjustment, and the conventional digital scoring on the screen. Figure 11.5 shows the console for the Magnavox Odyssey 4000. The two joystick controls are removable, and the slide switch indicates which of the games is being played.

Technical Description   This is not a microprocessor-controlled game, but there are a number of specially designed ICs to provide such functions as ball-wall generation, video logic, digital score generation, etc. Because this is basically an analog type of game, a number of potentiometers are required for adjusting particular timing portions as explained in Chap. 3. The RF oscillator can be set to produce video on either channel 3 or channel 4, and the antenna switch does not control the power to the game. It is therefore necessary to turn the game off with a separate power switch. Either battery or ac-adaptor operation is possible with all three models.

Special Features Individual movement of players and a number of levels of difficulty are the main special features provided in the Magnavox Odyssey games.

Manufacturer Magnavox, 1700 Magnavox Way, Fort Wayne, IN 46804.

STUDIO II (RCA)

Studio II is a microprocessor-based TV game featuring plug-in cartridges which promise an almost unlimited range of games and TV activities. Five games—Doodle, Patterns, Bowling, Freeway (racing), and Addition—are built into the set and require no cartridges.

RCA offers three series of cartridges, each designed for a different type of TV activity. The TV Arcade series features games that are generally based on physical skill, such as tennis, baseball, and space war. The TV Schoolhouse series of cartridges, as the name implies, deals with mental skills, using the TV quiz format to teach math, social studies, and other subjects. Contestants usually compete for the highest score in answering multiple choice questions. The third cartridge series available is called TV Casino and provides games of chance.

As illustrated in Fig. 11.6, Studio II consists of a single console with keyboards *A* and *B*, each containing 10 keys. These push buttons serve a number of different functions. The numeral marked on each button may be entered, depending on the plug-in cartridge or game selected, as a number in the math quiz or fun with numbers

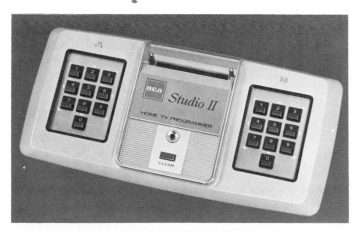

Figure 11.6 Studio II home TV programmer (RCA).

game. In Doodles, Patterns, or other games, each of the keys, except the center one (5), controls movement in one of eight directions, as indicated by the small arrows next to the respective keys. In addition, specific keys, on specific keyboards, select the programs and control the level of difficulty, handicap, and many other features of a game. In some games the time that a key is depressed determines distance, speed, etc. The main feature of these two digital keyboards is that they are directly interfaced with the microprocessor.

The RCA Studio II can provide TV signals on either channel 2 or 3.

Technical Description The microprocessor, RCA's CDF 1802, provides the central computer control for all of the games and educational programs. This is a CMOS, 8-bit, register-oriented microprocessor, operating at 5 V dc at a clock frequency of 1.76 MHz. The memory consists of 2048 kilobytes of ROM and 512 bytes of RAM, contained on eight separate ICs. The RAM stores TV refresh information, stack, and variable data, while the ROM stores 1024 kilobytes of programs for the five resident games and 1024 kilobytes of an interpreter language required for interfacing the cartridge. All cartridges contain their respective game programs in a ROM in compatible format.

A variable-tone beep sound is generated by the microprocessor-controlled timer-oscillator and can be switched off if desired. In the RCA Studio II, the game power supply is shut off when the antenna switch selects the TV antenna.

Special Features The versatility and almost unlimited programmability of RCA's Studio II is probably its most outstanding feature. RCA is in the process of adding cartridges which have educational rather than pure entertainment value. The unique dual-keyboard concept also can be considered a special feature. Because the keyboard readout is under control of the microprocessor, it can be used in a variety of different ways. The special features of this game can be summed up in one word: versatility.

Manufacturer RCA Distributor and Special Products Division, Deptford, NJ 08096.

CHANNEL F (Fairchild Camera and Instrument Corp.)

Channel F is a cartridge-based, microprocessor-controlled TV game featuring unique, hand-held joystick-type controllers. The basic con-

Figure 11.7 Channel F (Fairchild Camera and Instrument Corp.).

sole illustrated in Fig. 11.7 includes two games, hockey and tennis, and contains five push buttons, a *cartridge eject* lever, a receptacle for the cartridges, and a storage space for the controllers. A small speaker is mounted in the console. Fairchild offers a series of Video Cart plug-in cartridges which contain the programs for a series of games, such as Tic-Tac-Toe, Doodles, Blackjack, Space War, and a variety of math games.

Fairchild's unique controllers are held in one hand, while the other hand operates the knob somewhat in the manner of a joystick. The triangular control knob contains a recessed arrow which is pointed toward the screen. Each knob provides eight-way control: forward and backward, left and right, twist-to-the-left and twist-to-the-right, and push-down and pull-up. Pushing to the left causes motion toward the left of the screen. Pushing forward causes motion upward, while pushing backward causes motion downward. The push-and-pull action controls such things as firing a tank cannon or choosing another card in Blackjack.

One of the five push buttons on the console resets the control circuits. The remaining four buttons provide multiple functions, depending on the cartridge plugged in. Selection of one game out of several on a cartridge is one function. It is also possible to set the time limit for a game at 2, 5, 10, or 20 minutes or to select certain special game modes. In general, these buttons set up the mode or rules for a particular game, and the hand controls are then used for the game itself.

All of the games available through Channel F are in full color.

Technical Description As the name indicates, this TV game is based on the Fairchild F8 microprocessor, which is implemented here with a Type 3850 CPU and a Type 3851 used as a program storage unit (PSU). Control inputs from the console switches and the right controller go to the CPU, while the left controller is connected to the PSU. This IC also provides the control for the audio generator. Another Type 3851 contains the program and data for the two console-contained games, tennis and hockey. The plug-in cartridge busses go directly to the three ICs mentioned above.

A 3.58-MHz crystal oscillator provides the color subcarrier and also serves as master clock for the horizontal and vertical sync generators. Four 4096 RAM ICs contain all of the video data, and conventional logic is used to combine video, sync, and the color subcarrier. A single-transistor RF oscillator and a diode modulator provide the modulated RF output for channel 3. The power supply consists of two separate, regulated sources for +5 and +12 V. An additional −5-V source serves the RAMs.

Special Features The Fairchild Video Cart cartridges each contain a spring-loaded door which covers the contacts. When the cartridge is inserted in the system console, the contacts are not visible at all and a special *eject* button must be pressed to remove the cartridge. This method protects the contacts both of the cartridge itself and of the mating connector in the system console.

Another unique feature is a *hold* button that permits the player to either freeze the action of a console game in progress or, after freezing the action, change the time, the speed, or both of the remaining game without altering the score. A third unique feature is the fact that the microprocessor will generate certain symbols with a question mark in setting up each game. When the *reset* button is depressed, "G?" appears. When the game is selected by means of one of the four buttons on the central console, "S?" appears. Depending on the game selected, the microprocessor may then ask the player to select a time period by displaying "T?" or to select a certain mode by displaying "M?" With games such as Blackjack, the display on the TV screen may ask "CUT?" "BET?" or "HIT?" In a similar manner, the microprocessor displays the results as well as the scores in alphanumeric characters on the screen.

Manufacturer Fairchild Consumer Products, 4001 Miranda Avenue, Palo Alto, CA 94304.

VIDEO COMPUTER SYSTEM (Atari)

Video Computer System is a cartridge-based, microprocessor-controlled TV game featuring different sets of hand controllers for different types of games. In contrast to some other cartridge games, there are no games resident in the console, but the game is supplied with one cartridge, the "Combat Game Program." As illustrated in Fig. 11.8, the console contains a *power* switch, a *game reset* switch, and a *game selection* switch. In addition, there is a TV-type switch which selects either color or black-and-white operation. Separate switches arc available to select the degree of difficulty for the left and right players. The controls for racing games use a digital encoder coupled to the "steering" knob, with an additional "throttle" switch to speed up the racing vehicle. For tennis-type games a paddle position controller is supplied, which also contains a push button to put English on the ball after it has been hit by the paddle. Two joystick-type controls are available for controlling the tanks in tank battle games. These handles can be moved in eight directions and contain separate push buttons for firing a cannon or missile. At the rear of the console there are two separate receptacles which hold the connectors for either type of control. In the Atari Video Computer System,

Figure 11.8 Video computer system (Atari, Inc.).

the sound for any of the games is transmitted over the TV channel and will therefore come from the TV speaker.

Technical Description   The microprocessor and its associated ICs are part of the 6500 series manufactured by MOS Technology and Rockwell. Atari, Inc. has declined to supply any additional technical information.

Special Features   The use of different controllers for different games is unique to the Atari Video Computer System. Besides the versatility of additional cartridges, it is also conceivable that, in the future, Atari will offer different controllers for unique, as yet unheard of, video entertainment.

Manufacturer   Atari, Inc., Consumer Division, 1195 Borregas Avenue, Sunnyvale, CA 94086.

TELSTAR ARCADE (Coleco Industries)

This microprocessor-based color TV game is unique in that it uses a three-sided control console for the three different basic games for which it is designed. A matching triangular cartridge, located at the top of the control console as shown in Fig. 11.9, controls road race, tennis, or quick-draw, a target-shooting game. Additional cartridges are available for such games as hockey, handball, target, for one to four players, and a variety of pinball and other target-shooting games.

The roadrace game, a realistic steering wheel moves the player's car out of the way of the onrushing smaller cars, and a two-position gearshift lever controls the speed. When a collision occurs, the cars will go in the reverse direction and there is a 3 to 6 second penalty. Restart after a crash must be in first gear. Both the mileage score and a countdown score appear in digital form on the TV screen.

The tennis game control panel also contains the game selector knob and allows two levels of skill for playing. In addition to the right and left paddle position control, a button can be depressed to put English on the ball.

The quick-draw game includes a holstered pistol—with the conventional photoelectric pickup and optics. For each shot the target starter must be depressed and the pistol pulled from its holster as fast as possible. The figure of the outlaw representing the target must be bright pink or white so that the photoelectric system of the pistol can pick it up. The digital score on the TV screen indicates the number of

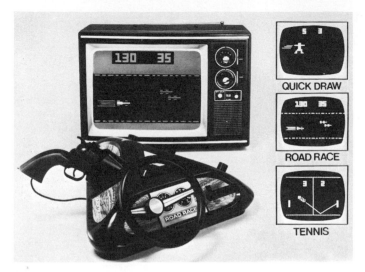

Figure 11.9 Telstar Arcade (Coleco Industries, Inc.).

shots fired and the number of hits. After each shot, the pistol must be replaced in the holster and the target starter depressed again.

Coleco Industries also produces two other games which are not cartridge-controlled. Telstar Ranger is a conventional tennis, hockey, handball, jai alai, skeet, and target game, while Combat is a tank battle game with realistic controls for maneuvering each tank and firing its cannon.

Technical Description The manufacturer does not release technical data.

Manufacturer Coleco Industries, Inc., 945 Asylum Avenue, Hartford, CT 06105.

TIC TAC QUIZ (Sega of America)

This coin-operated game is available either in a table or an upright model and features a combination of a quiz game and tic-tac-toe as shown in Fig. 11.10. A single player can play against the machine, or two players can play against each other. Questions appear on the screen, apparently selected at random, and the players have a time limit, usually 30 seconds, to either agree or disagree. If the correct push button is selected, the player is permitted to enter a 0 or an ×, in the usual tic-tac-toe format. One player has all nine × switches in a keyboard, while the other has the corresponding 0s. The tic-tac-toe

Figure 11.10 TIC TAC QUIZ (Sega of America).

pattern on the screen is then updated accordingly. The player who gets three in a row or five of a kind wins. Options, such as a free game or credit, are possible for those who finish the game in a specified number of moves. In the table model the entire cover is sealed by glass, and in the upright version the control panel is at a slant, with the display being vertical.

Technical Description   This game is controlled by a National Semiconductor SC/MP microprocessor, and its block diagram is shown in Fig. 11.11. The computer includes the microprocessor and all of the RAM, ROM, I/O, and other ICs. A total of 84 ICs, 6 transistors, and miscellaneous diodes are used in this computer board. Each of the two keyboards contains eight ICs, one transistor, and two diodes. One of the interesting features is the use of a tape deck, a Clarion 12-V dc automobile stereo cartridge deck that plays in either direction. All of the 2500 test questions are stored, in digital form, in a special format on the magnetic tape and are played back at a baud rate of 1844. Each question data block (256 characters) is stored in 2 kilobits of RAM and is then converted into alphanumerics by the character generator. Between questions the tape deck is turned off to reduce the wear of the tape and tape heads. Another 2 kilobits of RAM provide storage for the CPU, and the entire game program is in 12 kilobits of ROM. Almost all of the ICs are National Semiconductor TTL low-power Schottky Standard types. A Motorola 23-in TV monitor is used to display the tic-tac-toe pattern as well as the questions and answers. The computer portion of the tic-tac quiz controls the various lamp signals and accepts keyboard information.

Manufacturer Sega of America, 2550 Santa Fe Avenue, Redondo Beach, CA 90278.

"FONZ" (Sega of America)

This coin-operated game simulates the action of a speeding motorcycle, and, as in most racing games, the object of the player is to go as fast as possible without colliding with oncoming vehicles or the roadside railing. The realistic motorcycle handlebars as shown in Fig. 11.12, the roar of the engine, and the view of the moving road ahead are key features in the popular appeal of this arcade-type game. Dotted lines indicate the railing, and these lines move from

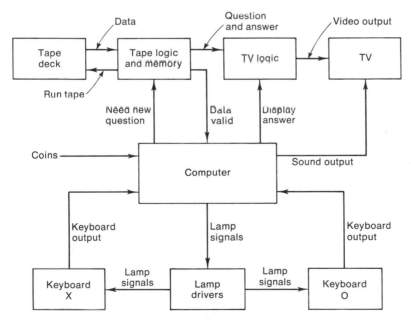

Figure 11.11 Block diagram of TIC TAC QUIZ (Sega of America).

top to bottom, creating the illusion of the roadway flashing by. As the handlebar is turned, the motorcycle on the screen swerves and banks accordingly. When the throttle control handle is twisted, the dotted lines move faster, the motorcycle moves toward the top of the screen, and the roar of the engine sounds louder and faster. Both the road and the motorcycle are shown in perspective, with everything at the bottom, closest to the player, larger than at the top. The picture tube is mounted lengthwise so that the screen is longer than it is wide, further strengthening the illusion of the roadway fading into the distance.

When the image on the screen collides with another vehicle or the railing, a crashing noise is heard, the handlebars shake, and the motorcycle image is reversed. Each collision results in lost time and slower start-up speed. The score is continuously displayed on four numerical indicators, and the elapsed time is shown on two indicators. When the score reaches 1000, the "extended play" lamp indicates that the player has earned another, free, 30 seconds of playing time. The amount of extended play time as well as the time limit and the time lost for each collision can be adjusted on the electronics chassis.

Figure 11.12   FONZ (Sega of America).

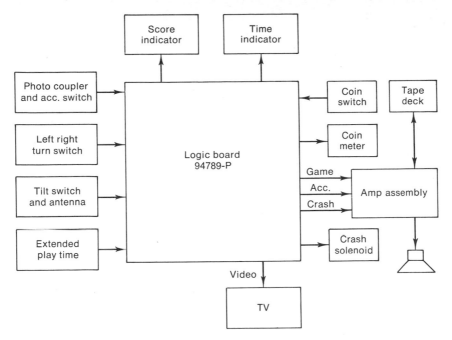

Figure 11.13   Block diagram of FONZ (Sega of America).

Technical Description   This is not a microprocessor-controlled game, but over 40 ICs, plus many discrete transistors and diodes, provide all of the logic and display functions necessary to generate the realistic video and audio effects. Standard TTL logic is used, except for a special ROM which serves as character generator for the motorcycle images. The different views of the motorcycle are stored in this ROM and provide the realistic swerve and tilt. Size changes are implemented by changing clock frequency so that more or fewer lines are used for the image. An audio tape deck is used for the recorded sounds of the motorcycle engine and the sound of crashes. The chassis contains a power transformer and an elaborate, regulated power supply which drives the logic board and the audio section. A 23-in (diagonal) TV monitor is used to display the picture. As in most coin-operated games, there are *interlock* switches for the front and back doors, a coin meter, a "tilt" switch, and an extended-play timer.

Manufacturer   Sega of America, 25550 Santa Fe Avenue, Redondo Beach, CA 90278.

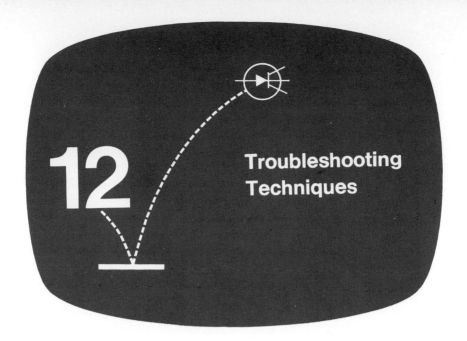

12.1 BASIC TROUBLESHOOTING TECHNIQUES

A sound, logical, and methodical approach is absolutely essential for all electronics troubleshooting. The haphazard probing, testing, and parts replacement of the screwdriver mechanic just won't work with any of the electronic games The importance of planning the troubleshooting and following a logical technique cannot be emphasized enough. Four basic troubleshooting techniques have proved highly successful in all areas of electronics, and their application to electronic games is the subject of this chapter. Most experienced troubleshooters are already using some of the techniques described here, but the full benefit of these techniques can only be obtained by applying the right technique at the right time. The *symptom-function* technique can be considered the first of three or four steps in a complete troubleshooting routine. First, we localize the defect to a subassembly; then, by using the *signal-tracing* method, we further localize the defect to one or several components. As a third step, we can find the defective component by the *voltage and resistance* technique. Verification of the defect and ultimate repair involve the *substitution* method.

Ninety-five percent of all defects in electronic games and in most other electronic devices can be located by the application of these four techniques. The remaining 5 percent are either intermittent or so rare that a very special approach must be taken. These problems are covered at the end of the chapter.

Symptom-Function Technique The scientific method of investigation relies on a connection between cause and effect. In troubleshooting electronic games, the cause is a defect within the game, and the effect is an unsatisfactory display, sound, or control action. Here is an example of the symptom-function technique. The TV picture looks normal when TV stations are received but appears very noisy and weak when the antenna switch is set to the "game" position. All game patterns and functions are OK, but, regardless of which game is tried, the pictures are always weak and noisy and they have a tendency to lose synchronization. Figure 12.1 is a block diagram of a typical TV game. It is clear from the symptom observed that the TV set, the tuner, and the antenna itself are OK. The controls, the logic, the display circuits, and the power supply appear to be functioning correctly according to the display on the TV screen. Clearly, the trouble is most likely to be somewhere in the RF oscillator and modulator, in the antenna switch, or in the connection between the

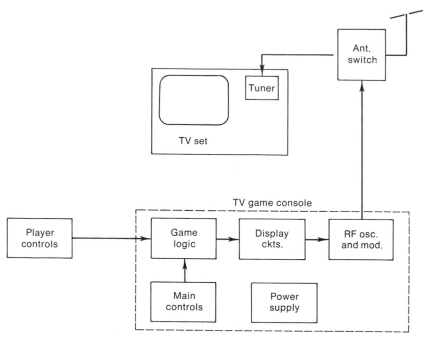

Figure 12.1 TV game block diagram.

oscillator and the antenna switch. Checking the output of the RF oscillator is not a simple matter, but the continuity of the coax cable from the RF oscillator to the antenna switch can be checked by a simple ohmmeter test. In this example, a poor ground on the coaxial connector at the TV game output caused the particular defect.

The symptom-function technique, in short, depends largely on understanding the major functions of the electronic game and how they affect what we can see and hear. For most troubleshooting with this technique, we don't even need test equipment. This trouble-shooting technique does not always find the defective part itself but helps localize the defect to a particular subassembly.

Signal Tracing   This technique usually involves some electronic test equipment and consists of tracing a signal through circuits where the defect is most likely to be located. A good example of the signal-tracing technique would be the case of a microprocessor-controlled TV game in which cartridge-operated games function well but the resident games do not work at all. The symptom-function technique tells us that the trouble must be in the resident game circuits since the controls, the microprocessor, the display circuits, and all the other functions seem to operate correctly. Signal tracing with the oscilloscope to check all of the signals going to and from the resident game ROM determines that the "read" signal does not reach the correct pin of the resident game ROM. The oscilloscope shows that the proper "read" command is present at the microprocessor but is absent at the ROM. We conclude from this that there is an open circuit between these two points. Visual inspection reveals that a crack in the conductive path of the PC board is present.

Signal tracing can take many different forms, and in some instances it is necessary to inject a test signal and then trace it through the system, usually with the oscilloscope. For microprocessor-controlled games and for those using extensive logic circuits, the signal-tracing method may require special logic probes or even the powerful, new logic analyzer. More will be said about this approach in Sec. 12.3.

Voltage-Resistance Technique   This method invariably requires a volt-ohm milliammeter (VOM) or its more sophisticated equivalent, the digital multimeter (DMM). One simple way of using the voltage-resistance technique is to measure all B-plus and test point voltages on the PC board to which the defect has been isolated. The same approach can be taken by measuring all resistances of the suspected circuit with the power turned off. Very often it is possible to locate open or short circuits in this manner. Leaky capacitors can also be found quickly by use of this method.

The use of the voltage-resistance technique can be illustrated by the example described earlier for the symptom-function technique (see Fig. 12.1). We can determine that the defect lies between the RF oscillator and the TV tuner by simply measuring the resistances of the RF cable and of the connectors and grounds between the RF oscillator and the antenna switch. The bad ground assumed to be the defect in the earlier example would be found in this way. If we suspect that the RF oscillator output is low, we can use the voltage-resistance technique to check the voltage on all dc points in this circuit. Low B-plus voltage, possibly due to a leaky bypass capacitor, would result in low oscillator output and, probably, the wrong frequency.

The voltage-resistance technique is most useful when the defect has already been localized to a relatively small circuit area. If an entire section or the whole game is inoperative, the defect is obviously due to power supply problems and we will use the voltage-resistance technique immediately.

Substitution Substituting a component known to be good for one suspected of being defective is a method obviously limited to the case where the trouble has been isolated to a few components. In some electronic equipment, plug-in PC boards permit substitution of entire circuit sections, but this is not usually the case in electronic games. Substituting other ICs is often the only way to determine that a suspected IC is defective.

Most electronic games do not use plug-in ICs, and, as everyone knows who has tried it, unsoldering and resoldering a 14- or 22-pin IC is quite a delicate and difficult task, even if you have all of the proper tools. Later in this chapter we shall discuss a variation of the substitution technique which permits us to compare the operation of two ICs without actually replacing the suspected one.

12.2 SYMPTOM-FUNCTION TECHNIQUE FOR ELECTRONIC GAMES

While it is not possible to present all of the applications of this technique, some typical uses for the three basic types of electronic games are described below. The key to successful use of the system-function technique lies in understanding how each function of the game affects the display or its accompanying sound. A few minutes spent in logical analysis, sometimes with the aid of pencil and paper, will save hours of tedious troubleshooting.

Typical Uses in Board Games We know from Chaps. 9 and 11 that board games are usually based on a hand-held device similar to a pocket calculator. The symptoms are displayed on numerical LEDs and are somehow related to the functions controlled by the push-button keyboard. Figure 12.2 shows a simple symptom-function chart for a calculator-based game like the Texas Instruments Calculator Squares or Checkout. Many of the symptoms listed in this chart and many of the functions likely to be defective apply also to pocket calculators or other board games. When the symptom consists of dark or dim displays or of inoperative player controls, this is almost invariably due to a defect in the battery, the power supply, or in the B-plus filter circuits. Similarly, when one display digit remains dark, there is a defect either in that particular display or its driver circuit, or else there is a loss of B-plus to that digit. When one push button does not work, a poor contact or open lead is obviously the trouble. A whole row or column of keyboard switches can only fail in those devices where a mechanical switch assembly is used with horizontal

Symptoms	Functions likely to be defective
1. Display dark or dim; player controls have no effect.	Battery, power supply, B+ filter
2. One display digit is dark.	B+ to that digit missing, driver IC defective, display defective
3. One pushbutton doesn't work.	Poor contact, open lead
4. One row or column of keyboard switches doesn't work.	Mech. switch assembly, open lead
5. One function (+, −, ×, %) doesn't work.	Open lead, no contact, or logic defect
6. None of the functions (+, −, ×, %) work.	Defective clock circuit, logic defect
7. Random errors on all functions.	Major logic defect
8. Constant error on some functions.	Minor logic defect
9. Decimal point missing	Defect in decimal logic
10. Answers increase until all digits are 9s.	Loss of reset signal

Figure 12.2 Symptom-functions for a calculator-based game.

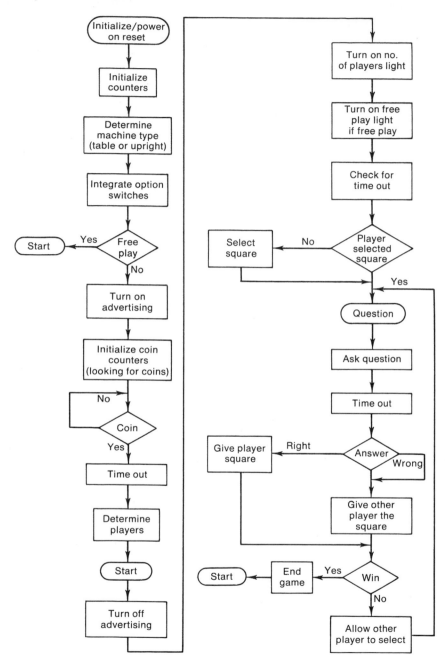

Figure 12.4 Program flowchart for TIC TAC QUIZ (Sega).

tom-function technique is to decide whether the defect is connected with the operation of the TV set itself or whether it is due to the game. This is relatively simple in most cases since we can demonstrate TV-set operation from broadcast stations and then show the operation with the TV game separately. If the same defect, such as poor horizontal synchronization, is present in both modes of operation, it is logical to assume that the defect is in the TV set and not in the game. Conversely, if vertical rolling occurs only when the TV game is connected, we must believe that the defect is due to a poor vertical synchronization signal generated by the TV game. In some situations it is necessary to turn off the TV game, disconnect the antenna switch, and connect the TV set directly to the antenna to demonstrate beyond any doubt where the defect originates. This kind of problem usually occurs when TV stations are received poorly or when the RF signal generated by the TV game is close to and interfering with a local station.

Once the trouble has been isolated to the game itself, we can consider each of the game functions, listed in Fig. 12.5, as potential troublespots. Some of the symptoms that we will observe can easily be matched to this list. If one of the player controls is defective, it obviously will not work properly with the game. Similarly, if the vertical, horizontal, or color sync circuits are not working properly, the result will be incorrect vertical, horizontal, or color synchronization at the TV receiver—defects which will occur only when the game is connected and not when broadcasts are received. Some games have specific circuits which act as character generators, score counters, motion generators, and contact detectors. Clearly, when one of these functions is defective, the symptoms can easily be related to it. If, for example, the scoring display does not work but alphanumeric characters are displayed, the scoring counters are defective. If the game characters appear but cannot move, this must be due either to the player controls or the motion-generating circuits.

One way to apply the symptom-function technique to TV games is to observe the symptoms and then check the list of TV game functions shown in Fig. 12.5 to see which functions, if defective, could result in the observed symptoms. In some instances, several different functions can account for a particular symptom. Loss of the color sync signal right at the crystal oscillator, for example, may mean that the horizontal and vertical synchronizing signals cannot be formed. In that event, it is not possible to obtain any sort of picture on the TV set. It often helps if we can look at a block or circuit diagram of the TV game while trying to apply the symptom-function technique.

Power (batteries, ac adapter, switches, and fuses)

Game selection (resident, cartridge)

Cartridge (plug-in contacts)

Time selection

Option selection

Player controls (cables and connectors)

Antenna switch (power switch)

RF oscillator (frequency, output power)

Modulator

Vertical sync generator

Horizontal sync generator

Color sync burst circuits

Color phase gating

Character generator

Score counters

Motion generator

Contact detector

Video combiner

Control logic or microprocessor

Clock circuits

Reset circuits

Audio circuits

Figure 12.5   TV game functions.

12.3   SIGNAL-TRACING TECHNIQUES FOR ELECTRONIC GAMES

The signal-tracing method can be applied either by injecting a test signal and following it through the circuit or by tracing a signal that is already available in the circuit. One simple example of how this method is used in electronic games is illustrated in Fig. 12.6 for the vertical stripe generator described in Chap. 3 and shown in Fig. 3.4. Assume that the symptom-function technique has shown that the ball in Tennis or Hockey is a horizontal stripe instead of a dot. Since we know that the function that makes a dot out of a horizontal stripe is the vertical stripe generator, we focus our attention on that circuit. We know from Chap. 3 that the horizontal synchronizing pulse is applied as trigger to the first one-shot. By connecting the oscilloscope probe to test point 1, we can check to make sure that a trigger signal appears. Assume for the moment that we can see the horizontal synchronizing pulse at test point 1. We next move the oscilloscope probe to test point 2, where we should see the output of the one-shot. If we do not see this output at that point, we know the defect is probably in the one-shot, a portion of an IC. We can trace the various signals, as they are described in Fig. 3.4, through each of the test points in Fig. 12.6. Whenever a signal is missing or greatly reduced in amplitude, we know that the defect is probably in the preceding circuit.

Often we can also determine what kind of defect exists by analyzing the waveform. The waveform must be quite different at point 3 than at point 2. Figure 3.4 illustrates the effect of differentiation. If one of the resistors or capacitors of the differentiating circuit is open or shorted, the correct waveform will not appear. Finally, we will check with the oscilloscope that the waveforms at points 4 and 5 appear added at point 6.

When the signal is missing at the output of one circuit, it is not always safe to assume that the defect is definitely in the preceding circuit. It often happens that the input to the next stage is shorted, causing such a bad impedance match that the signal is lost. For that reason it is important to measure the impedance (a simple ohmmeter test for most ICs) before we can be sure where the defect really is. We have assumed that the oscilloscope probe will have an input impedance of at least 1 MΩ. This is quite satisfactory for all logic ICs but may become a problem in some high-impedance circuits or in RF oscillators, where the capacity of the test probe can shift the frequency of the oscillator.

When signal tracing uses an injected signal, some source of signal, a pulse generator or logic analyzer, must be connected to the circuit

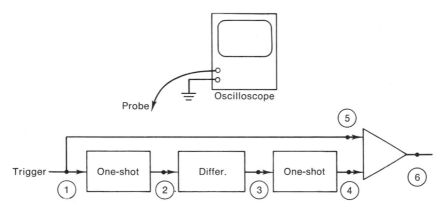

Figure 12.6 Signal tracing the vertical-stripe generator.

under test. For this application, impedance matching is extremely important in order to obtain correct test results. Be sure to check the output impedance of any signal or pulse generator and then compare it with the input impedance of the circuit to which it is to be connected. When you connect a very-high-impedance source to a low-input impedance, this may tend to load down the source and result in incorrect signal amplitudes. Similarly, when you connect a very-low-impedance signal generator output to a high-input impedance, the signal generator will load down the circuit under test. The best impedance match is obtained when both impedances are the same value.

Oscilloscope Signal Tracing   Next to proper impedance matching, the correct synchronization is most important if we want to see the signal under test. In the example of Fig. 12.6, where the trigger signal is at the horizontal sweep rate, 15.75 kHz, the oscilloscope must be synchronized to at least twice that frequency in order to show us two horizontal sync pulses. Oscilloscopes can be synchronized, internally by the signal they receive, in which case the first pulse is usually not fully visible. They can also be synchronized to an external signal, such as the output of the sync generator in the TV game logic. Wherever convenient, external sync will provide simpler troubleshooting.

In TV games the signal amplitudes, except for the RF oscillator, range between 2 and 8 V. The oscilloscope's vertical input gain must be adjusted to present the proper picture. Most oscilloscopes have an internal calibrator which permits us to make a good amplitude measurement of the observed signal.

When properly used, signal tracing with the oscilloscope permits us to not only confirm the presence of signals but also determine their waveform, a feature that is particularly important when differentiation, sawtooth-waveform, and other nondigital signals are present. When the circuits operate strictly in the digital mode, all signals are either zeros or ones, and the oscilloscope loses some of its effectiveness. In troubleshooting microprocessors, for example, we want to observe the data input and output, and this cannot be done as effectively with a simple oscilloscope as with a logic analyzer. The key difference is that with a logic analyzer the oscilloscope output can show many different channels simultaneously and the output can be in the form of zeros or ones, as described below. An oscilloscope capable of multitrace displays can be quite helpful, however, even without the aid of a logic analyzer.

Using Logic Probes For signal tracing in digital circuits, a simple logic probe is often very useful. The basic circuit for such a device is shown in Fig. 12.7 and consists of two inverter amplifiers, each driving an LED indicator. If the test leads are connected to a zero voltage, a voltage close to the ground potential, the LED labeled "0" will light up and the other one will remain dark. If the voltage reaches the minimum triggering level of the amplifier, the LED labeled "1" will light up and the other LED will remain dark. If the signal sensed by the test leads changes faster than about 20 times per second, i.e., if it is a square wave of more than 20 Hz in frequency, then both LEDs will be illuminated. Clearly, this relatively simple circuit can be quite useful for checking the presence or absence of all sorts of digital signals.

A variety of commercial logic probes are available for different logic families or different frequencies. Some even have a numerical indication like the test probe shown in Fig. 12.8. This unit obtains its V_{cc} from a terminal in the circuit under test. It will indicate a 0 logic level when the voltage is less than 30 percent and a 1 logic level when the voltage is more than 70 percent of V_{cc}. Any voltage between 30 and 70 percent results in no display at all. Its input impedance is greater than 2.7 MΩ, more than ample to prevent circuit loading in any kind of logic family. One of the options available with this probe is a gating feature which allows input from two channels so that the pulse indicator displays only when both inputs are in coincidence. Another option provides memory or stretch modes, the ability to capture high-speed pulse trains, and "latching," as well as the ability to detect individual high-speed pulses.

Another popular type of logic probe is able to test an entire IC. As

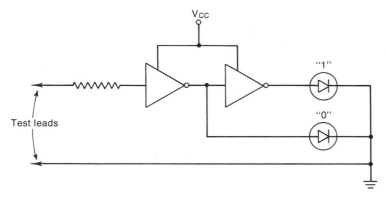

Figure 12.7 Basic logic-probe circuit.

illustrated in Fig. 12.9, the probe itself consists of a clothespin-type device in which the smaller end is clamped to the pins of a DIP IC. The larger end consists of 16 or more LEDs, each one corresponding to a pin on the IC under test. A separate power supply is located in the control box, which also contains a selective trigger threshhold to match the precise characteristics of the logic family under test. In order to use this type of logic probe effectively, we must know what signals are supposed to be present at which pin of the IC under test. It often helps to draw a separate diagram showing the expected signals and waveforms and their relationships. With this arrangement it is possible to observe gate inputs rising and falling, and pulses going from one circuit to another. Flip-flops may be seen changing states, and decoders and encoders can be seen accepting and recording information. Of course, we can observe changing signals only if their rate of change is not faster than the resolution capability of the human eye, i.e., usually less than 20 times per second.

Word Generators and Logic Analyzers These rather complex and expensive pieces of test equipment are usually found only in service departments that specialize in digital equipment and computer

Figure 12.8 Logic probe (Kurz-Kasch, Inc.).

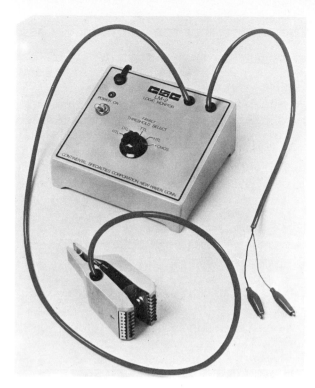

Figure 12.9 Logic monitor (Continental Specialties Corp.).

troubleshooting. Word generators are essentially pulse generators which are able to deliver digital signals corresponding to one or more bytes, complete words, or a series of words. Logic analyzers are usually capable of accepting 16 or more simultaneous inputs and often contain their own word generators. Many logic analyzers can be programmed to apply specific test words or word groups to equipment and then analyze the simultaneous response of many different outputs. In effect, a logic analyzer performs the entire signal-tracing process of a complex digital circuit automatically. It is capable of detecting specific errors, stopping the input when errors occur in the output, and then pinpointing the logic section in which the error apparently originates. Logic analyzers often require sophisticated programming and are able to display the input and/or output signals in terms of 0 and 1. An oscilloscope usually provides the display. For a more detailed description of the application of logic analyzers, we refer the reader to *Complete Guide to Digital Test Equipment* by Walter H. Buchsbaum, Prentice-Hall, 1977.

12.4 VOLTAGE-RESISTANCE TECHNIQUE FOR ELECTRONIC GAMES

As indicated at the beginning of this chapter, this technique is most useful in pinpointing a defective component once the defect has been localized to a specific circuit. Voltage measurements are particularly effective in troubleshooting power supply defects. When measuring battery voltage and the output voltage of AC adaptors, voltage regulators, and RC decoupling networks, it is important to remember that the voltage may vary as the circuit load varies. Batteries may appear to supply adequate voltage when they are removed from the circuit but may show a considerable voltage drop when the electronic game is drawing maximum current. The same applies to the electronic power supply and its various outputs. Temperature effects often change the current drastically, a good reason to measure voltage both under cold and warm-up conditions. A defective voltage-regulator IC may show up as defective only after the game has been on for a while and the IC has been allowed to heat up.

The ohmmeter measures resistance and is useful to check not only resistors but also capacitors, diodes, transistors, and even, though to a limited extent, ICs. Where potentiometers are used, either as player controls or as adjustments in the game circuits, the ohmmeter measurement should be made with the potentiometer varied over its entire range.

Capacitors that are larger than 1.0 mF can be tested by first shorting the capacitor and then connecting it across the ohmmeter, which should be set to one of the higher resistance scales. As the capacitor is charged, the ohmmeter reading should go from near zero to almost open circuit. If the capacitor is either shorted or open, the ohmmeter will indicate this. If the capacitor is leaky, the ohmmeter will show little charging effect and the final resistance reading will be low.

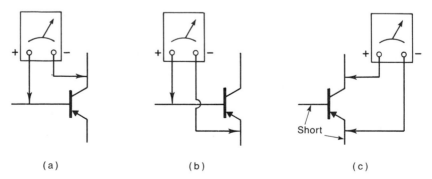

(a)   (b)   (c)

Figure 12.10 Ohmmeter tests of transistors.

Diodes are tested by measuring their forward and backward resistance, and, as a simple rule of thumb, the ratio between the two should be at least 10:1. If it is not, the diode is defective.

Transistors can be represented as two-diode devices and can be tested by that same principle. Three basic tests are illustrated in Fig. 12.10. One diode test is shown in Fig. 12.10*a*, the ohmmeter being applied between the base and collector with the polarities indicated. This should result in a high resistance reading. If the ohmmeter leads are now reversed, the resistance reading should be low. The ratio between these two readings should be at least 100:1 to indicate that this junction of the transistor is good. The base-emitter diode is tested by the circuit of Fig. 12.10*b*. With the polarities indicated here, the resistance reading should be high, and when the test leads are reversed, the reading should be low. Again, a 100:1 ratio of the two resistance readings indicates that the base-emitter diode is good. One measure of the overall operation of the transistor can be obtained by the simple test circuit of Fig. 12.10*c*. By shorting the base to the emitter, possibly with a clip lead, the resistance reading with the polarities indicated should be high. When the short circuit is moved from the emitter to connect the base to the collector, the resistance reading should be low. These three simple tests will quickly find open or shorted transistors.

Resistance tests are only of limited utility when we are dealing with LSI ICs. We can check the input and output resistance of specific leads but cannot in any way determine what any of the other logic elements are like. In many instances, however, the defect in the IC is due to an open circuit between the pin and the internal connection to the semiconductor strip. This type of defect can be picked up by the resistance technique. If we know the input and output impedance of all of the logic elements on a particular IC, we can check with the ohmmeter to make sure that they are correct. In general, ICs are better tested by different methods.

12.5 SUBSTITUTION TECHNIQUE IN ELECTRONIC GAMES

Substituting a good part for a suspected part is one sure way of finding out if we have really located the trouble. Unfortunately, the substitution technique has only limited application in electronic games because relatively few components can be substituted easily, quickly, and inexpensively. Depending on what we have concluded from the application of the symptom-function technique, we may decide to substitute new batteries, laboratory power supplies, fuses, cables, etc. If a particular electronic game operates erratically with its AC adaptor but performs perfectly well when connected to a well-regulated laboratory power supply, chances are there is some component in the AC adaptor power supply which is marginal. If we find that one of the player controls does not operate correctly, we may be able to interchange controls by interchanging connectors and cables. This will help us to localize the defect to the control itself or, possibly, to the connector. Capacitors, particularly those used as B-plus filters, can be easily substituted by disconnecting one side of the capacitor and connecting one known to be good.

Unfortunately, it is not as simple to substitute ICs if they are soldered into the PC board. A variety of special tools are now on the market which are specifically designed for removing ICs from a PC board with minimum damage to the IC and to the PC board itself. Even with the right tools, however, removing an IC and replacing it on a PC board is still laborious and time-consuming. One method of testing ICs in the circuit, without removing them, is a comparison testing technique such as the one available with the Fluke Trendar equipment. This device includes a clothespin-type clamp similar to the one shown in Fig. 12.9, which connects to the IC under test by means of spring pressure. A plug-in socket on the unit holds a duplicate IC known to be good. A set of LED indicators, one for each pin, shows the difference between the logic states of each pin on the unit under test and the one known to be good. The substitute IC receives the same input signals as the suspected unit, and its output signals are presumably correct. If all of the output signals are the same on both ICs, it must be assumed that the unit under test is good. This approach works well as long as none of the input gates are shorted to ground, in which case some of the gates would simply not be tested. If the signals applied to the IC under test are the wrong signals, the test, of course, is not very helpful. When using this substitution or comparison technique, it is best to start with the one IC that we are sure has the correct signals on all inputs and outputs. This comparison method is quite helpful in coin-operated games where large numbers of standard ICs are used.

12.6 MOST FREQUENT DEFECTS IN ELECTRONIC GAMES

Electronic equipment is quite reliable by itself but depends, to a great extent, on such mechanical portions as connectors, switches, cables, etc. The vast majority of defects originate in these mechanical parts. It can be argued that any kind of defect in electronic equipment, even a defect in the IC itself, is mechanical in nature since it means a change in the mechanical structure of the electronic circuits. For our purposes, however, we will consider mechanical defects to be those which we can clearly see or check with an ohmmeter. When we use the symptom-function technique to isolate a defect to a specific functional area, we should always consider open and short circuits as well as intermittent contacts in all mechanical parts such as switches, connectors, and cables. In addition to these mechanical trouble sources, the following listing of frequently found defects will help the troubleshooter to work with electronic games of all types.

Display Defects Defects in LEDs or other numerical displays are quite rare. Dim individual segments or a dead LED are obvious defects which can only be repaired by substituting a new unit. Where the display is a TV set or a monitor, the following six basic types of defect are most frequent, in the order of their listing.

1. *Horizontal oscillator and flyback circuit.* Defects in this section frequently result in total loss of the TV raster. When the horizontal oscillator does not work properly, it does not supply the flyback pulses and this, in turn, results in loss of the high voltage required for the second anode or ultor of the picture tube. Whenever the screen is dark, check to see that the filaments of the picture tube are illuminated, and then you can assume that the defect is in the horizontal oscillator and flyback section. Occasionally a defect is found in the high-voltage section itself.

2. *Vertical sweep.* Defects in this section frequently show up either as a single horizontal line or as vertical nonlinearity. When you observe a single horizontal line instead of the normal raster, the vertical sweep signal is probably missing from the deflection yoke. The most likely trouble source is the vertical oscillator itself. When the pictures appear compressed at the top or expanded at the bottom, or vice versa, the most likely defect is a misadjustment of the vertical linearity and height controls. Similarly, if the picture does not fill the screen at the top or bottom, these controls are either misadjusted or the circuits connected to them are defective. Another occasional defect connected with the vertical sweep section is loss of vertical synchronization. This is apparent when the picture seems to roll through the screen in a vertical direction. The sync circuits may be defective or, very likely, the sync separator section of the TV monitor or receiver is attenuating the vertical synchronizing signal. Occasionally, when these circuits operate marginally, TV pictures transmitted over

the air may synchronize better than those originating in a TV game. The vertical synchronizing signal generated by the TV game should be checked before suspecting the sync separator section.

3. *TV Tuner Contacts.* Mechanical channel selection is used in the vast majority of home TV receivers, and the contacts required to accomplish this often wear and become intermittent. When a channel is not normally used, the contacts for that channel may become corroded so that they operate only intermittently when a TV game is connected and displayed. If you have to jiggle the channel-selector switch in order to get the best picture and sound, you know that the tuner contacts need cleaning and tightening. Another defect of the channel-selector section can be due to misadjustment of the internal fine tuning. This is particularly true when you first connect the set to the game and tune for channel 2, 3, or 4, which have never been previously used. It may be necessary to fine-tune for this channel by means of the internal alignment screws.

4. *Interference.* The problem of interference with TV reception can be quite troublesome, and its solution goes beyond the scope of this book. When a TV set is connected to an electronic game, most interfering signals are shut out by the antenna switch. In some rare cases, however, interference can be picked up by the TV game itself and will then appear on the screen. This type of interference is invariably due to outside sources like automobile or truck ignition systems, CB or amateur radios, diathermy (heat-sealing) machines, etc. We can often determine the source of the interference by observing its duration and the time when it occurs. If you live near a doctor's office and receive interference only when the doctor has office hours, chances are it is due to the diathermy machine or some other equipment in the office. Amateur and CB radio interference always occurs in short bursts, corresponding to the transmissions of the offending operator. Automobile or truck ignition interference can usually be correlated with the engine noise itself. The first approach in such situations is to contact the owner of the interfering device and point out the FCC-imposed obligation not to interfere.

5. *Control Defects:* Since player controls often receive fairly rough handling, they are more likely to become defective than the main console controls. Some of the defects will be quite obvious. If someone spills coffee into a hand-held joystick control or into the main console, we can expect poor and intermittent contact to result. When the cable to the player control is frayed, nicked, or badly bruised, defective connections are likely to result. The spot at which controls most frequently become defective is at the connectors. TV game owners as well as those using the coin-operated games tend to be careless with the player controls, the cables, and the connections. We have seen many instances of connectors where pins are bent or broken or where pieces of metal have become stuck in the connector and have shorted out pins. In summary, almost all of the control defects are due to mechanical wear and tear.

6. *Logic Defects:* While anything can happen to the delicate and sensitive ICs mounted on a PC board, defective connectors, particularly PC board edge connectors, are the most frequent trouble source. Next in frequency of occurrence are defects in the PC board itself. Usually these are due to cracks in the conductors, to open circuits, or to short-circuits between conductors. This latter type of defect is fairly rare when the PC boards are coated with an insulating material, but "bare" PC boards can easily develop short circuits. Iron filings, pieces of solder, or tiny pieces of wire from cut-off components have a way of wedging themselves in between adjacent conductors and causing short-circuits. Defects in the IC pins or in through-plated holes on the PC board are fairly rare, but if they occur, hairline breaks or cold solder joints are the most likely trouble. A defect in the IC itself is the least likely of the troubles we can look forward to when we have isolated a defect to the logic section itself.

12.7 INTERMITTENT AND HARD-TO-FIND DEFECTS

The reader who has a fair amount of experience in troubleshooting electronic equipment will remember instances where all of the techniques, all of the tests, all of the repairs and substitutions, have failed to cure the trouble. Just as frustrating as these hard-to-find defects are intermittent defects. In this case the defect occurs only at certain times and then disappears. When everything else has failed, we recommend the following last-resort method.

Arrange to heat the equipment that contains the hard-to-find or intermittent defect up to the temperature limit of its most sensitive component, usually the ICs. Commercial grade ICs can usually withstand temperatures up to 45°C. When this temperature is reached, carefully repeat the tests you have previously performed. Write down the results of each test. When all measurements are done and the equipment is still working correctly, attempt to lower the temperature as quickly as possible. This can be done by blowing cold air on it with a fan or blower, or by using one of the "freezer" spray cans. Most ICs are rated to operate satisfactorily at 0°C, and this temperature can usually be achieved without too much trouble. Repeat this entire test procedure and again write down the results of every test. In the course of this work you may find that some components have developed specific defects. Replace them and repeat the test procedure. You have, in theory at least, found the defective or marginal component.

If the hot and cold temperature cycling does not result in locating the true defect, you might try mechanical vibration—shaking or jiggling the equipment for 10 or 15 minutes at a stretch—alternated with hot and cold temperature cycling. The theory behind this method is that the intermittent or hard-to-find defect is due to some marginal component which is likely to fail under the stresses of heat and/or mechanical vibration. From time to time it is a good idea to interrupt the temperature cycles and carefully go over the suspected circuitry with detailed voltage, frequency, amplitude, waveform, and other measurements, which are compared, step-by-step, with the manufacturer's technical data. This method is time-consuming, but eventually the defective part will be located.

Appendix

The following is a list of the subroutines used with the Blackjack
game program given in Chapter 10.

Hexadecimal code			Mnemonic		
Address	Instruction	Label	Instruction		Comment
1020	C5	GEN CARD:	PUSH	B	Save selected card.
21	CD0001		CALL	OUTLINE	Generate card outline.
24	014100		LXI	B,#0041	Correct screen position to
27	09		DAD	B	start suit display.
28	C1		POP	B	
29	CD6010		CALL	SUIT SELECT	Uses B to form suit address.
2C	C5		PUSH	B	
2D	CD3101		CALL	PATTERN DISP	Final screen address in DE.
30	EB		XCHG		
31	C1		POP	B	
32	CD8010		CALL	POINT SELECT	Uses B to form point address.
35	2B		DCX	H	
36	2B		DCX	H	
37	C5		PUSH	B	
38	CD3101		CALL	PATTERN DISP	
3B	C1		POP	B	
3C	C9		RET		
1060	C5	SUIT SELECT:	PUSH	B	Most significant hex in B
61	E5		PUSH	H	determines suit.
62	78		MOV	A,B	*MSH Suit Suit address*
63	E6F0		ANI	#F0	01 heart 0151
65	0F		RRC		02 spade 015D
66	0F		RRC		03 diamond 0169
67	0F		RRC		04 club 0175
68	0F		RRC		

Figure A-1   Blackjack subroutines.

Hexadecimal code			Mnemonic		
Address	Instruction	Label		Instruction	Comment
1069	214501		LXI	H,#0145	Suit address base number.
6C	110C00		LXI	D,#000C	Suit address movement number.
6F	19	LOOP:	DAD	D	
70	3D		DCR	A	Modify address to correspond
71	C26F10		JNZ	LOOP	to particular suit.
74	EB		XCHG		
75	E1		POP	H	
76	C1		POP	B	
77	C9		RET		
		POINT			
1080	C5	SELECT:	PUSH	B	Pattern for ace at 0200, two
81	E5		PUSH	H	at 020C, three at 0218, etc.
82	78		MOV	A,B	
83	E60F		ANI	#0F	Strip off point valve.
85	21F401		LXI	H,#01F4	Initialize point address base number.
88	110C00		LXI	D,#000C	Point address increment number.
8B	19	LOOP:	DAD	D	Modify address to correspond
8C	3D		DCR	A	to pattern for selected point.
8D	C28B10		JNZ	LOOP	
90	EB		XCHG		
91	E1		POP	H	
92	C1		POP	B	
93	C9		RET		
0100	3E1B	OUTLINE:	MVI	A,#1B	Top line of card outline.
02	160B		MVI	D,#0B	Repeat counter.
0104	77	LOOP2:	MOV	M,A	
05	23		INX	H	
06	15		DCR	D	
07	C30401		JNZ	LOOP2	
0A	3E07		MVI	A,#07	Right side of card outline.
0C	014000		LXI	B,#0040	
0F	1606		MVI	D,#06	
11	77	LOOP3:	MOV	M,A	
12	09		DAD	B	Add line number to move.
13	15		DCR	D	
14	C21101		JNZ	LOOP3	
17	2B		DCX	H	Bottom line.
18	01C0FF		LXI	B,#FFC0	Subtract line number (2s complement).
1B	09		DAD	B	
1C	3E36		MVI	A,#36	
1E	1608		MVI	D,#08	
20	77	LOOP4:	MOV	M,A	
21	2B		DCX	H	
22	15		DCR	D	
23	C22001		JNZ	LOOP4	
26	3E38		MVI	A,#38	Left line
28	1606		MVI	D,06	
2A	77	LOOP5:	MOV	M,A	
2B	09		DAD	B	

Figure A-1 (Continued)

Hexadecimal code		Mnemonic			
Address	Instruction	Label		Instruction	Comment
2C	15		DCR	D	
2D	C22A01		JNZ	LOOP5	
30	C9		RET		
0131	23	PATTERN DISP	INX	H	Correct screen address.
32	23		INX	H	
33	EB		XCHG	D	
34	013C00		LXI	B,#003C	Next line increment.
37	C5		PUSH	B	Save line increment.
38	0603		MVI	B,#03	
3A	0E04	NEW LINE:	MVI	C,#04	
3C	7E	NEX GRAPHIC:	MOV	A,M	Put graphic in A.
3D	23		INX	H	Increment graphic address
3E	EB		XCHG		pointer.
3F	77		MOV	M,A	Put graphic on screen.
40	23		INX	H	
41	EB		XCHG		
42	0D		DCR	C	
43	C23C01		JNZ	NEX GRAPHIC	
46	E3	LINE CHECK:	XTHL		Any more lines to display.
47	EB		XCHG		
48	19		DAD	D	
49	EB		XCHG		
4A	E3		XTHL		
4B	05		DCR	B	
4C	C23A01		JNZ	NEW LINE	
4F	C1		POP	B	
50	C9		RET		
1040	210011	FORM DECK:	LXI	H,#1100	Initialize deck location.
1043	1E10		MVI	E,#10	Suit pointer.
45	1601	LOOP 6:	MVI	D,#01	Face value pointer.
47	7B	LOOP 7:	MOV	A,E	
48	82		ADD	D	
49	77		MOV	M,A	
4A	2C		INR	L	Next location
4B	14		INR	D	Next card
4C	7A		MOV	A,D	
4D	FE0E		CPI	#0E	Any more cards in suit?
4F	C24710		JNZ	LOOP7	
52	7B		MOV	A,E	
53	C610		ADI	#10	⎫ Change to next suit.
55	5F		MOV	E,A	⎭
56	FE50		CPI	#50	Any more suits?
58	C8		RZ		
59	C34510		JMP	LOOP6	
1F20	46	PACK DECK:	MOV	B,M	Save selected card.
21	23	PACK MORE:	INX	H	⎫
22	5E		MOV	E,M	⎬ Push card beneath into
23	2B		DCX	H	⎪ vacated space.
24	73		MOV	M,E	⎭
25	23		INX	H	⎫
26	79		MOV	A,C	⎬ Any more cards
27	BD		CMP	L	⎪ to pack?
28	C2211F		JNZ	PACK MORE	⎭

Figure A-1 (Continued)

Hexadecimal code		Mnemonic			
Address	Instruction	Label	Instruction		Comment
1F2B	0D		DCR	C	
2C	C9		RET		
1F40	110088	MESSAGE:	LXI	D,#8800	Screen start position.
43	7E	NEX CHAR:	MOV	A,M	
	C				
44	FE0		CPI	#C0	Check for end of message—
46	C8		RZ		the "@" symbol.
47	EB		XCHG		
48	77		MOV	M,A	
49	23		INX	H	
4A	13		INX	D	
4B	EB		XCHG		
4C	C3431F		JMP	NEX CHAR	
					Places character struck
1F00	CD101F	INPUT:	CALL	KBD IN	on KBD into A.
03	FED3		CPI	#D3	Check for "S."
			DEALER		
05	CA801E		JZ	CARDS	
08	33		INX	SP	} Get RANDOM address
09	33		INX	SP	} off stack so can return
0A	C9		RET		to proper point in MAIN.
1F10	DB89	KBD IN:	IN	#89	}
12	E601		ANI	#01	} Check for key press
14	C2101F		JNZ	KBD IN	} signal.
17	DB88		IN	#88	
19	F680		ORI	#80	
1B	C9		RET		
		RANDOM			
1F50	0E33	INIT:	MVI	C,#33	Initialize deck size to 52
52	41	RANDOM:	MOV	B,C	cards.
53	DB89	LOOP:	IN	#89	Check if key struck.
55	E601		ANI	#01	
57	CC001F		CZ	INPUT	} Loops generating random
5A	05		DCR	B	} numbers from 1 to current
5B	C2531F		JNZ	LOOP	} deck size until key is
5E	C3521F		JMP	RANDOM	} struck.
1F63	21D188	BET:	LXI	H,#88D1	Initialize to screen location
66	CD101F	NEX CHAR:	CALL	KBD IN	of bet display.
69	FEC5		CPI	#C5	Check if "E" struck.
6B	CA731F		JZ	STORE	
6E	77		MOV	M,A	Place entry on screen
6F	23		INX	H	if not an "E."
70	C3661F		JMP	NEX CHAR	
73	21D188	STORE:	LXI	H,#88D1	Load bet into bet register.
76	7E		MOV	A,M	
77	CD9000		CALL	PACK	} Packs first 2 characters
7A	23		INX	H	} together into single byte.
7B	7E		MOV	A,M	
7C	CD9000		CALL	PACK	}
7F	32A210		STA	#10A2	

Figure A-1 (Continued)

Hexadecimal code		Mnemonic			
Address	Instruction	Label		Instruction	Comment
82	23		INX	H	Packs next two characters.
83	7E		MOV	A,M	
84	CD9000		CALL	PACK	
87	23		INX	H	
1F88	7E		MOV	A,M	
89	CD9000		CALL	PACK	
8C	32A110		STA	#10A1	Store results.
8F	C9		RET		
0090	E6OF	PACK:	ANI	#0F	Convert ASCII to HEX.
92	4F		MOV	C,A	
93	78		MOV	A,B	B contains partial packed result.
94	E6OF		ANI	#0F	
96	07		RLC		
97	07		RLC		
98	07		RLC		
99	07		RLC		
					Packs in new character on right.
9A	81		ADD	C	
9B	47		MOV	B,A	Save result in B.
9C	C9		RET		
00C0	F5	UNPACK:	PUSH	PSW	Save word.
C1	0F		RRC		
C2	0F		RRC		Convert 4 MSBs to proper ASCII character
C3	0F		RRC		
C4	0F		RRC		
C5	E6OF		ANI	#0F	
C7	F6BO		ORI	#B0	
C9	77		MOV	M,A	Display it.
CA	23		INX	H	
00CB	F1		POP	PSW	Convert 4 LSBs to proper ASCII code.
CC	E60F		ANI	#0F	
CE	F6B0		ORI	#B0	
D0	77		MOV	M,A	Display it.
D1	23		INX	H	
D2	C9		RET		
1FA0	2AA110	CHECK BET:	LHLD	#10A1	Bring in bet.
A3	EB		XCHG		Store bet in DE.
A4	2AA310		LHLD	#10A3	Bring bankroll into HL.
A7	7C		MOV	A,H	If H > D, bet OK.
A8	BA		CMP	D	If D > H, bet NG.
A9	CAB01F		JZ	CHECK L	If D = H, check L and E.
AC	D0		RNC	BET OK	
AD	C3B51F		JMP	BET NG	
B0	7D	CHECK L:	MOV	A,L	
B1	BB		CMP	E	
B2	D0		RNC		Bet OK
B3	21B113	BET NG:	LXI	H,#13B1	Message: "I'M SORRY, YOU'RE
B6	CD401F		CALL	MESS	BET MORE MONEY THAN . . ."

Figure A-1 (Continued)

Hexadecimal code			Mnemonic		Comment
Address	Instruction	Label		Instruction	
B9	3AA410		LDA	#10A4	
BC	21D188		LXI	#88D1	Display bankroll as part
BF	CDC000		CALL	UNPACK	of previous message.
C2	3AA310		LDA	#10A3	
C5	CDC000		CALL	UNPACK	
C8	CD631F		CALL	BET	
CB	C9		RET		
1FD0	CD521F	CREATE:	CALL	RANDOM	Generate card number
D3	68	SUB CREATE:	MOV	L,B	Remove card from deck.
D4	2611		MVI	H,#11	
D6	CD201F		CALL	PACK DECK	
D9	78		MOV	A,B	Check for picture card—
DA	E60F		ANI	#0F	if picture card, replace
DC	FE0A		CPI	#0A	point value by 10.
DE	F8		RM		
DF	3E10		MVI	A,#10	
E1	C9		RET		
					Initialize to first byte in video
00F2	210088	CLR SCRN:	LXI	H,#8800	RAM.
F5	3E3F	LOOP 8	MVI	A,#3F	Put a blank in A.
F7	77		MOV	M,A	
F8	23		INX	H	
F9	7C		MOV	A,H	Check for end of screen.
FA	FE8C		CPI	#8C	
FC	C2F500		JNZ	LOOP 8	
FF	C9		RET		

Figure A-1   (Continued)

Index

Access time, 154
A/D (analog-to-digital) conversion, 200–202
AFC (automatic frequency control), 22
ALU (arithmetic/logic unit), 79–81
Anharmonic signals, 54
Antenna switch, 30, 49, 51
Application program, 103
Architecture, microprocessor, 81–84
   8080, 95–102
Aspect ratio, 14
Assembler, 84
Assembly language, 84, 104
Audio carrier, 12
Autorace (game), 286–288

Ball games, 228
Battle games, 229
BCD (binary-coded decimal) arithmetic, 123
Binary counter, 36
Bits, 79
Black level, 19
Blackjack (game), 262–281
  main routine description, 274–275
  memory map for, 269
  on-screen message generator, 272
  software description, 268
  subroutines used in: listing of, 325–330
    summary of, 266–267
  video card generator technique, 270
Blanking pulse, 18–20
Blue lateral magnet, 25
Board games, troubleshooting technique for, 307–308
Breakpoints for program debugging, 148–149
Brightness, 22
Burst gate (color), 40
Byte, 79

Calculator Squares (game), 238
Cassette recording:
  modified, 174
  unmodified, 172–174
Cathode-ray tube (CRT), 187–189
Channel F (game), 292–294
Character generator ROM, 189
Check Out (game), 238
Chess Challenger (game), 234, 285–286, 308
Code Name: Sector (game), 283–285
Coin-operated games, troubleshooting technique for, 308–309
Color display circuits, 43–45
Color phase modulator, 43
Color picture tubes, 22–25
Color reference burst circuit, 43
Color subcarrier, 25–28, 39–40, 43
Color TV signals, 25–28
Computer, 79
  (See also Microprocessors)
Computer program, 83
  (See also Instruction sets)
Control defects, 323
Convergence coil, 24
CPU (central processing unit), 79–81
Crystal-controlled clock, 38
Current-voltage waveforms, 15

Data recording (see Digital data recording)
Decoders, programmable, 36–38
Defects:
  intermittent and hard-to-find, 323–324
  logic, 323
  most frequent, 320–323
Definition (resolution), 17
Deflection yoke, 15, 24
Delta system, 24
Differentiating network, 20

Digital counters, 36–40
Digital data recording on magnetic tape, 167–178
  direct, 174–178
  on unmodified audio cassette recorder, 172–174
Digital video generator, 39, 40
Diode modulators, 31–32, 49, 51
Display circuits, 8–9, 33–52
  color, 43–45
  defects in, 321–323
  for fixed patterns, 33–40
  for moving patterns, 40–43
  special effects, 45–48
  troubleshooting, 50–52
  typical, 48–50
Display control, 39, 40
Dividers, digital, 36–40
DMA (direct memory access), 93–95
Draw poker (game), 235–236
Dynamic RAM, 156

EAROM (electrically alterable read-only memory), 153, 162
Editor program, 106
Educational games, 238–241
8080 microprocessor, 95–102
  instruction set, 112–134
    arithmetic group, 121–123
    branch group, 127–131
    data transfer group, 114–121
    description of, 112–114
    listing of, 98–101
    logical group, 123–127
    stack, I/O, and machine control group, 131–134
  interfacing to magnetic serial I/O devices, 182
  memory interfacing techniques, 165, 168
  system status signals, 102
Electron guns, 14, 22–25
EPROM (erasable programmable read-only memory), 153, 162

Federal Communications Commission (FCC) approval, 10, 30
Field, TV, 16–18, 36

Filters, 66
  output, 31
  voltage-controlled, 66, 67
Flip-flop, 36–37
Flowchart symbols, 108
Flowcharts, programming, 87, 107–112, 310
Flyback circuit, 321
Flyback transformers, 18
FONZ (game), 299–301, 308, 309
Football (game), 286–288
Fourier series components of waveform, 56–59
Frequency response, 19

Game block diagram, TV, 4–7, 29–33, 304
Games:
  of chance, 235–238
  educational, 238–241
  of mental skill, 232–235
  of physical skill, 227–232, 296–297
  war, 228–230, 236
  (See also specific game)
Gas-discharge devices, 9
Graphics ROM, 192–194
Guess the Number (game), 233–234

Hardware-software trade-offs, 199–211
  analog joystick interface, 199–203
  keyboard interface, 203–205
  LED multidigit display, 205–208
  software UART, 208–211
Hexadecimal number system, 83
High-frequency response, 19
Horizontal automatic frequency control (AFC), 22
Horizontal blanking period, 33
Horizontal blanking pulse, 20
Horizontal equalizing pulse, 20
Horizontal oscillator, 321
Horizontal sync pulses, 20–22, 314
Hue, 22, 43

IC (integrated-circuit) color phase generator, 44
IF (intermediate-frequency) bandwidth, 19

IF (intermediate-frequency) signal, TV, 13
Impedance matching, 314
Indy 500 (game), 288–289
In-line system, 24
Instruction sets, microprocessor, 82–83
    8080 (*see* 8080 microprocessor, instruction set)
Integrating network, 20
Intercarrier sound IF signal, 13
Interfacing:
    displays to microprocessor, 205
    joystick control, 199–203
    keyboard (*see* Keyboard interfacing)
    magnetic tape recorder to microprocessor, 178–185
    microprocessor memory, 163–167
    software UART, 208–211
    UART to microprocessor, 182
    video RAM to microprocessor, 197
Interference, 30, 322
Interlaced scanning, 17, 20
Intermittent defects, 323–324
Interrupt, 93–94
    vectored, 94
I/O (input/output) ports; 80, 90–94
IR (instruction register), 81, 82

Joystick control interfacing, 199–203
    in Pit and the Pendulum, 258–261

Keyboard interfacing:
    keyboard encoder ROM, 157, 158
    software implementation of, 203–205
    techniques of, 94

LCD (liquid-crystal display), 9
LED (light-emitting diode) driver system, 8
LED (light-emitting diode) scanning implementation in software, 205–207
Logic analyzers, 316–317
Logic defects, 323
Logic monitor, 317
Logic probes, 315–316
Low-frequency response, 19
LSI (large-scale integration), 39, 80

Machine language, 83
Magnetic deflection, 15
Magnetic tape:
    digital data recording on, 167–178
    I/O devices, 178–185
    properties of, 174
MAR (memory address register), 82
Masking, 125
Memory addressing techniques, 82, 159, 160, 163–167
Memory interfacing:
    to 8080 microprocessor, 165, 168
    to microprocessors, 163–167
Memory map for Blackjack program, 269
Microprocessors, 79–102
    control of video effects (*see* Video effects, microprocessor control of)
    execution of a sample program, 86–90
    interfacing to I/O devices, 90–92, 178–185
    (*See also* Interfacing)
    internal architecture of, 81–84
    memory interfacing to, 163–167
    microprogrammable instruction sets, 83
    (*See also* 8080 microprocessor)
Missile Attack (game), 286–287
Modulators (*see* Diode modulators)
Monochrome picture tube, 14–16
Monochrome video signals, 18–19
Monte Carlo wristwatch, 235
Motion signals for dot generator, 41
Multiplication (game), 238–239

Nim (game), 232–233
Nonvolatility, 153
Number system, hexadecimal, 83
Numbers:
    picture-tube type, 14
    random, 3

Odyssey series (games), 48, 290–291
OR gate, 37
Oscillators
    horizontal, 321
    RF, 31, 49, 51
    voltage-controlled, 56, 61
Oscilloscope signal tracing, 314

Output filter, 31
Output waveforms, 38

Patching programs, 151, 152
PC (program counter), 81–82
Phase modulator, 40
Phosphor screen, 14
Piano sound, 60
Picture-tube cross section, 14
Picture-tube-type numbers, 14
Picture tubes:
  color, 22–25
  monochrome, 14–16
Pit and the Pendulum (game), 243–262
  hardware version of, 243–252
    generation of moving bar, 247
    generation of on-screen scoring, 250
    generation of player video image, 246
    joystick interfacing, 258–261
  software version of, 252–262
    flowchart for, 253
Poker, draw (game), 235–236
Primary colors, 22
Program storage techniques, 153–185
  (*See also* RAM; ROM)
Programmable decoders, 36–38
Programming, 103–152
  8080 microprocessor (*see* 8080
    microprocessor, instruction set)
  examples, 134–152
    Blackjack (*see* Blackjack)
    deck packing for card games, 138–142
    electronic craps, 143–146
    Pit and the Pendulum (*see* Pit and
      the Pendulum)
    random-number generator, 136–138
    time delay, 146–148
  flowcharts, 107–112
  playing card selection, 111, 141
PROM (programmable read-only
  memory), 161–162
Propeller-driven aircraft sound, 55, 74–76
Purity magnet, 25

Racing games, 228, 230–231
RAM (random-access memory), 155–172
  dynamic, 156
  static, 155
Random-number generator, 136–138, 143
Random numbers, 3
Randomness, 3
Raster, 15
Raster scans, 187–199
Rectangular dot generator, 35
Red, green, and blue (RGB) dot pattern, 22–25
Resolution, 17
Retrace period, 18
  vertical, 20
RF (radio-frequency) interface for TV
  games, 31
RF (radio-frequency) oscillator, 31, 49, 51
Roadrace (game), 230–231
ROM (read-only memory), 80, 153–172
  addressing schemes, 159, 160, 163–167
  character generator, 189
  graphics, 192–194
  keyboard encoder, 157, 158
  multibit-per-word, 161
RWM (read/write memory), 153, 154, 162

Saturation (color), 22, 43
Scanning, horizontal and vertical, 16–18
Schmitt trigger, 61–63
School House (game), 239–240
Serial access devices, 171
Serial data transmission, 180
Serial I/O interfacing to 8080
  microprocessor, 182
Shadow mask, 23, 24
Signal tracing, 305, 312–317
  oscilloscope, 314
Software debugging methods, 148–152
Software design rules, 105–107
Software-hardware trade-offs (*see*
  Hardware-software trade-offs)
Sound effects, 53–77
  microprocessor-controlled, 219–225
    complex sound generator ICs, 223
    digital white noise, 220, 221
    table look-up methods for special
      sounds, 222
Sound-generator circuits, 69–77
  explosions from cannon fire, 72
  gunshots, 70–72

jet airplane, 73
propeller-driven aircraft, 74–76
spacecraft, 76
Sound synthesizer, 54, 59
Special display effects, 45–48
Spectral characteristics of waveform, 56
Stack, memory, 85–86, 131–134
Static RAM, 155
Studio II (game), 49, 233, 291–292
Subroutines, 84–86, 138–142
nested, 85
(*See also* Blackjack, subroutines used in)
Sync pulse, 19
horizontal, 20–22, 314
Sync separator circuits, 13, 20–21
Synchronization, 20–22

Telstar Arcade (game), 296–297
Tennis (game), 228–229
Three-gun picture tube, 23
Tic-Tac Quiz (game), 234, 297–299, 309, 310
Tint (color), 22
Trace routines for program debugging, 150
Troubleshooting techniques, 303–324
defects, 320–324
display circuits, 50–52
signal tracing, 305, 312–317
substitution, 306, 319–320
symptom-function, 304–311
voltage-resistance, 305–306, 318–319
TV bandwidth, 19
TV channel, 12
TV channel spectrum, 11
TV field, 16–18, 36
TV frames, horizontal and vertical scanning, 16–18
TV game block diagram, 4–7, 29–33, 304
TV games, troubleshooting technique for, 309–311
(*See also* Games)
TV IF signal, 13
TV picture tubes:
color, 22–25
monochrome, 14–16
TV receiver block diagram, 13

TV receiver functions, 11–14
TV tuner contacts, 322

UART (universal asynchronous receiver-transmitter), 180–185
data format, 180
interfacing to a microprocessor, 182
internal structure of, 181
software implementation, 208–211
Ultor, 23

VCO (voltage-controlled oscillator), 56, 61
Vectored interrupt, 94
Vertical retrace period, 20
Vertical-stripe generator, 34
signal tracing, 313
Vertical sweep, 321–322
Vestigial sideband suppression, 12
Video carrier, 12
Video Cart, 293, 294
Video Computer System (game), 295–296
Video effects, 29–52
microprocessor control of, 211–219
adding color to display, 216–219
collision of objects, 215–216
inverting the video, 212
moving object, 211
rotation of objects, 213
Video RAM display, 188
interfacing to microprocessor, 197
Video signals:
color, 25–28
monochrome, 18–19
Voltage-controlled amplifier, 68, 69
Voltage-controlled filter, 66, 67
Voltage-controlled oscillator, 56, 61
Voltage-resistance troubleshooting technique, 305–306, 318–319

War games, 228–230, 236
White level, 19
White-noise sources:
conventional, 64
digital, 220
Word generators, 316–317